The European Union and South Korea

The European Union and South Korea

The Legal Framework for Strengthening Trade, Economic and Political Relations

Edited by James Harrison

EDINBURGH
University Press

Edinburgh University Press Ltd
22 George Square, Edinburgh EH8 9LF
www.euppublishing.com

Typeset in 10/12 Goudy Old Style by
Servis Filmsetting Ltd, Stockport, Cheshire, and
printed and bound in Great Britain by
CPI Group (UK) Ltd, Croydon CR0 4YY

A CIP record for this book is available from the British Library

ISBN 978 0 7486 6860 1 (hardback)
ISBN 978 0 7486 6861 8 (webready PDF)
ISBN 978 0 7486 6862 5 (epub)
ISBN 978 0 7486 6863 2 (Amazon ebook)

Contents

PART III Beyond Trade and Economic Cooperation: Wider Issues in EU–Korea Relations

Acknowledgements

The idea for this book arose from a joint symposium organised by Edinburgh Law School and Sungkyunkwan Law School in May 2011, which looked at the legal aspects of EU–Korea relations. I am grateful to both institutions, which gave generous financial support to allow the symposium to take place. I would also like to thank all the staff and students who took part in the event, not all of whom could be involved in the subsequent book project.

I am indebted to John Watson at Edinburgh University Press for his support and encouragement in developing the outline for this book. Finally, I would like to acknowledge the valuable assistance of Charlotte Lelong, who helped edit various contributions to this volume.

Contributors

Colin Brown is a lawyer with the Directorate General for Trade of the European Commission. He provides legal advice on a range of issues, including the EU's FTAs, and he was deeply involved in the final stages of the negotiation and ratification of the EU–Korea FTA. He is also a visiting lecturer in international economic law at the Université Catholique de Louvain. He is a graduate of the Faculty of Law of the University of Edinburgh, the Bologna Center of the School of Advanced International Studies, John Hopkins University and the College of Europe, Bruges.

Dr Gracia Marín Durán is a Lecturer in international economic law and Director of the LLM programme in international economic law at the University of Edinburgh since February 2011. She has published in the areas of EU external relations law, international trade law and development law, including a co-authored book on *Environmental Integration in the EU's External Relations – Beyond Multilateral Dimensions* (2012). She was awarded the 2009 Jacqueline Suter Prize (ECJ/EUI) for her doctoral thesis, which deals with the interactions between the EU external trade and sustainable development policies. Prior to joining academia, she served as a trade officer at the EU delegation in South Africa, from 2008 to 2011, and, previously, worked in the legal affairs division of the World Trade Organization (2007).

Dr James Harrison is a lecturer in international law at the University of Edinburgh. He has written broadly on international economic law, international law of the sea, international environmental law and international dispute settlement. In 2010, he served as the United Kingdom National Reporter on the Protection of Foreign Investment for the 18th International Congress of Comparative Law. Prior to entering academia, he worked for a small non-governmental organisation, as a researcher on international trade law and policy.

Dr Hae-Won Jun is an assistant professor at the Institute of Foreign Affairs and National Security of the Korea National Diplomatic Academy (KNDA). Her main areas of research are the European Union, legislative politics and the EU–Asia relationship. Prior to joining the KNDA, she worked at Hanyang University and Sogang University in Seoul as a research professor. She holds an MSc from the London School of Economics and a DPhil from the University of Oxford.

Professor Il Hwan Kim is a Professor of Law at Sungkyunkwan University, where he specialises in data protection law. He completed his undergraduate education in Korea, and he obtained a PhD from the University of Mannheim in Germany.

Dr Younsik Kim is a senior researcher at the Korean Constitutional Research Institute. He has obtained a PhD in law at the University of Edinburgh. He also holds an LLM (Law) from the University of Chicago and an LLM (Public Law) and an LLB (Law) from Korea University. His research interests include constitutional law, legal theory and international investment law. In particular, he is currently focusing on the relationship and between international investment law and national constitutional law, under the concept of global law.

Young Lo Ko is a PhD candidate in EU law at the University of Edinburgh. Before starting his PhD, he was a desk officer for European affairs at the Ministry of Foreign Affairs and Trade, in the Republic of Korea. His main research interests are EU external relations law and international institutional law.

Justyna Lasik is an official with the Directorate General for Trade of the European Commission. For the last five years, she was responsible for trade relations with the Republic of Korea and, in particular, for the EU–Korea FTA. Recently she has started working on EU trade relations with Japan. She holds a Bachelor degree in European studies from Warsaw University and Masters degrees in international economic relations from the Warsaw School of Economics and in WTO/EU trade law from the Europa Kolleg Hamburg.

Dr Elisa Morgera is lecturer in European environmental law and Director of the LLM programme in global environment and climate change law at the University of Edinburgh. She has written widely on international and EU environmental law. Her recent publications include: *Environmental Integration in the EU's External Relations: Beyond Multilateral Dimensions* (2012) as co-author, and *The External Environmental Policy of the European Union: EU and International Law Perspectives* (2012) as editor.

Boris Rigod is a PhD candidate in international trade law at the European University Institute in Florence. His current research focuses on the law and economics of risk regulation under WTO law. Before joining the PhD programme, he worked as a research and teaching assistant at the University of Göttingen, as an intern at the German–Uruguayan Chamber of Commerce in Montevideo and as an intern at a boutique law firm in Geneva, specialising in WTO law. Boris holds a first state examination in law and a MLE from the University of Göttingen, as well as a LLM from the European University Institute.

David Rossati is a PhD candidate at the University of Edinburgh. His current research focuses on the institutional aspects of the global climate finance regime. Before joining the PhD programme, he worked in Amsterdam as an associate legal counsel for Climate Focus – an international consultancy in the field of climate change. David holds an LLM in international law from the University of Edinburgh, a Masters degree in institutional law and a Bachelor degree in law from the LUISS Guido Carli University in Rome.

Professor Jae Ho Sung is a Professor of Law at Sungkyunkwan University, specialising in international law. He has a particular interest in international economic law and international environmental law. Professor Sung is Director of the Korean Association of International Law, Director of the Korean Association of International Economic Law and Director of the Korean Branch of the International Law Association. He is also a member of the Committee of International Legal Counsel, which advises the Korean Ministry of Foreign Affairs and Trade.

Figures and Tables

Principal Treaties

1966 International Convention on the Elimination of All Forms of Racial Discrimination (UNTS, vol. 660, p. 195)

1966 International Covenant on Civil and Political Rights (UNTS, vol. 999, p. 171)

1966 International Covenant on Economic, Social and Cultural Rights (UNTS, vol. 993, p. 3)

1969 Vienna Convention on the Law of Treaties (UNTS, vol. 1155, p. 331)

1970 Treaty on the Non-proliferation of Nuclear Weapons (UNTS, vol. 729, p. 161)

1971 Ramsar Convention on Wetlands of International Importance (UNTS, vol. 996, p. 245)

1973 Convention on International Trade in Endangered Species (CITES) (UNTS, vol. 993, p. 243)

1979 Convention on the Elimination of All Forms of Discrimination against Women (UNTS, vol. 1249, p. 13)

1983 International Convention on the Harmonised Commodity Description and Coding System (UNTS, vol. 1503, p. 168)

1984 Convention against Torture and Other Cruel, Inhumane or Degrading Treatment or Punishment (UNTS vol. 1465, p. 113)

1985 Convention for the Protection of the Ozone Layer (UNTS, vol. 1513, p. 293)

1987 Montreal Protocol on Substances that Deplete the Ozone Layer (UNTS, vol. 1522, p. 3)

1989 Basel Convention on the Transboundary Movement of Hazardous Wastes (UNTS, vol. 1673, p. 57)

1989 Convention on the Rights of the Child (UNTS vol. 1577, p. 3)

1992 Convention on Biological Diversity (UNTS, vol. 1760, p. 79)

1992 United Nations Framework Convention on Climate Change (UNTS, vol. 1771, p. 107)

1994 Marrakesh Agreement establishing the World Trade Organization (UNTS, vol. 1867, p. 4)

1996 Framework Agreement for Trade and Cooperation between the European Community and its Member States on the one hand and the Republic of Korea on the other hand ([2001] OJ L 90/46, 30 March 2001)

1997 Agreement on Cooperation and Mutual Administrative Assistance in Customs Matters ([1997] OJ L121/14, 13 May 1997)

1997 Kyoto Protocol (UNTS, vol. 2303, p. 148)

1998 Convention on Prior Informed Consent Procedure for Certain Hazardous Chemicals and Pesticides in International Trade (UNTS, vol. 2244, p. 337)

2000 Cartagena Protocol on Biosafety (UNTS, vol. 2226, p. 208)

2001 Stockholm Convention on Persistent Organic Pollutants (UNTS, vol. 2256, p. 119)

2006 Agreement on Scientific and Technological Cooperation ([2007] OJ L106/44, 24 April 2007)

2007 Treaty of Lisbon amending the Treaty on European Union and the Treaty establishing the European Community ([2007] OJ C306/1, 17 December 2007)

2009 Agreement concerning Cooperation on Anti-competitive Activities ([2009] OJ L202/36, 4 August 2009)

2010 Free Trade Agreement between the European Union and its Member States of the one part, and the Republic of Korea of the other part ([2011] OJ L127/6, 14 May 2011)

2010 Framework Agreement between the European Union and its Member States on the one part, and the Republic of Korea, on the other part

PART I

The Legal and Policy Context for EU–Korea Relations

1

An Introduction to the Legal Framework for EU–Korea Relations

James Harrison

1 INTRODUCTION

In 2010, the European Union (EU) and the Republic of Korea[1] launched a strategic partnership, through which they agreed to closer cooperation on a range of matters, spanning trade, investment, sustainable development and international peace and security.[2] This book is concerned with the nature and depth of this cooperation and how the partnership is likely to develop over time. More specifically, it will focus on the proliferation of legal instruments, which has accompanied the strengthening of trade, economic and political relations between the EU and Korea.

Particular attention will be paid to two instruments, which were concluded at the same time as the launch of the strategic partnership in 2010, namely the EU–Korea Free Trade Agreement (FTA)[3] and the EU–Korea Framework Agreement.[4] These agreements are the legal foundation of EU–Korea relations, and it is, therefore, necessary to appreciate their scope and substance, in order to understand how they may influence the development of the strategic partnership. To this end, the book will explore the nature of the obligations undertaken by the parties in the FTA and the Framework Agreement, as well as other relevant instruments. It will consider what is required of the parties in order to comply with their commitments, and what questions of interpretation are likely to arise in the application of the FTA and the Framework Agreement, as well as how these might be answered. Moreover, it will ask what factors are likely to determine the successful implementation of the agreements in question and what obstacles may need to be overcome.

---

[1] Throughout this book, the Republic of Korea will be referred to as South Korea or simply Korea.

[2] See European Union, *EU–Republic of Korea Summit Joint Press Statement*, Document MEMO/10/461, Brussels, 6 October 2010.

[3] Free Trade Agreement between the European Union and its Member States of the one part, and the Republic of Korea of the other part (EU–Korea FTA) [2011] OJ L127/6, 14 May 2011.

[4] Framework Agreement between the European Union and its Member States on the one part, and the Republic of Korea, on the other part (EU–Korea Framework Agreement), www.eeas.europa.eu/korea_south/index_en.htm (accessed 20 April 2012).

More generally, the book will also consider the place of bilateral coopera-tion between the EU and Korea in the context of the broader international legal framework. Several questions arise in this context. Firstly, in what ways do the agreements concluded between the EU and Korea interact with other international treaties on similar issues? Secondly, what can a closer partner-ship between these two actors add to existing cooperation at the multilateral level? In addressing these questions, it is hoped that the contributions to this book will not only be relevant to EU–Korea relations, but that they may also offer broader insights into the emergence of a multipolar world, where international actors are increasingly cultivating bilateral relations as a supple-ment, or sometimes as an alternative, to multilateralism.

The purpose of this introductory chapter is threefold. Firstly, it will explain the trend towards bilateralism and regionalism in international relations, thus providing a broader context for the examination of the rela-tionship between the EU and Korea. Secondly, it will trace the historical evolution of EU–Korea relations, up to the conclusion of the FTA and the Framework Agreement in 2010. Thirdly, it will conclude by highlighting the key issues that are likely to arise in the implementation of the EU–Korea strategic partnership and the related themes that will be addressed in more detail throughout this book.

2 BILATERALISM AND REGIONALISM IN INTERNATIONAL RELATIONS

The launch of the EU–Korea strategic partnership, along with the con-clusion of the FTA and the Framework Agreement, can be seen as part of a broader trend towards bilateral and regional cooperation in recent years. It is true that states have always been involved in bilateral and regional initiatives, largely because 'the relative homogeneity of the inter-ests or outlooks of actors will then ensure a more efficient or equitable implementation of the relevant norms'.[5] Nevertheless, the recent trend is also linked to the fact that it has become increasingly difficult to solve common challenges at the multilateral level. This phenomenon is, perhaps, most clearly illustrated by recent developments in international economic relations.

The establishment of the World Trade Organization (WTO) in 1995 was, arguably, the crowning success for multilateralism, which had been the dominant approach to economic cooperation since the conclusion of the General Agreement on Tariffs and Trade (GATT) in 1947. The WTO pro-vides a multilateral framework for pursuing its goal of substantially reducing tariffs and other barriers to trade and eliminating discriminatory treatment

---

[5] International Law Commission, *Report of the Study Group on the Fragmentation of International Law*, Document A/CN.4/L.682, paragraph 205.

in international trade relations.[6] There is no doubt that the WTO continues to play a central role in the international trading regime. Yet, its dominance has come under challenge, by a proliferation of bilateral and regional trade deals concluded over the past two decades.

It has been said that 'bilateralism . . . returned with a vengeance', soon after the establishment of the WTO.[7] According to WTO statistics, 'as of 15 January 2012, some 511 notifications of RTAs (counting goods and services separately) had been received by the GATT/WTO'.[8] Whilst preferential trading regimes are not, themselves, new,[9] the speed at which they are being concluded is notable. More than two-thirds of these notifications have taken place since 2000.[10] Moreover:

> this most recent wave of regionalism covers a much wider network of participants – including bilateral, plurilateral and cross-regional initiatives – and encompasses countries at different levels of economic development – including 'developed-developed', 'developing-developing', and 'developed-developing' alliances. And although these new agreements, like previous PTAs, also involve preferential tariff reductions, they focus even more on WTO-plus type issues, such as services, capital flows, standards, intellectual property, regulatory systems (many of which are non-discriminatory) and commitments on labour and environment issues.[11]

This increase in RTAs is partly a result of the failure to make progress on key outstanding issues at the multilateral level.[12] The disparate interests of an increasing number of WTO Members means that trade negotiations, at the international level, have become increasingly difficult. At the time of writing, multilateral trade negotiations remain gridlocked, with several deadlines for completion having been missed.[13] In response, states and other

---

[6] Agreement establishing the World Trade Organization, Preamble.

[7] S. Lester and B. Mercurio (eds), *Bilateral and Regional Trade Agreements: Commentary and Analysis* (Cambridge: Cambridge University Press, 2009), p. 3.

[8] See www.wto.org/english/tratop_e/region_e/region_e.htm (accessed 15 June 2012).

[9] For a historical perspective on the conclusion of preferential trade agreements, see World Trade Organization, *World Trade Report 2011* (Geneva: World Trade Organization, 2011), pp. 48–54.

[10] For a list of RTAs and their entry into force dates, see www.rtais.wto.org/UI/publicPreDefR epByWTOLegalCover.aspx (accessed 3 July 2012).

[11] World Trade Organization, *World Trade Report 2011*, p. 53.

[12] See, for example, D. Evans, 'Bilateral and plurilateral PTAs', in S. Lester and B. Mercurio (eds), *Bilateral and Regional Trade Agreements: Commentary and Analysis* (Cambridge: Cambridge University Press, 2009), p. 54; F. A. Abbott, 'A new dominant trade species emerges: is bilateralism a threat?', *Journal of International Economic Law* vol. 10 (2007), pp. 573–5.

[13] The so-called Doha Development Round of multilateral trade negotiations was launched at the fourth WTO Ministerial Conference in November 2001, with an initial deadline for completion as of 1 January 2005; for more information, see the Doha Ministerial Declaration, Document WT/MIN(01)/DEC/1, adopted on 14 November 2001, paragraph 45. This deadline was extended by a WTO General Council Decision of 1 August 2004,

actors have looked to other forums in order to achieve any progress on trade liberalisation, hence, leading to the proliferation of bilateral and regional trade agreements described above.

The EU and Korea have been at the forefront of this process of regionalisation in trade relations. As explained in Chapters 2 and 3 of this volume, bilateralism and regionalism in economic affairs have been key policy priorities for both the EU and Korea since the mid-2000s. Whilst both actors still support, at least rhetorically, the ongoing multilateral trade negotiations in the WTO, most of their efforts and energies have been directed towards the development of bilateral or regional relations. Indeed, the EU–Korea strategic partnership is an excellent illustration of the increase in bilateral trade deals, which take place outside strict geographical regions.[14]

This trend towards bilateralism and regionalism is not necessarily limited to the trade and economic context. There are other policy areas where the international community has struggled to achieve consensus at the multilateral level, but where progress has been possible between smaller groupings of like-minded actors. The EU–Korea relationship clearly demonstrates the opportunities that are available for bilateral cooperation, in areas such as climate change,[15] environmental protection[16] and personal data protection.[17]

Once it has begun, 'the trend towards preferential arrangements is self-reinforcing',[18] because states enter into an increasing number of new agreements in order to avoid missing out on the opportunities that others are enjoying. In the trade context, one author observes that:

> the proliferation of bilateral/regional trade agreements is driven by the race for leadership for some, and the fear of exclusion for others . . . [and] [t]he best illustration of the geopolitical dimension of trade, and the role of bilateral/regional agreements, is the race for power between the EU and the US.[19]

Thus, 'even countries that continue to advocate the benefits of multilateralism over bilateral or plurilateral alternatives have, out of necessity, focused

---

Document WT/L/579, paragraph 3. A new deadline for completing negotiations in 2006 was set at the fifth WTO Ministerial Conference in December 2005 (see Document WT/MIN(05)/DEC, adopted on 18 December 2005, paragraph 1), but this deadline was also missed. Negotiations continue.

14 D. Evans, 'Bilateral and plurilateral PTAs', in S. Lester and B. Mercurio (eds), *Bilateral and Regional Trade Agreements: Commentary and Analysis* (Cambridge: Cambridge University Press, 2009), p. 55.

15 See Chapter 13 of this volume.

16 See Chapter 12 of this volume.

17 See Chapter 14 of this volume.

18 Abbott, 'A new dominant trade species emerges: is bilateralism a threat?', p. 578.

19 O. Cattaneo, 'The political economy of PTAs', in S. Lester and B. Mercurio (eds), *Bilateral and Regional Trade Agreements: Commentary and Analysis* (Cambridge: Cambridge University Press, 2009), p. 42.

increasingly on [Preferential Trade Agreements]'.[20] In this regard, the sustainability impact assessment of the EU–Korea FTA, conducted on behalf of the European Commission, stressed that:

> the potential impact of the Korea–EU FTA must be assessed in the context that if the bilateral FTA is not concluded, that both partners will continue to develop bilateral trade agreements with other partners and that bilateral trade and investment relations will be attenuated by preferences both sides grant to the other partners.[21]

In this light, it is perhaps no surprise that the decision to negotiate the EU–Korea FTA quickly followed the conclusion of the Korea-United States FTA in 2007.[22]

Such geopolitical rivalries, it would appear, can be decisive factors in influencing cooperative strategies. They can dictate not only the initiation of an agreement, but also the nature and level of commitments that are undertaken. As the number of bilateral and regional agreements grows, existing agreements will also come under scrutiny to ensure that they continue to offer sufficient advantages. This factor requires bilateral relations to remain dynamic, responding to the activities and policies of competitors and related developments.

Without doubt, the proliferation of agreements at the bilateral level increases the complexity of the international legal framework and leads to, what Lester and Mercurio have referred to as, 'a mish-mash of overlapping, supporting, and possibly conflicting, obligations'.[23] Yet, there is also a danger that they pose a threat to the multilateral framework, by undermining its importance.[24] There is a particular concern, in the context of the WTO regime, that 'the unregulated proliferation of [Preferential Trade Agreements] tend to create vested interests that may make it more difficult to attain meaningful multilateral liberalization'.[25]

Yet, it is not always the case that bilateralism is opposed to multilateralism.

---

[20] Evans, 'Bilateral and plurilateral PTAs', pp. 54–5.

[21] IBM Belgium, in association with DMI, TAC & TICON, *Trade Sustainability Impact Assessment of the Free Trade Agreement to be negotiated between the European Community and the Republic of Korea: Final Report*, Report prepared for the European Commission, June 2008, p. 18.

[22] The United States is also intensely aware of the consequences of the EU–Korea FTA, for its own relations with Korea. For more information on this issue, see W. H. Cooper, R. Jurenas, M. D. Platzer, and M. E. Manyin, *The EU–South Korea Free Trade Agreement and its Implications for the United States*, Congressional Research Service (CRS) Report for Congress, 1 December 2011.

[23] Lester and Mercurio (eds), *Bilateral and Regional Trade Agreements: Commentary and Analysis*, p. 4.

[24] Abbott, 'A new dominant trade species emerges: is bilateralism a threat?', p. 581. See, generally, R. Baldwin and P. Low (eds), *Multilateralizing Regionalism: Challenges for the Global Trading System* (Cambridge: Cambridge University Press, 2009).

[25] See Report by the Consultative Board to the Director-General Supachai Panitchpakdi, *The Future of the World Trade Organization* (Geneva: World Trade Organization, 2004), paragraph 84.

In some areas, bilateral arrangements provide an opportunity to pursue international cooperation, where there are no meaningful opportunities for cooperation at the multilateral level. This is the case in the area of investment and competition, where any negotiations within the context of the WTO or other multilateral regimes have been rejected, at least in the short-term.[26] Thus, bilateralism can play a gap-filling role, which does not necessarily harm the multilateral framework.

Alternatively, bilateral and regional initiatives can also be used as stepping-stones for developments in the multilateral regime. This would appear to be the case in certain areas of trade policy, such as intellectual property rights and government procurement, where the pursuit of these topics at the bilateral level has not prevented subsequent plurilateral agreements.[27] Indeed, this is not only observable in the economic area; bilateral and regional cooperation can also be used in other spheres to support the implementation of existing multilateral agreements or to build consensus for ongoing or future multilateral negotiations.[28] In this context, bilateral or regional agreements are instrumental; they are not an end in themselves, rather, they are a means to influence broader political processes at the multilateral level.

3 THE EVOLUTION OF EU–KOREA RELATIONS

3.1 *The EU and Asia*

Although it stands out today as one of the key strategic partners of the EU, Korea's relationship with the EU must be understood in the context of the latter's wider policy on external affairs and its Asian policy, in particular. The EU has always pursued a policy of close bilateral and regional cooperation with other states in its own region[29] and with its former colonies and dependencies,[30] as well as with strategically important third states in other regions. However, the EU's engagement with Asia, traditionally, has '[lagged] well behind other regions'.[31] This can be attributed, in part, to the fact that

---

[26] See Chapters 6 and 7 of this volume.

[27] See Chapter 4 of this volume.

[28] See, in particular, the discussion of environmental cooperation between the EU and third states in Chapter 12.

[29] This includes both the EU Enlargement Policy, see www.ec.europa.eu/enlargement/index_en.htm (accessed 3 July 2012), as well as the so-called European Neighbourhood Policy, see www.ec.europa.eu/world/enp/index_en.htm (accessed 3 July 2012).

[30] See, for example, the Partnership Agreement between the members of the Africa, Caribbean and Pacific Group of States of the one part, and the European Union and its Members States on the other part [2000] OJ L317/3, 15 December 2000. For background information concerning the Partnership Agreement and related instruments, see www.europa.eu/legislation_summaries/development/african_caribbean_pacific_states/r12101_en.htm (accessed 5 April 2012).

[31] European Commission, *Communication on Europe and Asia: A Strategic Framework for Enhanced Partnership*, Document COM (2001) 469 final, 4 September 2001, p. 12.

Asia was a geopolitically sensitive region during the years of the Cold War, with the USSR and the US jostling for influence. This changed in the 1990s, when 'the Cold War's end encouraged new political-security thinking . . . [and] the rise of Asia's "tiger economies" encouraged both sides to look at each other's relevance anew'.[32]

The EU adopted its first major policy on Asia in 1994, with an acknowledgement that 'the European Union needs to accord Asia a higher priority than it has done in the past'.[33] The 1994 Communication committed the EU to a broad set of policy objectives, including strengthening the EU's economic presence in Asia, as well as widening and deepening its political and economic relations with countries across Asia.[34] The strategy recognised that Asia was not a homogenous region[35] and that the objectives of the EU would have to be pursued at different levels and through different means, depending on the nature of the countries concerned.[36] Overall, the 1994 Communication covered 26 countries, but it expressly noted that cooperation, particularly economic cooperation, should be urgently extended to some countries in particular. Korea was highlighted as an emerging economic powerhouse in the region and, therefore, a potentially important partner for increased cooperation.[37] Whilst the EU and Korea continue to engage with one another as part of the Europe–Asia Meetings, which have taken place biennially since 1996,[38] they have also developed a dedicated bilateral dialogue, which has gradually been strengthened over the years.

3.2 The development of bilateral relations

At the time of the 1994 Communication, the EU had not concluded any agreements or other arrangements with Korea, unlike other significant

---

[32] R. E. Kelly, 'Korea–European Union relations: beyond the FTA?', *International Relations of the Asia–Pacific* vol. 12 (2012), p. 105.

[33] European Commission, *Communication: Towards a New Asia Strategy*, Document COM(94) 314 final, 13 July 1994, p. 13.

[34] European Commission, *Communication: Towards a New Asia Strategy*, p. 3.

[35] Ibid.

[36] See European Commission, *Communication on Europe and Asia: A Strategic Framework for Enhanced Partnership*, p. 20.

[37] European Commission, *Communication: Towards a New Asia Strategy*, p. 20. The Communication also stresses that: '[g]reater emphasis should be placed on pro-active economic cooperation. Top priority for this type of co-operation should go to the newly emerging Asian markets, largely, but not exclusively in East and Southeast Asia, namely South Korea, China, Macao, Taiwan, Hong Kong, Indonesia, Malaysia, Pakistan, Philippines, Singapore, Thailand and India'. Ibid. p. 24.

[38] See www.eeas.europa.eu/asem/index_en.htm (accessed 31 January 2012). See, also, I. Medvidgy, *Economic and Trade Relations between the European Union and South Korea* (Saarbrücken: Verlag Dr Müller, 2008), pp. 40–3.

economic actors in the Asian region, such as India, Pakistan, ASEAN and Japan.[39] Yet, plans to formalise the relationship between the two partners were already hinted at in the 1994 Communication.[40]

The first step in strengthening relations between the EU and Korea was the conclusion of a Framework Agreement for Trade and Cooperation between the European Community and its Member States, on the one hand, and the Republic of Korea, on the other hand, on 28 October 1996.[41] This instrument is a so-called 'third generation' cooperation agreement,[42] meaning that it promotes broad cooperation on topics ranging from trade and economic policy to, *inter alia*, justice and home affairs.

Korea is not the only country in Asia to have such an agreement with the EU,[43] but it was the first *developed* Asian country to enter into a legally binding cooperation agreement. In contrast, relations with other developed countries in the Asia–Pacific region (that is, Japan, Australia and New Zealand) are governed by political declarations.

The 1996 Framework Agreement, itself, contains few substantive obligations. Much of the agreement is concerned with reiterating the commitments that the two parties had recently entered into at the conclusion of the Uruguay Round, which established the WTO on 1 January 1995. Thus, the preamble to the Agreement recalls that both the EU and Korea have committed themselves to the principles of free trade and market economy, through their participation in GATT and the Agreement establishing the World Trade Organization, and the parties further confirm their rights and obligations, under the WTO's Most-Favoured Nation principle,[44] the WTO Government Procurement Agreement,[45] the WTO Agreement on Sanitary and Phytosanitary Measures,[46] the WTO Agreement on Trade-related Aspects of Intellectual Property Rights[47] and the WTO Agreements on Anti-dumping and Anti-subsidy Measures.[48]

Other than these substantive commitments, the 1996 Framework Agreement sets an agenda for cooperation in economic and related fields. The parties commit themselves to 'establishing economic cooperation in

---

[39] For a list of cooperation and other agreements in place at the time of the 1994 Communication, see European Commission, *Communication: Towards a New Asia Strategy*, Annex III.

[40] Ibid. p. 4.

[41] Framework Agreement for Trade and Cooperation between the European Community and its Member States on the one hand and the Republic of Korea on the other hand (1996 Framework Agreement) [2001] OJ L90/46, 30 March 2001.

[42] See, for example, European Commission, *Communication* on *Europe and Asia: A Strategic Framework for Enhanced Partnership*, p. 12.

[43] Similar agreements have been entered into by Nepal, Laos, Cambodia, India and Pakistan.

[44] 1996 Framework Agreement, Article 4.

[45] Ibid. Article 5(4).

[46] Ibid. Article 6(3).

[47] Ibid. Article 9(2).

[48] Ibid. Article 11(2).

fields of mutual interest, including scientific and technological cooperation and industrial cooperation'.[49] The Agreement also goes beyond economic cooperation, and it provides that:

> a regular political dialogue, based on shared values and aspirations, shall be established . . . [which] shall take place in accordance with the procedures agreed in the Joint Declaration between the European Union and the Republic of Korea on this subject.[50]

Moreover, specific articles of the Framework Agreement mandate cooperation on a wide range of policy issues, including drugs and money laundering,[51] energy,[52] environmental matters,[53] development assistance[54] and culture, information and communication.[55]

As well as promoting cooperation between the parties themselves, the 1996 Framework Agreement is also aimed at 'facilitating cooperation between businesses by facilitating investment on both sides and by promoting better mutual understanding'.[56] In order to achieve this, the parties undertook to promote 'exchange of information between economic operators and industrial cooperation between enterprises'[57] and to organise 'trade and investment visits'[58] and 'general and single industry trade fairs'.[59]

Given the lack of substantive obligations, the most important aspect of the 1996 Framework Agreement is, perhaps, the creation of institutional machinery to oversee the implementation of the Agreement and the development of stronger ties. A Joint Committee is established, under Article 19 of the Agreement, composed of representatives of the EU and Korea. The Joint Committee is charged with ensuring that the Agreement operates properly and making recommendations for promoting further expansion in trade and cooperation between the two parties. The institutional framework allowed the parties to build up the mutual trust and understanding which was necessary, in order to further develop their relations in a more substantive manner.

Following the conclusion of the 1996 Framework Agreement, the parties entered into several other sectoral agreements, designed to further cooperation

---

[49]   Ibid. Article 2(b). See, also, Articles 12 and 14.
[50]   Ibid. Article 3.
[51]   Ibid. Article 13.
[52]   Ibid. Article 16.
[53]   Ibid. Article 15.
[54]   Ibid. Article 18.
[55]   Ibid. Article 17.
[56]   Ibid. Article 2(c).
[57]   Ibid. Article 5(2)(b). See, also, Article 12.
[58]   Ibid. Article 5(2)(i).
[59]   Ibid. Article 5(2)(j).

in specific areas. In 1997, they concluded an Agreement on Cooperation and Mutual Administrative Assistance in Customs Matters,[60] the objective of which was to assist each party in the prevention and investigation of operations in breach of customs legislation. In 2006, they entered into an Agreement on Scientific and Technological Cooperation.[61] The purpose of this instrument was to facilitate cooperation and joint projects in the fields of science and technology to the mutual benefit of both parties. Then, in 2009, the parties concluded the Agreement concerning Cooperation on Anti-Competitive Activities,[62] which was aimed at contributing to the effective enforcement of competition laws in each party, through cooperation and exchange of information.

The entry into force of the 1996 Framework Agreement in 2001 was also quickly followed by the establishment of high-level summits between the parties, which took place in Copenhagen in 2002, Hanoi in 2004, Helsinki in 2006, Seoul in 2009 and Brussels in 2010. The first four of these meetings took place on the sidelines of the Europe–Asia Meeting. However, in 2010, the strategic partnership was formally launched at the first stand-alone EU–Korea summit. This indicated a change in emphasis, whereby Korea was no longer treated as a strand of the EU's Asia strategy, but, rather, as a priority partner. As noted above, this coincided with the conclusion of two other agreements, which, today, form the main pillars of the legal framework for EU–Korea relations, namely the Free Trade Agreement and a new Framework Agreement. It is these agreements which will form the focus of inquiry throughout this book, in order to determine what implications they have for EU–Korea relations.

4 DEVELOPING THE EU–KOREA STRATEGIC PARTNERSHIP

4.1 What is a strategic partnership?

Korea is the latest in the list of strategic partnerships entered into by the EU. It joins the ranks of the United States, Russia, China, South Africa, India, Japan, Mexico and Canada as emerging powers, with which the EU is seeking a strategic relationship.[63] The effect of this classification is to:

---

[60] Agreement between the European Community and the Republic of Korea on cooperation and mutual administrative assistance in customs matters [1997] OJ L121/14, 13 May 1997.

[61] Agreement on the Scientific and Technological Cooperation between the European Community and the Government of the Republic of Korea [2007] OJ L106/44, 24 April 2007.

[62] Agreement between the European Community and the Government of the Republic of Korea concerning cooperation on anti-competitive activities [2009] OJ L202/36, 4 August 2009.

[63] See T. Renard, 'Strategy wanted: the European Union and strategic partnerships', *EGMONT Security Policy Brief No. 13*, September 2010, p. 1.

automatically raise the status of the third country, which is to say that the EU recognizes the growing importance and influence of the strategic partner, but it also acknowledges its new responsibilities and obligations as a global player.[64]

To this end, the preamble to the 2010 Framework Agreement acknowledges 'the growing role and responsibility assumed by the Republic of Korea in the international community'.[65]

The establishment of strategic partnerships can also be seen as a way in which the EU seeks to assert its own authority for the conduct of international relations. This is increasingly important, as more and more powers are transferred by the Member States to the EU. A significant development, in this regard, took place with the entry into force of the Lisbon Treaty on 1 December 2009, which formally conferred international legal personality on the EU[66] and which introduced new powers and procedures for the exercise of its external relations.[67] Reflecting these developments, the preamble to the 2010 Framework Agreement explicitly makes reference to 'the accelerated process whereby the European Union is acquiring its own identity in foreign policy and in the field of security and justice'.[68]

Apart from the symbolic nature of the relationship, the nature and consequences of a strategic partnership remains ambiguous. To be sure, such partnerships would seem to be comprehensive in scope,[69] as well as going beyond mere bilateral issues, to include global challenges.[70] Beyond that, there is room for each partnership to develop in its own particular way, reflecting the particular needs and characteristics of the partners, as well as the EU's own interests and priorities in each case. The following sections will seek to identify some of the key features, which are likely to influence the development of the EU–Korea strategic partnership, and which will be discussed in more detail by various contributors to this volume.

---

[64]   Ibid. p. 3.
[65]   EU–Korea Framework Agreement, Fourth Preambular Paragraph.
[66]   Consolidated Version of the Treaty on the European Union (TEU) [2010] OJ C83/13, 30 March 2010, Article 47.
[67]   In particular, the reforms introduced a new High Representative of the Union for Foreign Affairs and Security Policy (TEU, Article 18(1)) and the European External Action Service (TEU, Article 27(3)). For a more detailed explanation of the reforms, see, for example, J. C. Piris, *The Lisbon Treaty: A Legal and Political Analysis* (Cambridge: Cambridge University Press, 2010), Chapter 7; M. Cremona, 'External relations and external competence of the European Union: the emergence of an integrated policy', in P. Craig and G. de Búrca (eds), *The Evolution of EU Law* (2nd edn) (Oxford: Oxford University Press, 2011), pp. 217–68.
[68]   EU–Korea Framework Agreement, Third Preambular Paragraph.
[69]   G. Grevi, 'The rise of strategic partnerships: between interdependence and politics', in G. Grevi and A. de Vasconcelos (eds), *Partnerships for Effective Multilateralism: EU Relations with Brazil, China, India and Russia*, Chaillot Paper No. 109 (Paris: EU Institute for Security Studies, 2008), p. 147.
[70]   T. Renard, 'EU strategic partnerships: evolution of a concept from Amsterdam to Lisbon', *EU–China Observer*, Issue 5 (2010), pp. 17, 20.

4.2 The legalisation of EU–Korea relations

One of the features of the EU–Korea strategic partnership is its foundation upon a number of legal instruments. In other words, rather than pursuing cooperation on a purely political basis, the parties have decided to create a legal framework for their partnership. This legalisation of EU–Korea bilateral relations distinguishes it from many of the other strategic partnerships entered into by the EU, where partner countries have been 'reluctant to enter binding commitments in their relations with the EU and to accept, for example, social or human rights clauses are attached to economic agreements'.[71]

Of course, the degree of legalisation in EU–Korea relations varies, from policy area to policy area. Generally speaking, the FTA displays a greater degree of legalisation than the Framework Agreement, particularly in terms of the specificity of its provisions. Nevertheless, both of the agreements contain dispute settlement procedures, which allow differences to be settled by a third party.[72] These procedures not only apply to subjects who have traditionally been subject to dispute settlement at the multilateral level, but they also extend to new subject areas, where it is less common to have independent adjudication.[73] It follows that the legal framework demonstrates a broad acceptance by the parties that their relationship will be governed by law and not just by politics.

Arguably, legalisation plays a particularly important role in EU–Korea relations, because it is a partnership that brings together actors from different sides of the world, who do not share long-standing historical or cultural ties.[74] Therefore, it has been necessary for the EU and Korea to explicitly identify and agree, at the outset, on the common interests and shared values, which underpin their relationship. By expressing their expectations in legal form, the parties establish a stable foundation for the development of the partnership, by providing a common reference point for future cooperation.[75] It also means that the interpretation and

---

[71] Grevi, 'The rise of strategic partnerships: between interdependence and politics', p. 151. However, it should be noted that the EU has entered into legally binding arrangements with some of its less developed strategic partners, such as South Africa and Mexico. Thanks to my colleague, Gracia Marín Durán, for pointing this out.

[72] There are, of course, important exceptions to this. For a more detailed discussion of dispute settlement in the FTA, see Chapter 4 of this volume. For an overview of the dispute settlement procedure in the Framework Agreement, see Chapter 9 of this volume.

[73] In Chapter 5 of this volume, Rigod gives the example of extending dispute settlement to the topic of trade facilitation, which is not subject to dispute settlement at the multilateral level.

[74] This is in contrast to many other cooperation arrangements entered into by the EU, with former colonies or with neighbouring states in the same region.

[75] See J. Goldstein, M. Kahler, R. O. Keohane and A. M. Slaughter, 'Legalization and world politics', *International Organization*, vol. 54 (2000), p. 393.

application of the agreements will not be subject to the sole discretion of the parties, but may be decided by independent adjudicators. In turn, this fact makes it significantly more important to conduct a legal analysis of the relationship.

4.3 Promoting coherence in EU–Korea relations

Throughout the course of the book, it will become clear that neither the Framework Agreement nor the FTA is designed to be a static instrument. Rather, they both foresee the continual development of the legal and policy framework, within which EU–Korea relations will take place. This evolution may take place either through the conclusion of additional agreements or through other institutional processes. To this end, both the Framework Agreement and the FTA establish political institutions, which are central to the ability of the partners to develop their relationship over time, in order to respond to new and evolving challenges.[76] These political organs are able to adopt decisions, therefore forestalling problems which might arise in the implementation of the agreements, as well as making suggestions on issues of common interest, where future action may be appropriate.

A key challenge in the development of the strategic partnership will be the management of relations and the interactions between different instruments adopted by the parties. The Framework Agreement itself stresses the comprehensive nature of the relationship and the need for 'maintaining overall coherence in this regard'.[77] Although all of the existing agreements fall within a 'common institutional framework',[78] there is plenty of room for tensions to arise between the different policy objectives.

Coordination is necessary, because there is an inevitable overlap between the various agreements and policy dialogues, which together form the common institutional framework. As a result, actions taken in one policy area may have implications for other policy areas. Climate change cooperation under the Framework Agreement provides a good example, as measures taken to mitigate carbon emissions may have significant economic implications, potentially clashing with rules and principles contained in the FTA.[79] The parties must be able to manage such tensions, and it is in this respect that the institutional framework will also play an important role.

The need to balance the various policy goals is also reflected in the concept of sustainable development, which features prominently in the Framework

---

[76] EU–Korea Framework Agreement, Article 44; EU–Korea FTA, Chapter 15. See, further, Chapters 4 and 9 of this volume.

[77] EU–Korea Framework Agreement, Article 2(5).

[78] Young Lo Ko considers the nature of the common institutional framework in Chapter 10 of this volume.

[79] See, for example, the observations of Rossati in Chapter 13 of this volume.

Agreement[80] and the FTA.[81] According to the general understanding of the concept, sustainable development requires decision-makers to integrate economic growth, social development and environmental protection.[82] It is a concept which should guide the parties in the furtherance of their strategic partnership and help them achieve coherence in their bilateral relations.[83]

4.4 Other factors influencing the development of EU–Korea relations[84]

One aspect of the evolving EU–Korea relationship that cannot be ignored is the unique legal nature of the EU as an international actor. Although it has its own legal personality,[85] the EU is effectively a conglomeration of twenty-seven Member States and, with the important exception of trade matters, is not exclusively competent in all matters relating to international affairs. Questions concerning the division of competence between the EU and the Member States are important for determining with whom Korea must negotiate and cooperate on particular issues. Yet, there are areas where the answers to these questions are not clear.[86] Moreover, the ability of the EU to respond to challenges is limited by its own internal procedures for decision-making.[87]

The nature of the EU as an international actor must also be taken into account, in the context of dispute settlement under the legal framework. Both the FTA and the Framework Agreement are mixed agreements, meaning that the EU and the Member States are contracting parties. However, it will be necessary to determine who has competence over a particular issue, in order to determine who bears responsibility for a breach of the agreements.[88] This is a complex issue, which may require further clarification or the develop-

---

[80] EU–Korea Framework Agreement, Article 1(3): 'The Parties reaffirm their commitment to promoting sustainable development in all its dimensions'.

[81] EU–Korea FTA, Chapter 13. Marín Durán analyses these provisions in Chapter 8 of this volume.

[82] See, for example, World Commission on Environment and Development, *Our Common Future* (Oxford: Oxford University Press, 1987), pp. 37–41. For a recent affirmation of the three pillars of sustainable development, see United Nations Conference on Sustainable Development (Rio +20 Conference), *The Future We Want*, UN Document A/CONF.216/L.1, 22 June 2012, paragraph 1.

[83] On environmental integration, see the observations of Morgera, in Chapter 12 of this volume.

[84] Thanks to my colleague, Gracia Marín Durán, for her valuable comments on this section. Any mistakes, however, remain attributable to the author.

[85] TEU, Article 47.

[86] To this end, see the discussion of competence in Chapters 7 and 8 of this volume.

[87] The internal procedures for EU decision-making are explained by Brown and Lasik in Chapter 2 of this volume.

[88] See, generally, P. J. Kuijper, 'International responsibility and mixed agreements', in C. Hillion and P. Koutrakos (eds), *Mixed Agreements Revisited – The EU and its Member States in the World* (Oxford: Hart Publishing, 2010), pp. 208–28.

ment of a procedural mechanism, in order to identify the appropriate litigant in particular circumstances.

It must also be remembered that Korea has its own legal and policy framework for international relations.[89] Although it has often been noted that '[o] ne very striking feature of cooperation and economic integration agreements over the last twenty years has been the extent to which the [EU] is engaged in exporting its norms and standards',[90] it is debatable whether this is a factor in the development of closer relations between the EU and Korea. It cannot be assumed that the EU can dictate the content of the strategic partnership to Korea. This is a partnership between two developed countries.[91] Whilst it is true that the EU is vastly bigger, in terms of territory, population and overall economic power, the economic gap appears to be closing. According to the Trade Sustainability Impact Assessment carried out on behalf of the EU, although Korea's GDP is slightly below the average of the original EU Member States, it has a per capita GDP above many of the new Member States, and 'the process of convergence between Korea and the EU in per capita GDP is likely to continue'.[92] Moreover, Korea also has other attributes, which reaffirm its position as a developed country, not least its membership of the Organisation for Economic Cooperation and Development since 1996 and its participation in the G20 group of major economies. Thus, there is no doubt that Korea is on a stronger footing than many other states, with which the EU has concluded economic cooperation and partnership agreements. This helps to explain why some of the provisions in the EU–Korea agreement differ from similar agreements concluded by the EU with other countries.[93] It is important to take such contextual factors into account, when considering the future development of EU–Korea relations, as well as when drawing comparisons with other EU partners.

5 OUTLINE OF THE BOOK

The conclusion of the Framework Agreement and the FTA in 2010 was the latest step in the process of developing trade, economic and political

---

[89] For a discussion of Korean policy on trade and economic relations, see Chapter 3 of this volume.

[90] Cremona, 'External relations and external competence of the European Union: the emergence of an integrated policy', p. 237.

[91] Indeed, the FTA confirms the status of Korea as a developed country, by expressly excluding any reliance on special and differential treatment provisions in the WTO Agreements; see EU–Korea FTA, Articles 2.12 and 6.12.

[92] IBM Belgium, in association with DMI, TAC & TICON, *Trade Sustainability Impact Assessment of the Free Trade Agreement to be negotiated between the European Community and the Republic of Korea, Final Report*, pp. 15–16.

[93] See, for example, the comments of Marín Durán in Chapter 8, Hae-Won Jun in Chapter 11 and Morgera in Chapter 12 of this volume.

relations between the EU and Korea. However, it is clear that both of these instruments require measures to be taken by both sides, if they are to be fully implemented. Moreover, the two partners will also have to manage their ongoing relationship and deal with questions of interpretation and application, as they arise. Each policy area will have its own challenges, and the various contributions to this book will highlight key questions and issues that arise in particular policy areas.

Part 1 of this book is intended to give a background to the development of EU–Korea relations and the pursuance of trade and economic policy by each of these two actors. It considers the internal processes, which dictate the evolution of trade and economic policy. In Chapter 2, Justyna Lasik and Colin Brown introduce the trade policy framework of the EU and the steps that have been taken in negotiating and implementing a new set of RTAs, in light of the new institutional framework established by the Lisbon Treaty. They highlight the pioneering nature of the EU–Korea FTA, as the first RTA to be implemented under these new procedures. Chapter 3 then discusses the trade policy framework for the Republic of Korea. In this context, Younsik Kim contrasts the passage of the EU–Korea FTA with the Korea–US FTA, and he points towards the need for greater transparency in the treaty negotiation and implementation process, in order to avoid some of the problems that have arisen in the past.

The main focus of Part 2 of this book is bilateral trade and economic cooperation. This is, perhaps, the most prolific form of cooperation at the international and regional level. In terms of EU–Korea relations, this area is now governed by the FTA and related agreements. This part of the book will analyse the provisions of the FTA in the context of existing multilateral disciplines, as well as comparing the EU–Korea FTA to other examples of regional economic integration.

The contributions to this Part will also explore the innovative approaches that are taken by the FTA in relation to issues that are already addressed at the multilateral level, as well as those areas where the FTA goes beyond existing multilateral disciplines. Chapter 4 contains a broad overview of the content and structure of the FTA which is intended to set the scene for the more detailed analyses in subsequent chapters. This chapter also explains the dispute settlement procedures which apply to most disputes arising under the FTA, emphasising the legal nature of EU–Korea trade relations.

The other contributions in this Part look, in more detail, at particular aspects of EU–Korea economic relations. In Chapter 5, Boris Rigod considers the provisions of the FTA, which aim to liberalise trade in goods between the parties – a core objective of the Agreement. The chapter highlights the innovative nature of many of the FTA provisions on trade facilitation and non-tariff barriers, which are likely to lead to substantial economic integration over time. However, he also notes the 'incompleteness' of the FTA and the need to pursue ongoing cooperation on non-tariff barriers to trade, in order to ensure that the goals of the Agreement are fully achieved.

Chapters 6 to 8 deal with several of the 'WTO-plus' issues, which are addressed by the EU–Korea FTA. In Chapter 6, Jae Ho Sung looks at the provisions on subsidies and competition policy in the FTA and related instruments, whereas Chapter 7 considers the way in which investment promotion and protection is tackled, as well as the opportunities for future developments in this area. In Chapter 8, Gracia Marín Durán analyses those provisions of the FTA which are dedicated to trade and sustainable development. At the same time as explaining that this innovative part of the Agreement denotes a shift in EU policy towards the regulation of trade and sustainable development, Marín Durán deftly draws comparisons with the practice of other international actors in considering how to balance economic considerations with broader policy goals relating to labour rights and environmental protection.

Part 3 of this book moves beyond the realm of trade and economics, in order to look at other aspects of EU–Korea cooperation. The chapters in this Part emphasise the broad nature of the EU–Korea strategic partnership. They focus on the 2010 Framework Agreement, as the legal instrument which mandates cooperation across a range of topics. The contributions critically discuss what can be achieved at the bilateral level and how arrangements between the two partners will interact with their existing and overlapping commitments at the multilateral level.

Chapter 9 provides a general outline of the Framework Agreement and the types of obligations it contains, whereas Chapter 10 looks in more detail at the institutional framework, created by the Framework Agreement. In this regard, Young Lo Ko considers the links between the different agreements which underpin EU–Korea affairs, asking how we can achieve a coherent development of the strategic partnership. He also analyses the significance of the essential elements clause found in the Framework Agreement and how it can be used to uphold the values which underpin the relationship.

In Chapter 11, Hae-Won Jun considers the opportunities for cooperation between the EU and Korea in the fields of international peace and security, with particular emphasis on the non-proliferation of weapons of mass destruction, the non-proliferation of small arms and light weapons and counter-terrorism. She highlights that these are emerging areas for common action, but that cooperation will only be successful if the parties develop a relationship of mutual trust and a deeper understanding of their shared values.

Chapters 12 and 13 both reflect upon the scope of EU–Korea cooperation in relation to the protection of the environment. Elisa Morgera takes a general look at environmental cooperation, placing the EU–Korea relationship in the broader context of EU practice with third countries, whereas David Rossati undertakes a more detailed analysis of EU–Korea cooperation in the field of climate change. In Chapter 12, Morgera concludes that the EU has a tendency to use its bilateral partnerships to support the development and implementation of international environmental law, and she foresees the potential for the EU and Korea to build alliances on a range of environmental issues, which she outlines in some depth. In Chapter 13, Rossati also notes the commonalities in the positions of the EU and Korea on climate change mitigation and adaption. However, he warns that tensions could arise between action taken by the parties to promote climate change mitigation and adaption, on the one hand, and the rules and principles on trade liberalisation found in the FTA, on the other hand, and, therefore, he calls for close coordination between the various institutions created within the framework of EU–Korea relations, in order to avoid any conflicts.

The final chapter contains an analysis of the way in which the FTA and the Framework Agreement deal with personal data protection. This is an issue where states have taken different views on the correct balance to be achieved between competing policy goals. In Chapter 14, Il Hwan Kim describes developments in relation to data protection law in both the EU and Korea and outlines how the institutional provisions of the Framework Agreement can be used to harness compatibility between the regulations of the two parties. Thus, this policy area provides another example of an issue which could benefit from strengthened cooperation and which could lead to closer integration between the EU and Korea.

2

The EU–Korea FTA: The Legal and Policy Framework in the European Union

*Justyna Lasik and Colin Brown**

1 INTRODUCTION

The Free Trade Agreement (FTA) between the European Union and its Member States of the one part, and the Republic of Korea on the other part[1] is the most important trade agreement concluded by the European Union (EU) since the conclusion of the Marrakesh Agreement establishing the World Trade Organization (WTO) in 1994. This contribution seeks to place the EU–Korea FTA in respect to the policy and the legal framework of the European Union.[2]

In October 2006, the European Union announced its renewed trade strategy in the Global Europe Communication.[3] It established an integrated approach, detailing how to effectively combine internal and external policies, in order to create a favourable climate for the development of the EU's competitiveness. Among the most important elements of this new policy framework was the direction to launch Free Trade Agreements (FTAs) on an unprecedented scale in the EU. Based on this strategy, Korea emerged as one of the EU's priority FTA partners. Besides Korea, negotiations with other countries and regions in Asia and elsewhere followed. However, the negotiations with Korea were finalised first, and, thanks to its ground-breaking

---

* The views reflected in this contribution are personal and should not necessarily be attributed to the European Commission. This contribution is dedicated to the memory of our friend and colleague, Marjorie Niffe. Marjorie was the lawyer in the Directorate-General for Trade, responsible for the negotiations on the EU–Korea FTA. Her untimely passing came before the Agreement was provisionally applied.

[1] Free Trade Agreement between the European Union and its Member States of the one part, and the Republic of Korea of the other part (EU–Korea FTA) [2011] OJ L127/6, 14 May 2011, p. 6.

[2] The term 'European Union' or 'EU' is used throughout this contribution for the sake of clarity, even when, before the entry into force of the Treaty of Lisbon, the appropriate term would be 'European Communities'.

[3] European Commission, *Communication on Global Europe: Competing in the World. A Contribution to the EU's Growth and Job Strategy* (Global Europe Strategy), Document COM(2006)567 final, Brussels, 4 October 2006, endorsed by the Council of the European Union, 'Conclusions on Global Europe – Competing in the World' (14799/06) 13 November 2006.

provisions, the EU–Korea FTA created, if not a benchmark, then, at least, a reference point for any future FTA in the EU.

As regards the legal framework in the European Union, the Agreement is significant, in the sense that negotiations were initiated and completed before the entry into force of the Treaty of Lisbon,[4] while the signature, provisional application and conclusion of the Agreement took place, or will take place after the entry into force of the Treaty of Lisbon. This meant that there could be no doubt that the European Parliament should be involved, both in the procedure for ratification of the FTA, but also as co-legislator for the Safeguard Regulation, which accompanies the Agreement. It was also the first time in recent practice that the European Union adopted a Safeguard Regulation[5] accompanying the entry into force of an FTA.[6] Furthermore, the entry into the force of the Lisbon Treaty made further changes to the environment in which trade policy operated, notably, through the changes to the regime for the adoption of implementing and delegated acts.[7] The Safeguard Regulation was the first regulation in any policy field, and in trade policy, specifically, to be made subject to the new regime for implementing acts.

2 THE POLICY FRAMEWORK

2.1 Developments in EU trade policy

Whilst the idea of negotiating FTAs is not new for the EU, the considerations that accompanied the decision on how, and with whom, to negotiate have significantly evolved over time. Since the establishment of the European Common Commercial Policy, the EU has successfully negotiated many broader agreements, such as Association agreements with its neighbouring countries, which aimed at bringing these countries closer to the EU and included a free trade component. While the EU has engaged in talks with African, Caribbean and Pacific countries to negotiate Economic

---

[4] Treaty of Lisbon amending the Treaty on European Union and the Treaty establishing the European Community (Treaty of Lisbon) [2007] OJ C306/1, 17 December 2007.

[5] Regulation (EU) No. 511/2011 of the European Parliament and the Council of 11 May 2011 implementing the bilateral safeguard clause of the Free Trade Agreement between the European Union and its Member States and the Republic of Korea (Safeguard Regulation) [2011] OJ L145/19, 31 May 2011.

[6] The previous examples of such regulations being adopted concerned agreements with Turkey, Switzerland and Norway, in the late 1960s or 1970s. There are also regulations adopted to implement Stabilisation and Association Agreements with the Balkan countries, but these simply make a cross reference to the EU Safeguard Regulation (Regulation EC No. 260/2009 on the common rules for imports [2009] OJ L84/1, 31 March 2009), rather than create their own safeguard mechanisms.

[7] See the Consolidated Version of the Treaty for the Functioning of the European Union (TFEU) [2010] OJ C83/47, 30 March 2010, Articles 290, 291.

Partnership Agreements,[8] which were, undoubtedly, development-driven, it has also completed more commercially motivated trade agreements with both Mexico[9] and Chile.[10] However, many of these agreements, whilst serving legitimate objectives, were rather limited in scope and could not become a basis for improving the European Union's external competitiveness and help in creating much-needed jobs and growth in the twenty-first century.[11]

The EU focused on the multilateral system, from the creation of the Common Commercial Policy from the late 1960s onwards. Consequently, the WTO Doha Development Agenda (DDA), launched in November 2001, became the priority for the EU. This approach was further strengthened when Pascal Lamy, while serving as EU Trade Commissioner, put new bilateral trade initiatives on hold. The European Commission's belief was that new bilateral negotiations might weaken the negotiating power of the EU at the WTO level. However, the rather slow progress in the multilateral negotiations within the WTO, and the unlikeliness of reaching any swift conclusion, encouraged EU decision-makers to develop a new strategy, in order to address new challenges and reflect the changes in the geographical focus of trade. The EU was also fully aware that other countries, such as the United States, were moving ahead with their bilateral trade agenda and were focusing on regions with high economic growth and market potential, particularly in Asia. The EU could not afford to be left behind.

2.2 Renewed EU trade policy: Global Europe and the focus on the new generation of FTAs

On 4 October 2006, under the leadership of Peter Mandelson, then EU Trade Commissioner, the European Commission adopted its new trade policy.

The basis of this Communication was the renewed Lisbon Strategy of 2005, which set out the necessary actions that were required to deliver growth and jobs in the EU. The Global Europe Communication focused on the external aspects of how trade policy can contribute to boosting growth

---

[8] For an analysis of the EU–CARIFORUM EPA, including an overview of the process, see A. Beviglia Zampetti and J. Lodge (eds), *The CARIFORUM-EU Economic Partnership Agreement: A Practitioners' Analysis* (Alpen aan den Rijn: Kluwer Law International, 2011).

[9] Economic Partnership, Political Coordination and Cooperation Agreement between the European Community and its Member States, of the one part, and the United Mexican States, of the other part – Final Act – Declarations (EU–Mexico Agreement) [2000] OJ L276/45 28 October 2000.

[10] Agreement establishing an association between the European Community and its Member States, of the one part, and the Republic of Chile, of the other part – Final Act (EU–Chile Agreement) [2002] OJ L352/3 30 December 2002.

[11] European Commission, *Global Europe Strategy*, p. 11.

and creating jobs.[12] It also 'stressed the need to adapt the tools of EU trade policy to new challenges, to engage new partners, to ensure Europe remains open to the world and other markets open to us'.[13]

The Communication pointed out two critical and interlinked requirements, which were indispensable, in order to ensure the EU's competitiveness:[14]

> First having the right internal policies, which reflect the external competitive challenge and maintain our openness to trade and investment. Second, ensuring greater openness and fair rules in other markets, in particular our future major trading partners. Both must be underpinned by transparent and effective rules – domestic, bilateral and multilateral.

The Global Europe Communication proposed, *inter alia*, a specific action plan for EU external competitiveness, focusing on both EU internal and external dimensions. The launch of a new generation of FTAs, based on economic considerations, was high on the agenda.[15]

This renewed strategy also marked an important shift in the EU's trade policy. While reaffirming the importance of, and the EU's commitment to, the multilateral system and to the WTO DDA, it removed the *de facto* moratorium on launching new bilateral trade negotiations, which had existed under Pascal Lamy's leadership as EU Trade Commissioner, and the new strategy outlined the EU's plans to engage in a new generation of FTAs.[16]

The belief expressed by the European Commission was that the multilateral and bilateral negotiations can go hand-in-hand, and FTAs can complement the WTO system, if approached with care. According to the Global Europe Communication, to achieve a positive impact, the future FTAs had to: 1. be comprehensive in scope; 2. substantially liberalise all trade; and 3. go beyond the current WTO provisions.[17] The added value of FTAs, compared to the multilateral system, was expected to emerge from areas which were not yet ready to be the subject of multilateral discussions and, in fact, remained entirely or partially outside the scope of the WTO.[18]

---

[12] Ibid. p. 2.

[13] Ibid.

[14] Ibid. p.4.

[15] Besides the new FTAs, Global Europe proposed seven other specific areas where progress was expected with regard to EU external initiatives: WTO Doha Development Agenda (DDA), transatlantic trade and competitiveness, relations with China, enforcement of Intellectual Property Rights (IPR), renewed market access strategy, public procurement and the review of the Trade Defence Instruments; for more information see European Commission, *Global Europe Strategy*, pp. 10–14.

[16] European Commission Staff Working Document, Report on progress achieved on the Global Europe strategy, 2006–2010, Document SEC(2010) 1268 final, 9 November 2010, p. 3.

[17] European Commission, *Global Europe Strategy*, p. 10.

[18] These disciplines included investment, public procurement and regulatory issues, such as competition and IPR enforcement.

An important aspect of the new generation of FTAs was the focus on solid economic considerations when selecting new FTA partners. This was in contrast to previous EU agreements, where economic criteria were one of many factors and not the one single most important factor that was being analysed. The criteria included:

(a) market potential, in terms of the size of economy and the economic growth; and (b) the level of existing tariff and non-tariff barriers.[19]

An additional important aspect, in deciding with whom to negotiate, was the negotiations that the EU's potential FTA partners were conducting or envisaging with EU competitors and the likely impact of such negotiations on the EU's position in the market.

Despite the strong focus on economic criteria in selecting FTA partners, political considerations were not abandoned. It was stipulated in the Communication that FTA provisions should form 'an integral part of the overall relations with the country or region concerned'[20] and that 'the best way to achieve this within the wider institutional architecture will need to be established on a case-by case basis'.[21] In practice, this essentially implied that most, if not all, EU FTAs would be accompanied, where not already in place, by a political agreement, such as a Framework Agreement or a Partnership and Cooperation Agreement.

The content of the new generation of the EU FTAs, as stipulated in the Global Europe Communication, was intended to be comprehensive and ambitious in terms of coverage. The objective was to ensure the highest possible trade liberalisation, not only with regard to tariff and non-tariff barriers, but also in the area of services and investment. Additionally, the EU indicated that it would seek at least full parity with the FTAs that the prospective partners negotiated with EU's main competitors in a given market.[22]

In terms of scope, the future – so-called new generation – FTAs were supposed to, besides eliminating tariffs, deal with the existing non-tariff barriers, by ensuring or improving regulatory convergence. Strong provisions on Intellectual Property Rights (IPR), including enforcement, and competition were highlighted as key components of future EU FTAs. Additionally, in the Global Europe Communication, the Commission set out its aim of seeking simpler Rules of Origin in the new agreements, which would reflect the current reality, such as the changing patterns of supply chains,

---

[19] European Commission Directorate-General Trade, *EU–South Korea Free Trade Agreement: A Quick Reading Guide* (October 2010), p. 1, www.trade.ec.europa.eu/doclib/docs/2009/october/tradoc_145203.pdf (accessed 29 June 2012).

[20] European Commission, *Global Europe Strategy*, p. 12.

[21] Ibid.

[22] Ibid. p. 11.

due to globalisation. The EU's new FTA policy also insisted on the need to strengthen the provisions concerning correlation between trade and sustainable development.

The EU recognised the need for prospective FTA partners to share the EU's level of ambition, in terms of the content and scope of the Agreement, before the negotiations were launched, in order to avoid creating a discrepancy in expectations. The analysis of the substantive starting point for any future negotiations was to be made on a case-by-case basis. The decision to launch the negotiations took into consideration whether the objectives of the negotiations were implementable by both partners.

In pursuing the new policy, the EU has first targeted large emerging countries, as these were quickly becoming the new drivers of the world economy, while still maintaining some barriers to foreign competition. Based on the criteria stipulated in the Global Europe Communication, several countries and regions emerged as priority FTA partners. Korea, ASEAN and India, with their relatively high level of protection in terms of tariff and non-tariff barriers, combined with significant market potential, became priority partners for FTA negotiations. This was the first time that the EU was considering launching FTA negotiations with countries in Asia. From the choices made, it became clear that the EU, with its renewed trade policy, was turning to Asia.

The Global Europe Communication also identified other candidates which were suitable for FTA negotiations, but which were not located in Asia, such as Russia, and it reconfirmed MERCOSUR and the Gulf Co-operation Council (GCC) as potential partners.[23] It stipulated that although China met many of the criteria, special attention had to be paid to addressing both the opportunities and the challenges arising from the EU–China relations, via different channels than an FTA.[24]

2.3 Implementation of the Global Europe Strategy and new initiatives in the EU's FTA policy

As a result of the Global Europe Strategy, the European Commission has launched negotiations of several new generation FTAs.

Korea, with its offensive FTA policy initiated back in 2003[25] and its ongoing FTA negotiation with the United States,[26] was a natural priority and a suitable choice for an FTA partner, and it was ready to engage, almost immediately. The European Commission obtained negotiating directives

---

[23] The EU had already been negotiating with MERCOSUR and the GCC for some time.
[24] See European Commission Staff Working Document, *Report on Progress Achieved on the Global Europe Strategy, 2006–2010*, p. 15.
[25] See Chapter 3 of this volume.
[26] Korea and the United States announced the negotiations on 2 February 2006 and concluded the talks on 1 April 2007.

from the Council of the European Union to launch negotiations with Korea in April 2007, and, already, in May 2007, the negotiations between the EU and Korea were officially inaugurated. These were probably one of the fastest negotiations conducted by the EU to-date, as they were completed within two years of their launch. In parallel to the FTA negotiations, the EU and Korea also managed to upgrade their political relations and completed negotiations on an update of the existing Framework Agreement on Trade and Co-operation.[27]

The FTA negotiations with India and ASEAN followed suit and were also inaugurated over the course of 2007. However, they were not advancing as fast as the negotiations with Korea. At the time of writing, negotiations with India are still currently ongoing.[28] As far as ASEAN is concerned, in December 2009, the EU moved away from negotiating with the ten members of ASEAN as a group and started the process of initiating negotiations with individual members. Up to now, such talks have been launched with Singapore (negotiations are close to completion) and Malaysia, while others are expected to follow.

Besides re-launching negotiations with the GCC and MERCOSUR, in May 2009, the European Commission, based on negotiating directives from the Council, also launched negotiations with Canada. Although Canada had not previously been indicated as a priority partner, it fulfilled the economic criteria indicated in the Global Europe Communication. The Commission also managed to successfully complete negotiations with Peru, Colombia and Central America, in 2010.

The implementation of the Global Europe Strategy, in terms of FTAs, is not yet completed, but it can definitely be stated that the EU–Korea FTA became the first, and the most significant, deliverable to-date. Once all of the FTAs initiated since the Global Europe Communication are finalised, the proportion of EU trade covered by FTAs will move, from a quarter in 2006, to more than half.[29] The outcome of the negotiations and the implementation of the future agreements will prove whether they will deliver on the promise of ensuring greater market access for EU exporters, with the EU–Korea FTA being the first success story.

It is worth mentioning that in November 2010, the Commission presented an update of the EU's trade policy, in a document entitled *Trade, Growth and World Affairs, Trade Policy as a Core Component of the EU's 2020 Strategy.*[30] This

[27] See www.ec.europa.eu/trade/creating-opportunities/bilateral-relations/countries/korea/ (accessed 29 June 2012). For discussions of the negotiations of the 2010 Framework Agreement, see Chapters 9 and 10 of this volume.

[28] See www.trade.ec.europa.eu/doclib/docs/2006/december/tradoc_118238.pdf (accessed 29 June 2012).

[29] Calculation based on EU trade figures, available from EUROSTAT.

[30] European Commission, *Communication on Trade, Growth and World Affairs, Trade Policy as a Core Component of the EU's 2020 Strategy*, Document COM(2010) 612, 9 November 2010.

document, while building on the Global Europe Communication, reaffirmed the EU's commitment to the WTO, and, as one of the key goals, it stipulated the need to complete the ongoing FTA negotiating agenda. It also high-lighted the need to 'make good use of fast growing regional trade in East Asia and pursue our [the EU's] strategic economic interests in that region'[31] and announced the EU's plans to expand and conclude bilateral negotiations with ASEAN countries and deepen EU's trade and investment with the Far East.

3 THE LEGAL AND INSTITUTIONAL FRAMEWORK

3.1 Introduction

The legal and institutional background for the negotiation and implementa-tion of the EU–Korea FTA in the EU was of crucial importance for three reasons. Firstly, given that it was the first agreement in the field of trade to be subject to the new procedures, which were applicable as a result of the entry into force of the Treaty of Lisbon, a number of challenges were posed as regards untested procedures. Secondly, being the second largest trade agreement ever concluded by the EU, a number of substantive issues required attention during the process. These included the position of the European Parliament in safeguard investigations and the operation of certain provisions of the FTA. Thirdly, the procedure for ratification was closely watched, as the procedure was likely to set down the framework for the rati-fication of future FTAs. The various elements that make up the procedural and institutional framework are taken up in the following sections of this contribution.

3.2 The granting of negotiating authorisation and negotiating directives

Within the EU, the European Commission is responsible for the conduct of negotiations. The Commission can only formally start negotiations, once it has received negotiating authorisation from the Council. Furthermore, the process of ratification of an agreement only starts once the Commission has adopted a proposal to sign and conclude an agreement.

At the time that the Commission made the request for negotiating author-isation for an agreement with Korea, it was Article 133(3) of the Treaty establishing the European Communities, which was applicable:

> 3. Where agreements with one or more States or international organisations need to be negotiated, the Commission shall make recommendations to the Council, which shall authorise the Commission to open the necessary negotiations. The Council and the Commission shall be responsible for ensuring that the agree-

---

[31] Ibid. p.10.

ments negotiated are compatible with internal Community policies and rules.

The Commission shall conduct these negotiations in consultation with a special committee appointed by the Council to assist the Commission in this task and within the framework of such directives as the Council may issue to it. The Commission shall report regularly to the special committee on the progress of negotiations. The relevant provisions of Article 300 shall apply.

Negotiating authorisation for the EU–Korea FTA was granted on 23 April 2007. The Council also issued negotiating directives (based on a draft negotiating directives prepared by the Commission), which set out the framework for the EU's objectives in the negotiations.[32]

3.3 The conduct of the negotiations

The special committee, which the Commission was required to consult, was the '133 committee', renamed as the 'Trade Policy Committee' since the entry into force of the Treaty of Lisbon. This committee meets, at a minimum, once a week, and it is made up of Member State official, who are responsible for trade policy. It meets at the level of the most senior officials responsible for trade policy once a month.[33] Moreover, it has specific formations (for example, for services and investment), which are responsible for following developments on specific sectors of trade policy. During the FTA negotiations, the Commission reported regularly to the Committee, providing debriefings of negotiation sessions with Korea and consulting on draft negotiating texts.

Within the European Commission, the Directorate General for Trade was responsible for the negotiations, under the political guidance and responsibility of the European Commissioner responsible for Trade.[34] Within the Directorate General for Trade, the Directorate and unit responsible for bilateral trade relations with Korea was responsible for the overall coordination, while other units (and other Directorate Generals in the Commission) were responsible for negotiations on specific chapters, for example, non-tariff barriers and services.

Substantive negotiations were completed in March 2009. A legal review of the Agreement continued from then until September 2009, and the Agreement was formally initialled by Commissioner Ashton on 15 October 2009.[35] At this point, the Agreement was complete and could then be submitted for the respective ratification procedures.

---

[32] The negotiating directives are confidential.

[33] For the Commission, this is the Director General of the Directorate General for Trade.

[34] This was Mr Peter Mandelson, at the time of the initiation of negotiations, Mrs Catherine Ashton at the time of the completion of the negotiations, and Mr Karel De Gucht, at the time of the signature and provisional application of the Agreement.

[35] Press release: EU and South Korea initial free trade deal, Brussels, 15 October 2009, www.trade.ec.europa.eu/doclib/docs/2009/october/tradoc_145103.pdf (accessed 2 July 2012).

3.4 Signature and conclusion of the agreement

Article 218 of the TFEU sets out the framework for the ratification proce-dure for agreements negotiated by the EU. It provides, in relevant part:

> 5. The Council, on a proposal by the negotiator, shall adopt a decision authorising the signing of the agreement and, if necessary, its provisional application before entry into force.
> 6. The Council, on a proposal by the negotiator, shall adopt a decision conclud-ing the agreement. Except where agreements relate exclusively to the common foreign and security policy, the Council shall adopt the decision concluding the agreement:
> (a) after obtaining the consent of the European Parliament in the following cases:
> [. . .]
> (v) agreements covering fields to which either the ordinary legislative procedure applies, or the special legislative procedure where consent by the European Parliament is required. The European Parliament and the Council may, in an urgent situation, agree upon a time-limit for consent.

Given that ordinary legislative procedure is required for the adoption of legislation in the field of the Common Commercial Policy, the Parliament's consent for the EU–Korea FTA was required, in the wake of the Treaty of Lisbon, pursuant to Article 218(6)(a)(v). The EU–Korea FTA was, therefore, the first trade agreement, after the entry into force of the Treaty of Lisbon, requiring this consent. In reality, however, it was relatively likely that the Parliament's consent would have been required, even if the Agreement had been presented before the entry into force of the Treaty of Lisbon. This is because there was a requirement in Article 300 of the Treaty estab-lishing the European Community that the consent of the Parliament was required for 'agreements establishing a specific institutional framework by organising cooperation procedures'.[36] It is possible that the powers granted to the bodies established by the EU–Korea FTA would have meant that the FTA would have qualified under that heading, for the consent of the Parliament.

In any event, the EU–Korea FTA is widely regarded as being the first agreement subject to the Parliament's new powers, pursuant to the entry into force of the Treaty of Lisbon. The political sensitivities inherent in the new institutional balance, established by the Treaty of Lisbon, played a key part in the management of the EU–Korea FTA as regards the European Parliament.

---

[36] This is the provision which was used as the legal basis to request the consent of the European Parliament for the WTO Agreements.

3.5 Provisional application

One of the key issues, which rapidly emerged after the entry into force of the Treaty of Lisbon, was the question of whether the EU–Korea FTA would be provisionally applied, before the Parliament had voted on the Agreement. Article 218(5) of the TFEU permits the European Union to provisionally apply the Agreement, on the basis of a Council decision and, consequently, before Parliament has given its consent. The concern for Parliament was that if the Agreement was provisionally applied before Parliament had given its consent, the pressure on Parliament to accept the FTA would be increased, since the relevant administrations would have started to implement the Agreement, and, more importantly, economic operators would have started to adapt their operations to the new situation. This led to the Commission stating, in the Explanatory Memorandum accompanying the proposals for decision on signature and conclusion:[37]

> As Member States of the European Union will also be party to this Agreement because of certain commitments in the Protocol on Cultural Co-operation, it needs to be ratified by them according to their internal procedures. This will take a considerable period of time. In order to ensure prompt application of the Agreement pending full ratification by the Member States, the Commission proposes to provisionally apply it. In light of the significance of the Agreement, the Commission considers that the Council should send the notifications referred to in Articles 15.10(5)(a) and (b) only after a certain lapse of time so as to allow the European Parliament to express its views on the FTA. The Commission is ready to work with the Council and the EP so that the Agreement can be provisionally applied in 2010.

Additionally, the EU Trade Commissioner, in his intervention at the European Parliament's debate on 6 September 2010 concerning the bilateral safeguard clause in the EU–Korea FTA, indicated, on behalf of the Commission, a commitment to seek the consent of the European Parliament ahead of the provisional application of the FTA:[38]

> I cannot speak for the Council. I can say what the Commission's position is, and we will insist with the Council that it would only do this [i.e. approve provisional application of the FTA] once the safeguard regulation is adopted and Parliament has given its consent to the FTA. That is our clear position. Parliament should ask in the trilogue for the Council itself to engage on this and say that it will not do this before the final vote in Parliament.

---

[37] European Commission, *Proposal for a Council Decision authorising the signature and provisional application of the Free Trade Agreement between the European Union and its Member States and the Republic of Korea*, Document COM(2010)136 final, 9 April 2010, p. 4.

[38] See the full text of the EU Trade Commissioner's intervention, www.europarl.europa.eu/ (accessed 29 June 2012).

However, the Commission's statement was not binding on the Council, which could, of course, have decided to provisionally apply the Agreement before the European Parliament had given its consent. Indeed, it is the practice of the Council to seize the Parliament of an agreement, in order for it to give its consent, only *after* the Council has authorised the signature of the agreement.

In the end, the Council was strongly of the view that the Agreement could not be provisionally applied before the safeguard regulation implementing the Agreement was in place. Hence, Article 3(2) of the Council decision of 16 September 2010 on the signing, on behalf of the European Union, and provisional application of the Free Trade Agreement between the European Union and its Member States, of the one part, and the Republic of Korea, of the other part (2011/265/EU)[39] provided:

> In order to determine the date of provisional application the Council shall fix the date by which the notification referred to in Article 15.10.5 of the Agreement is to be sent to Korea. That notification shall include references to those provisions which cannot be provisionally applied.
>
> The Council shall coordinate the effective date of provisional application with the date of the entry into force of the proposed Regulation of the European Parliament and of the Council implementing the bilateral safeguard clause of the EU–Korea Free Trade Agreement.

This regulation, of course, had to go through the co-decision procedure (that is, it needed to be approved by both the Council and Parliament), and the Parliament arranged its proceedings, such that it approved the Safeguard Regulation and gave its consent to the Agreement in the same session. In any event, as part of the discussions leading to the adoption of the Council Decision on Signature, it was agreed that provisional application would start on 1 July 2011, provided that the Safeguard Regulation was in place at that time.[40] This gave the European Parliament time to complete its consent procedure, free from pressure from the Council.

3.6 Competence and the scope of provisional application

In making its proposal for the signature and conclusion of the EU–Korea FTA, the European Commission did not claim exclusive competence for the European Union. Had it successfully claimed exclusive competence, the Agreement would only require ratification in the EU system (that is, on the

---

[39] Council Decision of 16 September 2010 on the signing, on behalf of the European Union, and provisional application of the Free Trade Agreement between the European Union and its Member States, of the one part, and the Republic of Korea, of the other part (2011/265/EU) (Council Decision on Signature) [2011] OJ L127/1, 14 May 2011.

[40] See the Notice concerning the provisional application of the Free Trade Agreement between the European Union and its Member States, of the one part, and the Republic of Korea, of the other part [2011] OJ L168/1, 28 June, 2011.

basis of the Council decision on signature, the Parliament's consent and the Council decision, upon conclusion). Given that the Commission did not claim exclusive competence, this meant that the FTA also has to be ratified by the twenty-seven Member States of the European Union. At the time of writing, fourteen of twenty-seven Member States have sent their notification of ratification of the Agreement by their national parliaments.[41] The Council only adopts the decision on conclusion, hence, completing the ratification process in the EU, once all Member States have completed their individual ratification procedures.

However, the Commission only accepted that the Member State competence covered a limited number of areas. In the explanatory memorandum to the Commission's proposal, the Commission refers to 'certain commitments in the Protocol on Cultural Co-operation',[42] as falling under Member States competence. The question that was then posed was, given the Agreement would be provisionally applied before the Member State ratification process was advanced, what would be the extent of provisional application, assuming that it was defined?

The EU–Korea FTA marks a break from previous practice, because the Agreement specifically requires the identification of which parts of the Agreement will not be provisionally applied and, hence, by definition, those which will be provisionally applied. Specifically, Article 15.10(b) of the EU–Korea FTA provides:

> In the event that certain provisions of this Agreement cannot be provisionally applied, the Party which cannot undertake such provisional application shall notify the other Party of the provisions which cannot be provisionally applied. Notwithstanding subparagraph (a), provided the other Party has completed the necessary procedures and does not object to provisional application within 10 days of the notification that certain provisions cannot be provisionally applied, the provisions of this Agreement which have not been notified shall be provisionally applied the first day of the month following the notification.

This is the first trade agreement, in the recent practice of the EU, which requires an identification of those provisions which should *not* be provisionally applied. This evolution was linked to a clarification in the categorisation of competences within the European Union. Article 2 of the TFEU has clarified that in addition to exclusive competence, a number of other areas fall under the notion of shared competence. This is defined in Article 2(2) of the TFEU as:

---

[41] These are listed as Austria, Bulgaria, Cyprus, Czech Republic, Denmark, Estonia, UK, Hungary, Ireland, Latvia, Malta, Netherlands, Portugal and Slovakia. For more information, see www.consilium.europa.eu/policies/agreements/search-the-agreements-database?comman d=details&lang=en&aid=2010036&doclang=EN (accessed 10 June 2012).

[42] European Commission, *Proposal for a Council Decision authorising the signature and provisional application of the Free Trade Agreement between the European Union and its Member States and the Republic of Korea*, p. 4.

When the Treaties confer on the Union a competence shared with the Member States in a specific area, the Union and the Member States may legislate and adopt legally binding acts in that area. The Member States shall exercise their competence to the extent that the Union has not exercised its competence. The Member States shall again exercise their competence to the extent that the Union has decided to cease exercising its competence.

Article 4(2) TFEU lists those areas which are subject to shared competence. It is immediately obvious that to the extent that the provisions of the FTA were not covered by exclusive competence of the European Union, and, in particular, the EU's Common Commercial Policy, then they would be covered by the EU's shared competence. The result, looking at Article 2(2) of the TFEU, is that the Union could potentially act in all areas, other than simply those specifically reserved for the Member States. In the EU–Korea FTA, the only provisions which fell into that category were certain limited provisions of the Protocol on Cultural Co-operation. As a consequence, the Union was in a position to provisionally apply virtually all of the EU–Korea FTA, either as a matter of exclusive or shared competence. The only provisions which were not provisionally applied were the provisions of the Protocol on Cultural Co-operation and certain provisions on the criminal enforcement of intellectual property rights, given their perceived sensitivity for Member States. Consequently, Article 3(2) of the Council Decision on Signature reads:

> 1. The Agreement shall be applied on a provisional basis by the Union as provided for in Article 15.10.5 of the Agreement, pending the completion of the procedures for its conclusion. The following provisions shall not be provisionally applied:
> — Articles 10.54 to 10.61 (criminal enforcement of intellectual property rights),
> — Articles 4(3), 5(2), 6(1), 6(2), 6(4), 6(5), 8, 9 and 10 of the Protocol on cultural cooperation.

In order to provide that the extent of provisional application did not have a precedential effect, the Council Decision on Signature also included a recital, stating that the scope of provisional application should not be understood as affecting the division of competence between the Union and the Member States:

> (9) The provisional application foreseen in this Decision does not prejudge the allocation of competences between the Union and its Member States in accordance with the Treaties . . .

3.7 *The role of the European parliament in the implementation of the EU–Korea FTA*

The EU–Korea FTA also tested, at least in the field of the EU's Common Commercial Policy, precisely how the European Parliament's consent process would interact with the wider ratification process. As can be seen from Article 218(6) of the TFEU, the Parliament's role in the ratification process is limited to providing, or denying, its consent to the Agreement. Parliament cannot seek to amend the Agreement. This raises the question of if, and how, the Parliament can use its power to give consent to the Agreement to influence, for example, the later implementation of the Agreement.

Over the course of the consent procedure, numerous discussions took place between representatives of the European Parliament and the European Commission. This resulted in a Commission statement, which was recorded in the Parliamentary Resolution on the EU–Korea FTA, and in a Joint Declaration of the Parliament and the Commission on the EU–Korea FTA. These documents were published, as Annexes 1 and 2 to the Safeguard Regulation.[43]

In the Commission statement, the Commission outlines a number of actions that it will take and adopts interpretations of a number of provisions, both of the EU–Korea FTA and of the Safeguard Regulation. This statement could be considered broadly comparable to Statements of Administrative Action in the US system.[44]

The Joint Declaration is, arguably, even more striking. In it, the Commission commits to respond to the adoption, by the European Parliament, of a resolution calling for a safeguard investigation (normally, the Parliament would have no such role in issues relating to the implementation of Union law) and to report, at the request of the responsible committee, on Korea's implementation of the non-tariff barrier and sustainable development commitments. In both of these statements, the Parliament is placing itself in the system for implementing the EU–Korea FTA in the future, something which it is not, as a legislative body, normally called upon to do. However, the effect of the Joint Declaration is to give a structure to any requests by Parliament, for action on a particular issue.[45] Through the Statement and the Declaration, the Parliament has succeeded in using the leverage generated from the consent requirement to create a system, whereby it can ensure a certain oversight of the future implementation of the EU–Korea FTA. In so doing, a precedent for future FTAs has, undoubtedly, been created.

3.8 Direct effect

The Council Decision on Signature is the first decision, after the decision on the WTO Agreements, to address the issue of direct effect in EU law. Direct effect concerns the possibility that individuals may invoke the provisions of

---

[43] Safeguard Regulation, pp. 26–7.

[44] As an example, see the US Statement of Administrative Action on the WTO Agreement, H.Doc. 103-316 (1994), p. 659.

[45] Parliament can always request the Commission to act of its own volition.

the Agreement before Member State or EU courts, in order to argue that a particular law is inconsistent with the Agreement. After much discussion and litigation, the Court of Justice of the European Union decided, in its *Portugal* v. *Council* judgement, that the WTO Agreements did not have direct effect in the European Union.[46]

Given that the EU–Korea FTA incorporates many WTO obligations,[47] the Union institutions had to face the question of whether to take action to seek to prevent the Agreement having direct effect.[48] If the Agreement was considered to have direct effect, then Korean operators (or operators providing Korean goods) would be put in a better position than operators of other countries and EU operators, trading in anything other than Korean goods. Ultimately, the Commission proposed, and the Council accepted, that the Council Decision on Signature should state that the Agreement would not have direct effect. Hence, Article 8 of the Decision states:

> The Agreement shall not be construed as conferring rights or imposing obligations which can be directly invoked before Union or Member State courts and tribunals.

3.9 Use of Article 218(7) of the TFEU

Article 218(7) of the TFEU is a provision which permits the Council to authorise the Commission to approve limited amendments to agreements. The Council may, in so doing, set down the conditions for the Commission to approve such amendments. This is a provision which has been used sparingly in the past. However, the Decision on the signature of the EU–Korea FTA contains two uses of Article 218(7). It does so, firstly, in relation to the extension of the entitlement of Korean works to co-production rights, under EU policies promoting cultural diversity, and, secondly, in relation to the addition of new, protected geographical indications (GIs) to the list that is already established by the FTA. The procedure for the addition of new GIs is relatively unremarkable, since it uses an existing procedure to obtain the approval of new GIs, based on existing policy. The procedure for the entitlement for co-production is striking, however, since it requires unanimity in the Council to permit the continuation of the entitlement to co-production. This was considered appropriate, both because of the very sensitive nature of such matters and because the Agreement would, *de facto*, be concluded by unanimity, given that parts of the Protocol on Cultural Co-operation fall under the exclusive competence of Member States. The relevant excerpts from Recital 6 and Article 4(1) are instructive:

---

[46] Case C-149/96, *Portuguese Republic* v. *Council of the European Union* [1999] ECR I-08395.

[47] See, in particular, the discussion in Chapter 5 of this volume.

[48] The authors understand that in Korea, whilst international agreements can be invoked in domestic courts, they can also be overridden by subsequent legislation.

[. . .] The Commission should be authorised to bring about the termination of the entitlement to co-productions as provided for in Article 5 of the Protocol on Cultural Cooperation unless the Commission determines that the entitlement should be continued and this is approved by the Council pursuant to a specific procedure necessitated both by the sensitive nature of this element of the Agreement and by the fact that the Agreement is to be concluded by the Union and its Member States. [. . .]

The Commission shall provide notice to Korea of the Union's intention not to extend the period of entitlement to co-production pursuant to Article 5 of the Protocol on cultural cooperation following the procedure set out in Article 5(8) thereof unless, on a proposal from the Commission, the Council agrees four months before the end of such period of entitlement to continue the entitlement. If the Council agrees to continue the entitlement this provision shall again become applicable at the end of the renewed period of entitlement. For the specific purposes of deciding on the continuation of the period of entitlement, the Council shall act by unanimity.

3.10 *The adoption of the Korea Safeguard Regulation*

As noted above, the adoption and provisional application of the Agreement was accompanied by the adoption of a regulation setting out the procedures in the EU for applying the bilateral safeguard provisions contained in the FTA. Regulation (EU) No 511/2011 of the European Parliament and of the Council of 11 May 2011 implementing the bilateral safeguard clause of the Free Trade Agreement between the European Union and its Member States and the Republic of Korea (the Safeguard Regulation) entered into force on 1 June 2011 and was applied from the date of provisional application of the Agreement (that is, from 1 July 2011).

The Safeguard Regulation sets out the EU internal procedures for investigations and the eventual imposition of safeguard measures, in the event that the conditions for applying safeguard measures are met. It was considered necessary that this regulation be set in place before the FTA was provisionally applied. The most significant substantive change to the Regulation, from that proposed by the European Commission, was the addition of the possibility for EU industry to lodge a complaint, which, if it satisfies the requirements set down in the Regulation, would require the Commission to open an investigation. This is the first safeguard regulation in the EU which provides for that possibility. Previously, such a possibility was only available in relation to anti-dumping or countervailing duty investigations.

The Safeguard Regulation needed to be adopted by the Council and the European Parliament, on the basis of the ordinary legislative procedure.[49] It was the first major piece of trade legislation proposed and adopted

---

[49] TFEU, Article 294.

subsequent to the entry into force of the Treaty of Lisbon. Political agreement on the Regulation was reached in December 2010. The Parliament approved it on 17 February 2011, at the same time as it gave its consent to the Agreement itself. The Council then formally approved the Regulation on 11 April 2011.

The vote in Parliament was also accompanied by a Statement by the Commission and a Joint Declaration by the Commission and Parliament. These form Annexes I and II to the Regulation. In the latter document, the two institutions agreed that if the Parliament adopts a recommendation to initiate a safeguard investigation, then the Commission will carefully examine whether the conditions for the *ex officio* opening of investigations are fulfilled. If that is not the case, then it will report back to the European Parliament. The Commission Statement involved a number of commitments on implementation of the Regulation, but, more broadly, on other elements of the FTA, such as monitoring the sustainable development requirements of the FTA and the status of the processing zones on the Korean peninsula.

Possibly the most controversial issue during the legislative procedure for the Safeguard Regulation was neither the substantive standards, nor the possibility to permit the industry to lodge a complaint, but, rather, the decision-making scheme. The adoption of the Regulation was set against a broader and very controversial background debate on the decision-making procedures for trade defence measures. Most trade policy regulations, and, in particular, all trade defence regulations, fell outside the scope of the so-called 'Comitology Decision' of 1999.[50] The Commissioner for Trade, Karel De Gucht, in his confirmatory hearings before the Parliament in late 2009, had promised to bring trade policy under the new Comitology Regulation (later to be Regulation 182/2011).[51] The Commission made a proposal, in March 2010, which was intended to bring about such a result. However, it proved particularly controversial with Member States, a significant number of whom were concerned by the main practical effect of the Commission's proposal – changing the voting rule, in order to reject anti-dumping measures from requiring a simple majority of Member States to a qualified majority of Member States (the rule of qualified majority being the standard rule, applying to all other areas of EU decision-making procedures).

In the Commission proposal for the Safeguard Regulation, the

---

[50] Council Decision of 28 June 1999 laying down the procedures for the exercise of implementing powers conferred on the Commission (1999/468/EC) [1999] OJ L184/23, 17 July 1999, recital 12. See, also, Council Decision of 17 July 2006 amending Decision 1999/468/EC laying down the procedures for the exercise of implementing powers by the Commission [2006] OJ L200/11, 22 July 2006.

[51] Regulation (EU) No 182/2011 of the European Parliament and of the Council of 16 February 2011 laying down the rules and general principles concerning mechanisms for control by Member States of the Commission's exercise of implementing powers [2011] OJ L55/13, 28 February 2011.

Commission proposed that the 1999 Comitology Decision would apply (which would be automatically converted to the new system, set out in Regulation 182/2011 – see Article 13, thereof). The Comitology Decision provided for control by the Council and, to a lesser extent, the European Parliament of decisions taken by the Commission, where the Commission has been tasked with execution of legislation adopted by the Council and/ or Parliament.[52] Those Member States, which did not want the comitology regime to apply to trade defence measures at all, were consequently opposed to the Korea Safeguard Regulation being adopted with the references to the 1999 Comitology Decision. In November 2010, however, the outlines of an arrangement on the comitology issue, in general, emerged, with the result that it was accepted that the new Comitology Regulation (182/2011) would apply to trade defence instruments. This arrangement became known at the same time as the discussions between Parliament and the Council on the Korea Safeguard Regulation was coming to a head. In fact, the final negotiations on the Korea Safeguard Regulation took place the day after Parliament approved the new Comitology Regulation. This permitted the negotiators of Parliament and the Council to include references to the new Comitology Regulation in the Korea Safeguard Regulation. Consequently, this made it the first regulation in any EU policy, never mind the Common Commercial Policy, to have its decision-making procedures based on the new Comitology Regulation.

4   CONCLUSION

The EU–Korea FTA is the most significant FTA completed by the EU to-date, not only in terms of its content, but also in terms of the pioneering role that it played in the EU's policy and legal framework. The EU–Korea FTA is the first and, at the time of writing, the only new generation FTA delivered under the Global Europe Strategy. It was also the first trade agreement approved by the EU, under the new rules of the Lisbon Treaty and with the full involvement of the European Parliament. This FTA is the first trade agreement with its implementing provisions being subject to the ordinary legislative procedure, where the European Parliament and not only the Council, as was the case earlier, is involved.

At the EU level, the approval and ratification process of this FTA have undoubtedly created precedents for future EU FTAs to come and have paved the way for greater involvement of the European Parliament, throughout the procedure. The various Commission Declarations that accompanied the Council Decision on signing and provisional application of the FTA, as

---

[52] On the emergence and rationale of comitology, as well as the reforms introduced in the Lisbon Treaty, see P. Craig and G. de Búrca, *EU Law: Text, Cases and Materials* (5th edn) (Oxford: Oxford University Press, 2011), pp.134–41.

well as the Safeguard Regulation, have imposed certain obligations on the Commission, be it an additional reporting requirement or a commitment to include certain provisions in the future FTAs. The ratification process of later FTAs shows that the pattern set by the EU–Korea FTA was not only important in and of itself, but has set down the framework for future FTA ratification processes.[53]

Moreover, this chapter has shown that the complex institutional provisions governing the operation of the EU will continue to influence the oversight and implementation of the EU–Korea FTA. It is not only the Commission and the Member States (through the Council) which will be involved in this process, but the European Parliament has also carved out a role in relation to certain issues addressed by the FTA. The institutional balance between the Commission, the Council and Parliament must, therefore, be borne in mind when considering future developments in EU–Korea relations.

---

[53] The FTAs between the EU and Columbia/Peru and Central America (and their accompanying safeguard regulations), which are, at the time of writing, subject to the ratification process, are almost identical in institutional and legislative approach to the EU–Korea FTA.

3

The Policy and Institutional Framework for FTA Negotiations in the Republic of Korea

Younsik Kim

1 INTRODUCTION

The EU–South Korea Free Trade Agreement (FTA) is one of many FTAs to have been negotiated by the Korean government over the past decade. The purpose of this chapter is to provide an overview of Korea's policy and institutional framework for the negotiation of FTAs. It also makes some suggestions concerning measures that should be taken to ensure the smooth implementation of the EU–Korea FTA in Korea, in favour of the sound long-term development of EU–Korea relations.

Although Korea has negotiated many FTAs for its national prosperity over the last decade, some of these FTAs have provoked serious social conflict. Ironically, several political events related to the negotiation and conclusion of these controversial FTAs have made the Korean market and its society appear unstable to foreign investors and traders, despite the high levels of economic liberalisation achieved through the FTAs themselves. This chapter points out that this uncomfortable reality is created by a lack of democratic participation in the decision-making process for FTA negotiation. The Korean government has responded to the political turmoil created by FTAs, by updating the institutional framework for the negotiation and approval of FTAs. Nevertheless, this chapter argues that the current framework requires the incorporation of still more participatory measures, in order to overcome the fundamental problems rooted in the treaty-making process.

Sections 2 and 3 describe the development of the Korean FTA Road Map and its institutional framework for FTA negotiation. Through a critical evaluation of the current institutional framework, this chapter seeks to identify chronic problems in the treaty-making process. Section 4 will go on to compare the experience of the EU–Korea FTA and the Korea–US FTA, in order to examine how the deficiency in the current framework has influenced the negotiation and conclusion of these two FTAs differently, in accordance with their differing political and social contexts. This analysis implies that the deficiency in the institutional framework for FTA negotiation and conclusion poses a potential risk to the future implementation of the EU–Korea FTA. The chapter will conclude by identifying the general direction the Korean government should choose to take, in order to avoid such possible risks in the future.

2 THE KOREAN FTA ROAD MAP, IN THE CONTEXT OF KOREAN ECONOMIC POLICY

In 2003, Korea established an FTA policy Road Map to increase its access to foreign markets and attract foreign investment.[1] Whilst still participating in the progression of the WTO regime at the multilateral level, the Korean government also began to pursue the negotiation of bilateral FTAs. Having concluded its first FTA with Chile in 2003, Korea upgraded its Road Map to cope with the changing global economic situation. Korea found its access to foreign markets was being impeded by several external factors, including the proliferation of plurilateral or bilateral trade agreements, occasioned by the failure to make significant progress during the Doha Development Round.[2] This increase in trade agreements naturally leads to the emergence of regional economic blocs, as illustrated by the North American Free Trade Agreement (NAFTA). At the same time, Korean industry is losing its competitiveness, as emerging economies, like the BRICs (Brazil, Russia, India and China), became more attractive to global investors and importers. For example, as Korea has become increasingly democratic and developed, in line with OECD countries, it has ceased to enjoy the benefit of cheap labour costs. Moreover, FTA proponents and government officials have assessed that boosting national economic development using Korea's internal economic engine has become difficult, due to the fact that Korea now faces the challenges of a typical developed country: namely, an aging population, a declining workforce and economic polarisation that necessitates more welfare benefits for underprivileged classes.[3] In this situation, the Korean government elected to use FTAs as a means of boosting Korea's economy, by increasing access to foreign markets and attracting more global investments.[4] Consequently, the administration of President Roh Moo-Hyeon

---

[1] Official website for the Ministry of Foreign Affairs and Trade for the Republic of Korea, *FTA Status of ROK*, www.mofat.go.kr/ENG/policy/fta/status/overview/index.jsp ?menu=m_20_80_10 (accessed 15 March 2012).

[2] See the discussion of the current deadlock in WTO negotiations and its impact on bilateralism in Chapter 1 of this volume.

[3] Nakryoon Choi and Hongshik Lee, *A Sectoral Assessment of a Korea–US FTA and Policy Implications for the Korean Economy (Hanmi FTA Hyeobsang-ui Bun-yabyeol Pyeongga-wa Jeongchaeggwaje)* (Seoul: KIEP, 2007), pp. 43–5 (This explains the general scheme of Korean foreign trade and FTA policy). See, also, Hae-Young Lee, In-Kyo Cheong and Nam-Gu Jeong (eds), *KORUS-FTA: Conflicting Truths on One Treaty (Hanmi FTA Hana-ui Hyeobjeong Eosgallin Jinsil)* (Seoul: Sidaeui Chang, 2008) (This maps out the pros and cons of the economic development strategy through FTAs).

[4] Similar policy changes for economic development through liberalisation have been observable in many developing countries since the 1990s. See J. W. Salacuse, 'From Developing

(2003–8) established three principles for the conclusion of FTAs in the FTA Road Map: (1) the strategic, active and simultaneous pursuit of FTAs; (2) the negotiation of comprehensive FTAs; and (3) garnering public support for FTAs.[5]

In accordance with these principles, the Korean government signed a series of 'exploratory' FTAs with Chile and Singapore, on the assumption that they are not expected to have a negative impact on Korea's main industries or its legal system. Korean policy-makers determined whether or not Korea would maintain the FTA-driven development model, by assessing the outcome of these exploratory FTAs,[6] and they found them to have generated more mutual benefits than negative impacts.[7] Then, Korean policy-makers estimated that FTAs with major trading entities, like the EU and the United States (US), could produce even more positive benefits than the previous exploratory FTAs. This assertion is grounded in the fact that trade between Korea and these two major economies constitute a significant part of Korea's total foreign trade.[8] Against this backdrop, Korea and the US agreed to conclude a Free Trade Agreement in 2007, after around fourteen months of negotiations.[9] This Korea–US FTA generated critical momentum for the conclusion of the EU–Korea FTA in 2009.[10]

Countries to Emerging Markets: A Changing Role for Law in the Third World', *International Lawyer*, vol. 33 (1999), pp. 875–90.

[5] See Seongdae Cho, Eunmi Lee, Jinho Myeong and Jinu Park, *FTA Road Map in the Post One-Trillion-Dollar Trade Era (Post-mu-yeog 1jo Dalleo Sidae-ui FTA Lodeumaeb)* (Seoul: KIEP, 2011), pp. 1–6, www.kita.net/newtri2/report/iitreporter_view.jsp?sNo=848 (accessed 15 March 2012).

[6] See, generally, Wonhyuk Lim, 'KORUS FTA: A Mysterious Beginning and an Uncertain Future', *Asian Perspective*, vol. 30 (2000), pp. 175–7; Choi and Lee, *A Sectorial Assessment of a Korea-US FTA and Policy Implications for the Korean Economy*, pp. 41–78 (This explains the general scheme of Korean foreign trade and FTA policy).

[7] Korea Trade-Investment Promotion Agency (KOTRA) estimated that the bilateral trade volume between Korea and Chile increased by 454 per cent (from US$1.6 billion to US$7.2 billion), five years after the conclusion of the Korea–Chile FTA. See KOTRA, *Achievement and Issues of Korea-Chile FTA (Han-chille FTA Seonggwa-wa Sisajeom)* (Seoul: KOTRA, 2009).

[8] See Heungchong Kim, Changsu Lee, Gyuntae Kim, Jungu Kang, Sunchan Park, *An Analysis on the Economic Effects of A Korea–EU FTA and Policy Implications on The Korean Economy (Policy Analyses 2005–2009) (Haneu FTAaui Gyeongjejeog Hyogwa Bunseoggwa Jeongchaegjeog Dae-eungbang-an)* (Seoul: KIEP, 2005); see, also, Choi and Lee, *A Sectoral Assessment of a Korea–US FTA and Policy Implications for the Korean Economy*, pp. 55–77.

[9] The text of the Korea–US FTA is available at www.ustr.gov/trade-agreements/free-trade-agreements/korus-fta (accessed 11 June 2012).

[10] Free Trade Agreement between the European Union and its Member States of the one part, and the Republic of Korea of the other part (EU–Korea FTA) [2011] OJ L127/6, 14 May 2011.

3 THE DEVELOPMENT OF THE KOREAN INSTITUTIONAL FRAMEWORK FOR FTA NEGOTIATIONS

The Korean legislative branch does not usually become involved in the treaty-making process, until the executive branch submits the relevant bill for consent. In the Korean constitutional system, the president has the constitutional power to conclude and ratify treaties,[11] whereas the legislature only has a right to consent to some specifically constitutionally important treaties. These include: 'treaties pertaining to any restriction in sovereignty', 'treaties which will burden the State or the people with an important financial obligation' and 'treaties related to legislative matters'.[12] Although there is no clear doctrinal standard for defining a constitutionally important treaty,[13] in practice, the executive branch almost always submits a bill for legislative consent for FTAs to the National Assembly, because FTAs are considered as a typical type of constitutionally important treaty, which requires legislative approval. Yet, according to the general practice of treaty-making, the executive branch has taken all major steps towards the conclusion of the treaty in accordance with its internal procedures on treaty-making before legislative approval is sought.[14]

Since 2004, the Korean government has negotiated and concluded FTAs, mainly according to the 'Presidential Directive on the FTA Conclusion Procedure'.[15] This administrative rule has been revised to increase public and legislative participation, at times when FTAs have been expected to be controversial. In particular, this directive was amended by the 'Presidential Directive on Deliberations of FTA Conclusion and Implementation' (hereafter, FTA Directive), following the conclusion of the EU–Korea FTA, in

---

[11] Korean Constitution, Article 73: 'The President shall conclude and ratify treaties; accredit, receive or dispatch diplomatic envoys; and declare war and conclude peace'.

[12] Korean Constitution, Article 60: '(1) The National Assembly shall have the right to consent to the conclusion and ratification of treaties pertaining to mutual assistance or mutual security; treaties concerning important international organizations; treaties of friendship, trade and navigation; treaties pertaining to any restriction in sovereignty; peace treaties; treaties which will burden the State or people with an important financial obligation; or treaties related to legislative matters; (2) The National Assembly shall also have the right to consent to the declaration of war, the dispatch of armed forces to foreign states, or the stationing of alien forces in the territory of the Republic of Korea'.

[13] See, generally, Jibong Lim, 'Treaties Requiring the Consent of the Legislature in the Perspective of Constitutional Law – Focusing on the Korean Case (Heonbeopjeok Gwanjeomeseo bon "Gukhoeui Donguireul Yohaneun Joyak" – Urinaraui Gyeongureul Jungsimeuro)', *Public Law (Gongbeobyeongu)*, vol. 32 (2004), pp. 163–78.

[14] See Jibong Lim, 'Korean National Assembly's Control Power in Treaty-Making (Joyakchegyeore Gwanhan Gukhoeui Tongjegwon)', *Constitutional Law Study (Heonbeophagyeongu)*, vol. 14 (2008) pp. 133–42.

[15] Under Korean public law, this form of directive is categorised as an administrative rule or administrative order promulgated by the executive branch, in order to implement the procedures for a particular administration.

order to address certain weak points, such as scant public and legislative participation. However, despite frequent amendments to the administrative rules governing FTA negotiations, the Korean social movement has consistently criticised the participatory deficit, pertaining to the previous institutional framework. During the political debate over the Korea–US FTA, in particular, the Korean opposition parties criticised the secret negotiation and conclusion of the Treaty by a handful of high-ranking diplomats.[16] They argued for the enhancement of public participation and greater control over the overall institutional framework for FTA negotiation and implementation, by stressing more involvement of the National Assembly in decision-making.[17] They considered the passage of legislative statutes governing the FTA-making process as a first step to securing effective control over FTA policy, against the executive branch and the governing party. In January 2012, the governing party and executive branch agreed to pass the 'Conclusion Procedure and Implementation of a Trade Treaty Act' (hereafter, Korean Trade Procedure Act), in order to appease opposition parties. This new statute will be effective from 18 July 2012.

Under the FTA Directive and Korean Trade Procedure Act, the Ministerial Meeting on Foreign Economic Affairs (MMFEA) has the authority to initiate FTA negotiations between Korea and other states. The MMFEA, chaired by the Minister of Strategy and Finance, is composed of Cabinet ministers, who take charge of overall issues pertaining to national economic matters. The Free Trade Agreement Opportunity Committee (FTAOC), established under the FTA Directive, can also recommend that the MMFEA launch FTA negotiations.[18] The Minister for Trade chairs this committee, which is composed of assistant ministers from the relevant ministries, according to Article 5 of the FTA Directive.[19] Assistant ministers attending the FTAOC coordinate the various policies of each ministry, during FTA negotiations.[20] The Korean Trade Procedure Act requires the Minister of Foreign Affairs and Trade to assess the feasibility of concluding the relevant FTA.[21] Although the Korean Trade Procedure Act does not specify who exactly should perform this feasibility assessment, the Minster is likely to assign

---

[16] See Soun-Young Eum, 'The Globalization of Law: The Legal Character of the Treaty-Making Power and of the Consent of the Legislature to Treaty-Making (Beob-ui Segyehwa)', *Democratic Legal Studies (Minjubeophak)*, vol. 32 (2006), pp. 207–8.

[17] See Dong Suk Oh, 'A Critical Study on the Negotiation of Korea–US FTA (Minjujuui Gwanjeomeseo bon HanmiFTA Hyeopsanggwajeongui Munjejeom)', *Democratic Legal Studies (Minjubeophak)*, vol. 32 (2006), pp. 151–82.

[18] See FTA Directive, Articles 13–16.

[19] See, also, Jong Bum Kim, 'Korea's Institutional Framework for FTA Negotiations and Administration: Tariffs and Rules of Origin', in Seung Wha Chang and Won-Mog Choi (eds), *Trade Law and Regulation in Korea* (Cheltenham: Edward Elgar, 2011), p. 165.

[20] Ibid.

[21] See Korean Trade Procedure Act, Article 9.

this task to the FTAOC. This body deliberates on the general orientation of future FTA policy, as well as on the feasibility of concluding relevant FTAs and their national effects.[22] The FTA Directive allows the FTAOC to form a Private Advisory Committee, in which non-governmental trade experts can provide specialist advice.[23] The Private Advisory Committee of the FTAOC could serve as a channel, through which civil society interests may be represented at the inter-ministerial level. The FTAOC's chairperson can appoint advisory committee members from those with extensive knowledge and experience of the international economic sector or from those who can represent the opinions of relevant interest groups.[24] Before negotiations begin, the Minister of Foreign Affairs and Trade should establish plans concerning the conclusion of a trade treaty, known as a 'Trade Treaty Conclusion Plan'.[25] The current system requires a public hearing, before both the establishment of a Trade Treaty Conclusion Plan[26] and before the launch of a proposed FTA negotiation.[27] In addition, the Korea Trade Procedure Act requires the Minister of Foreign Affairs and Trade to establish a Trade Advisory Committee, within the Ministry of Foreign Affairs and Trade.[28]

Established under the control of the Minster of Strategy and Finance, the Free Trade Agreements Domestic Measures Committee (FTADMC) is also designed to obtain public support for the conclusion and ratification of FTAs, through cooperation between government and civil society.[29] The FTADMC provides the public with relevant information on the conclusion of FTAs and considers opinions from various strata of society, whilst supporting legislative activities associated with FTA conclusion, ratification and approval.[30] The FTADMC is supposed to generate a government-civil society partnership, and it is, therefore, composed of both officials and civilians (unlike the FTAOC). Additionally, the Committee is co-chaired by the Minister of Strategy and Finance, together with a civilian member, who is appointed by that Minister.[31] Like the FTAOC, the FTAMDC can form an advisory committee, when deemed necessary.[32] It should report

---

[22] See Kim, 'Korea's Institutional Framework for FTA Negotiations and Administration: Tariffs and Rules of Origin', p. 165.

[23] Ibid.

[24] FTA Directive, Article 10.

[25] Korean Trade Procedure Act, Article 6(1).

[26] Ibid. Article 7.

[27] FTA Directive, Article 12.

[28] Korean Trade Procedure Act, Article 21.

[29] See FTADMC official website, www.fta.korea.kr/kr/intro/greet/01/ (accessed 15 March 2012).

[30] Free Trade Agreements Domestic Measures Committee Decree (FTADMC Decree), Article 2.

[31] Free Trade Agreements Domestic Measures Committee Decree (FTADMC Decree), Article 3.

[32] Ibid. Article 6.

public opinion on FTAs to the President on a regular basis,[33] and it can request cooperation from relevant institutions and groups if it is in need of a specialist opinion or relevant information from government officials or civil experts.[34]

Despite the relatively frequent upgrades in the institutional framework for FTA negotiation, the executive branch could still be said to dominate FTA-making. The decision-making structure for negotiating and concluding these agreements is vulnerable to inappropriate influences from both politics and the economy. Although each ministry in the FTAOC is supposed to represent various social interests in the treaty-making process, they are homogeneous, in the sense that the committee is composed solely of internal government officials. Moreover, government officials must generally follow the political goals of the governing party or they may be ideologically aligned with major business actors. Consequently, urgent social needs tend to be distorted by a small number of government officials or experts, who are inclined to favour certain economic or political interests.

In response to this deficiency, the newly established Korean Trade Procedure Act prescribes that anyone can present opinions concerning a trade treaty or agreement.[35] However, it is unclear whether the authorities have any binding obligation to consider those opinions, because the Act allows the Government to consider such opinions: 'if the government finds the opinions reasonable'.[36] As such, the executive branch, in fact, has fundamental discretion over whether or not to accept public opinion.

Of course, this general clause can mainly be implemented through several committees, whose task is to consider the interests of civil society. However, several of these procedures for participation are used merely as instruments of support for the government decisions of techno-bureaucratic elites. Whilst there are a number of committees through which non-governmental experts can engage in FTA policy-making, there are no clear standards by which such committees can secure their independence or autonomy, as their members are appointed by government officials. As a result, the system remains relatively closed to direct input from civil society. Worse, those committees which are intended to promote government-civil society partnership do not appear to make a substantial contribution to democratic participation. In fact, it is unclear whether such committees have any meaningful influence on the FTA decision-making process. For example, the opinions of private advisory committees can only have a supportive role in government deliberations on FTA negotiations, because they have no legally binding force. In addition, it is not clear how the public opinion collected

---

[33] Ibid. Article 7.
[34] Ibid. Article 8.
[35] Korean Trade Procedure Act, Article 8.
[36] Ibid.

by the FTAMDC can be brought to bear on the decisions of government committees, like the FTAOC or MMFEA, who take practical charge of FTA matters, in any legally binding sense.

It follows that other relevant actors, such as trade unions or NGOs, take part in decision-making processes only as subordinate or even tokenistic partners, to give the appearance of democratic participation. Therefore, it is perhaps unsurprising that civil society views the numerous government measures designed to increase participation and transparency with extreme cynicism. At the same time, one cannot expect an independent committee to have the constitutional authority to bind democratically elected institutions to a given point of view.

In this context, the participation of the National Assembly, as another constitutional organ, could serve to alleviate the executive branch's domination of FTA practices. However, despite the constitutional function of the legislative branch in formally representing public opinion, the National Assembly plays a very limited role in the process of treaty-making. In fact, legislative controls are quite often impeded by lack of information and expertise. The legislature has a merely symbolic function, because it cannot reconsider the substantive details of the treaty, after its conclusion by plenipotentiaries from both sides of the negotiations. This leads to constitutional claims: some critics argue that the executive branch has infringed upon the powers of the legislature, in concluding the Korea–US FTA, because it unilaterally forged ahead with the treaty negotiations, showing reluctance to furnish the Korean public with the relevant information. It is said that: 'the administration has monopolized FTA-related information and carried out negotiations in a hasty, unfaithful and unilateral manner'.[37] As a result, twenty-three Korean law-makers raised a constitutional claim against the Korea–US FTA, based on a lack of transparent disclosure of negotiation information. Notably, they criticised the executive branch for monopolising FTA-related information and systematically hindering legislative intervention. However, the Korean Constitutional Court avoided a substantive review on this point, by deciding the case on the basis of a procedural requirement for constitutional claims. The Court held that the constitutional power of the National Assembly is granted not to individual members of the National Assembly, but to the National Assembly as an institution. Therefore, the Court argued that individual law-makers, as members of the National Assembly, have no legitimate standing to raise a constitutional claim of infringement upon the constitutional power of the National Assembly.[38]

The new Korean Trade Procedure Act seeks to respond to some of the

---

[37] Younhap News, 'Lawmakers Launch Lawsuit against South Korea–U.S. FTA Talks', *The Hankyoreh*, 7 September 2006, www.hani.co.kr/arti/english_edition/e_national/155156.html (accessed 15 March 2012).

[38] See 19-2 KCCR 436, 2006Hun-Ra5, October 25, 2007.

criticisms concerning the role of the National Assembly in treaty negotiations. Under the new framework, the government should present information about FTA negotiations and their implementation to the National Assembly and the public.[39] The Minister of Foreign Affairs and Trade should report plans concerning the conclusion of trade treaties[40] and other important issues.[41] In addition, the National Assembly can ask the executive branch to negotiate and conclude treaties, in accordance with the Korean Trade Procedure Act, in the case that the executive branch refuses to follow the Act, on the grounds that the relevant treaty is not a trade treaty defined under the Act.[42] It can also request the executive branch to submit a bill of approval for a treaty or agreement, if the National Assembly recognises it as a trade treaty.[43] The executive branch cannot, therefore, argue that a relevant agreement does not require legislative approval under Article 60(1) of the Korean Constitution, as long as the National Assembly defines that agreement as falling within the concept of 'trade treaty' under Article 2 of the Korean Trade Procedure Act. Furthermore, the National Assembly can present its opinions, regarding FTA issues,[44] and can establish a special committee to monitor the FTA negotiation process of the executive branch.[45] Although transparency towards the legislature has increased, the current system invites many questions, as to whether, or how, legislative inputs can be influential on the decision-making process of the FTA. Indeed, no special legislative committee has any formal legal authority to control negotiations themselves.[46]

4 COMPARING THE EXPERIENCE OF THE EU–KOREA FTA AND THE KOREA–US FTA

It has been seen in the previous section that the Korean process of negotiating FTAs suffers from the chronic and persistent problem that the institutional framework fails to garner public support in the initial phase of FTA-making. In the past, the executive branch has launched and pushed negotiations unilaterally, without sufficient participation or disclosure of

---

[39] According to Article 4 of the Korean Trade Procedure Act, the executive branch can keep some information confidential, if it is in the public interest and relates to a successful negotiation strategy. Nevertheless, the Government cannot refuse the disclosure of even sensitive issues, if the President of the National Assembly, based on a legislative resolution, asks the government to reveal the relevant information.

[40] See Korean Trade Procedure Act, Article 6(2).

[41] Ibid. Article 10(2); see, also, FTA Directive, Article 21.

[42] Korean Trade Procedure Act, Article 6(3).

[43] Korean Trade Procedure Act, Article 13(3).

[44] Ibid. Article 10(3).

[45] See Kim, 'Korea's Institutional Framework for FTA Negotiations and Administration: Tariffs and Rules of Origin', p. 167.

[46] Ibid.

information. Consequently, FTAs only come to public attention suddenly – at the eleventh hour of treaty-making – when they are discussed in the National Assembly for legislative approval. Indeed, if the Korean people discover that the FTA in question is expected to cause some social problems, then the legislative process could become deadlocked by severe opposition. It is possible to gain a greater understanding of this problem if one compares the experiences of the EU–Korea FTA and the Korea–US FTA. Both these FTAs face different kinds of social repercussions, because of their different political and social implications for Korean society.

It might be thought that vague fears, rooted in anti-American sentiment, have interrupted the negotiation and conclusion of the Korea–US FTA. Certainly, Korea has traditionally had an ambivalent attitude towards the US; Koreans have expected benefits from Korea–US relations, but have, at the same time, suffered from the sense of being victimised by America, because Korean people have experienced the unilateralism of the US as a superpower. Thus, the Korean officials responsible for foreign and trade policy have maintained a pro-American stance, in the belief that a stable economic and political alliance with the US benefits the Korean economy and national security, from the geopolitical perspective of East Asia.[47] At the same time, critical political groups have argued that the conclusion of the Korea–US FTA will exacerbate Korea's subordination to America. In this vein, opponents of the Korea–US FTA have accentuated the potential harm of the so-called 'poisonous clauses' in the Agreement, which they think are capable of forcing Korea to acquiesce in American social and economic interests, under the pretext of forming a stable economic and political alliance. Additionally, fear and antipathy towards the expansive power of global capitalism after the 2008 global economic crisis may further have fuelled this attitude towards the Korea–US FTA.[48]

In contrast, the EU–Korea FTA, negotiated with another strong political and economic entity, faced less social and political controversy than its US counterpart. Indeed, the conclusion of the EU–Korea FTA was mainly driven by economic interests. Even if trade with the EU has rapidly increased, its social and political influence is not significant enough to provoke social or economic conflicts. Additionally, it is questionable whether the conclusion of the EU–Korea FTA has any meaningful influence on East Asian geopolitics, as the EU does not appear, to Korean policy-makers, to be a major player, in this regard.

---

[47] See Joo-Hong Nam, *America's Commitment to South Korea: The First Decade of the Nixon Doctrine* (Cambridge: Cambridge University Press, 1986); T. Roehrig, *From Deterrence to Engagement: The US Defense Commitment to South Korea* (Lanham: Lexington Books, 2006) (This text describes the American influence on Korean foreign policy and national security).

[48] See the website of the Head Office of the Nationwide Campaign against KORUS-FTA, www.nofta.or.kr/ (accessed 15 March 2012).

Lack of public participation did not make any significant difference during the time when the officials launched the negotiation and concluded the Treaty. Upon requesting the legislative consent on the Treaty concluded by the executive branch, however, the Korea–US FTA faced more serious obstacles from the opposition parties and civil society, than the EU–Korea FTA. As the substantive details of the agreement was revealed to the public, people realised that they had not had enough knowledge of the Korea–US FTA, nor a sufficient chance to present their own views in the early stages of negotiation of the Korea–US FTA. While FTA opponents exaggerated the risks of the Korea–US FTA,[49] the Government downplayed those concerns, by labelling public opposition as a 'ghost story'.[50] An anonymous group raised a conspiracy theory on the web that the Government might be hiding something, in favour of US interests. This rumour spread very quickly through social networks, piggybacking on public disappointment over the incumbent Korean President. The Korean governing party eventually had to railroad approval of the Korea–US FTA through the National Assembly, as it has become embroiled in political turmoil.[51]

By contrast, although the negotiation and conclusion of the EU–Korea FTA began later than that of the Korea–US FTA, the EU–Korea FTA was more easily approved by the legislature, because it did not face any significant criticism. In fact, the Korean framework for FTA decision-making did not impede the EU–Korea FTA. However, this does not mean that the EU–Korea FTA's treaty terms were significantly more favourable to Korea, than those of the Korea–US FTA.[52] Ironically, the reason for the political amenability towards the EU–Korea FTA is that EU–Korea relations are still at an early stage, in terms of economic, political and social perspective. If the EU and Korea had already pervaded many aspects of everyday life, this agreement would have faced similar challenges to the Korea–US FTA.

This analysis leads to another uncertainty for the future of the EU–Korea

---

[49] See Gi-Ho Song, *Handbook of the KORUS-FTA: A Commentary of the KORUS-FTA for Government Officials (Hanmi FTA Haendeubug: Gongmu-won-eul Wihan Hanmi FTA Hyeobjeongmun Haeseol)* (Seoul: Noksaengpyeongnonsa, 2007); Gi-Bin Hong, *Investor-state Claims (Tujaja-gugga Jigjeob Sosongje)* (Seoul: Noksaengpyeongnonsa, 2006).

[50] The Korean Supreme Prosecutors' Office faced severe criticism, as it attempted to interrogate the internet users, who spread the 'anti-FTA rumours'. See Si-Soo Part, 'SNS Crackdown on FTA Rumors Sparks Backlash', *The Korea Times*, 9 November 2011, www.koreatimes.co.kr/www/news/nation/2011/11/116_98439.html (accessed 15 March 2012).

[51] Representative Sundong Kim, of the Democratic Labour Party, sprayed tear-gas into the Chamber, in order to stop the surprise vote on the Korea–US FTA. See Myo-ja Ser, 'KORUS FTA Ratified in Surprise Vote', *Korea Joongang Daily*, 23 November 2011, www.koreajoongangdaily.joinsmsn.com/news/article/article.aspx?aid=2944540&cloc=rss|newsjoongangdaily (accessed 15 March 2012).

[52] Hae-Yoeng Lee, 'Why are People Silent to Korea–EU FTA? (HantbsEU FTAneun Wae Ili Jo-yonghalkka?)', *Midiaus*, 29 April 2009, www.mediaus.co.kr/news/articleView.html?idxno=6468 (accessed 15 March 2012).

FTA; even a successful conclusion cannot guarantee its stable implementation. As observed in relation to Korea–US relations, the development of the EU–Korea relationship could increase the chances of stirring up resentment among Korean society, despite bringing significant mutual benefits to both countries. For example, the EU–Korea FTA is expected to promote the export of industrial products and reduce the living costs of urban residents, by reducing protective tariffs on imported agricultural products. However, this also means that Korean farmers will become less competitive in the Korean market.[53] Thus, if the implementation of the EU–Korea FTA were to cause social problems in the future, the long-term stable operation of the FTA could be undermined by public resistance, as illustrated by the so-called 'mad cow' row.[54]

The possible risks for Korea–EU relations cannot be ruled out on the basis of the experiences of the Korea–US FTA. The newly elected chairperson of Korea's main opposition party – the Democratic United Party – has vowed to press the Korean President to terminate the Korea–US FTA, if she wins the April 2012 general election.[55] She has already written to the US President and to the US Congress, in order to stop the implementation of the Korea–US FTA.[56] No one could deny the possibility that the EU–Korea FTA may face a similar future. This may be particularly true, if the EU and Korea decide to conclude a further agreement on investor protection.[57] In this context, public support becomes critical to successful negotiations and, ultimately, to the stable operation of FTAs, as the technical details of the Treaty can have a significant impact on the national interest and the lives of ordinary citizens.[58]

---

[53] See Jin-Seo Cho, 'FTA to Boost Auto Parts Makers', *The Korea Times*, 1 July 2011, www.koreatimes.co.kr/www/news/bizfocus/2012/02/330_90033.html (accessed 15 March 2012).

[54] In 2008, the newly elected President's trade policy was to deregulate imports of US beef, which other countries had barred, because of mad cow disease. This policy, enacted without public support, provoked a nationwide protest lasting for several months; the President was forced to apologise for his mistake. Korean public pressure eventually made the US administration consider an alternative policy regarding beef exports. See Seo-Soon Song, 'Study on Unconstitutionality of US Beef Deal (Soegogi Hyeobjeongt-ui Wiheon Yeobu-e Daehan Cochal)', *Studies of European Constitution (Yureopheonbeobyeongu)*, vol. 3 (2008), pp. 287–304.

[55] See Han Myeong-Sook, '"I Am a Pro-DJ" and "I Will Terminate the KORUS-FTA" (Hanmyeongsug "Naneun ChinDJ", "Hanmifta Bandeusi Pyegi")', *Chosun Ilbo*, 15 January 2012, www.news.chosun.com/site/data/html_dir/2012/01/15/2012011501366.html?news_topR (accessed 15 March 2012).

[56] See Sun-Young Lee, 'DUP to Ask Obama to Halt Korea FTA', *The Korea Times*, 3 February 2012, www.koreaherald.com/national/Detail.jsp?newsMLId=20120203000817 (accessed 15 March 2012).

[57] Harrison discusses the opportunities and challenges of negotiating an EU–Korea investment agreement in Chapter 7.

[58] See Soun-Young Eum, 'Democratic Control over the Globalization of the Law (Beob-ui Segyehwa-e Daehan Minjuju-uijeog Tongje)', *Democratic Legal Studies (Minjubeophak)*, vol. 28 (2005), pp. 136–59; Soun-Young Eum, 'The Globalization of Law: The Legal Character

5 CONCLUSION

Whilst the Korean government has actively pursued many FTAs, according to the Korean FTA Road Map, it has, arguably, not paid sufficient attention to public participation. This procedural deficiency has caused social conflict on some politically controversial FTAs, such as the Korea–US FTA. It would be impetuous to claim that all critical views concerning FTAs are unfounded. If one considers the Korea–US FTA ratification experience, it could nevertheless be said that unnecessary and extreme public resistance could be spared in advance, by delivering democratic participation and transparency to the public. In this context, Korea can fully enjoy the economic benefits of FTAs, only when they are founded on general public support and cooperation from civil society. The Korean government must be able to guarantee the stable operation of FTAs in practice, in order to attract more foreign investment and maximise the benefits of the agreements. However attractive the terms of an FTA may be, foreign actors will not expand their investment or trade into the Korean market, if the implementation of those terms is unstable.

To reduce the risk of such instability in implementation, Korea should take steps to establish a structural mechanism for overseeing the implementation of the EU–Korea FTA. Such a mechanism would aid both parties to circumvent and remedy any possible problems, before they become too serious. Korea's establishment of a new institutional framework to oversee the implementation of the EU–Korea FTA is a positive step. Indeed, the Korean Trade Procedure Act requires the Minister of Foreign Affairs and Trade to assess the implementation of any FTA that came into effect within the last ten years.[59] The Minister should assess the following: the economic effects of the trade agreement; the feasibility and reform of domestic measures to support vulnerable industries; issues discussed in the Trade Committee of the FTA; and any other issues that the Minister deems necessary.[60] In addition, Article 17 of the Korean Trade Procedure Act requires the Government to take appropriate measures, including renegotiation, in the case that the implementations of treaties cause unrecoverable domestic harm, in relation to a specific item for trading.

However, it is unclear how Korean civil society or the legislature could be involved in this process, because the Government has not yet provided any clear procedures for the conduct of the implementation assessment.

---

of the Treaty-Making Power and of the Consent of the Legislature to Treaty-Making'; Soun-Young Eum, 'The Globalization of Law and KORUS FTA: The Necessary Condition in Validity of Treaties and the Validity of KORUS FTA (Beob-ui Segyehwa-wa Hanmi FTA)', *Legal Studies (Beophagyeongu)*, vol. 15 (2007), pp.163–92.

[59] Korean Trade Procedure Act, Article 15(1).
[60] Ibid.

Indeed, the executive branch has discretion over how to shape the future institutional design of FTA implementation, by virtue of Article 15(3) of the Korean Trade Procedure Act, which allows it to prescribe specific procedural rules through a presidential decree, rather than through legislative enactment. Moreover, the Korean Trade Procedure Act fails to address whether, and how, civil society or the National Assembly can push the executive branch to propose a renegotiation of an FTA, if the assessment discovers serious problems concerning its implementation, notwithstanding Article 15.1.8 of the EU–Korea FTA.[61]

It is suggested that an institutional mechanism for FTA practice should allow civil society and the National Assembly to participate in any implementation assessment. Korean civil society should be allowed to effectively recommend that the executive branch initiate discussion about serious problems in the Trade Committee established under the FTA.[62] In this regard, Article 15.1.4 of the EU–Korea FTA states that the Trade Committee can 'communicate with all interested parties including private sector and civil society organisations'. Of course, a specific model of participation in the Trade Committee can be prescribed at the bilateral level, between the two contracting parties.[63] Nevertheless, the Korean government can, and should, take seriously the creation of an institutional link between international institutions, such as the Trade Committee, and the national procedures that promote public participation in trade and economic affairs.

---

[61] EU–Korea FTA, Article 15.1.8: 'Recognising the importance of transparency and openness, the Parties affirm their respective practices of considering the views of members of the public in order to draw on a broad range of perspectives in the implementation of this Agreement'.

[62] The Trade Committee under the EU–Korea FTA can discuss possible issues (including the amendment of the FTA), which are raised in relation to implementing the EU–Korea FTA. See EU–Korea FTA, Article 15.1. For a more detailed discussion of the institutions created under the FTA and the Framework Agreement, see Chapter 10 of this volume.

[63] See J. Harrison, 'Transparency and public participation in international economic law – A case study of the Korea–EU Free Trade Agreement', *Sungkyunkwan Journal of Science & Technology*, vol. 5 (2011), pp. 1–18 (This proposes a plausible institutional mechanism to secure participation in the Trade Committee at the bilateral level).

PART II

Trade and Economic Integration between the EU and Korea

4

Overview of the EU–Korea Free Trade Agreement

James Harrison

1 HISTORY AND SIGNIFICANCE OF THE FREE TRADE AGREEMENT

After eight rounds of negotiations, lasting almost two-and-a-half years, the Free Trade Agreement between the European Union and its Member States of the one part, and the Republic of Korea of the other part was initialled on 5 October 2009, and it was officially signed on 6 October 2010.[1] The Agreement was provisionally applied from 1 July 2011, pending its formal entry into force, which will occur when it is fully ratified by the EU, all twenty-seven Member States and Korea.[2]

In many senses, the Free Trade Agreement (FTA) is a logical progression from the Framework Agreement on Trade and Cooperation, concluded by the EU and Korea in 1996.[3] The reference to increased bilateral cooperation in the 1996 Framework Agreement[4] had already hinted at the possibility of negotiating closer economic ties between the two partners, and the speed with which the FTA was negotiated is testament to the close relations which the two partners had already developed.

Even before the full effects of the FTA have been felt, the EU and Korea are already significant trading partners. In 2011, the EU exported goods worth €32.4 billion and services worth €7.5 billion to Korea. Indeed, the EU is the second largest source of imports to Korea, only after China.[5] For its part, Korea exported goods worth €36.1 billion and services worth €4.5 billion to the EU,[6] making Korea the tenth largest trading partner of the

---

[1] Free Trade Agreement between the European Union and its Member States of the one part, and the Republic of Korea of the other part (EU–Korea FTA) [2011] OJ L 127/6, 14 May 2011.

[2] Ibid. Article 15.10.

[3] Framework Agreement for Trade and Cooperation between the European Community and its Member States on the one hand and the Republic of Korea on the other hand (1996 Framework Agreement) [2001] OJ L 90/46, 30 March 2001.

[4] Ibid. Article 5(2)(a).

[5] See www.trade.ec.europa.eu/doclib/docs/2006/september/tradoc_113448.pdf (accessed 7 June 2012).

[6] See www.ec.europa.eu/trade/creating-opportunities/bilateral-relations/countries/korea/ (accessed 20 April 2012).

EU.[7] The EU is among Korea's four largest export destinations, after China, Japan and the United States. The two partners also exchange significant levels of foreign direct investment.[8]

It is estimated that the FTA will further stimulate trade between the two economies, leading to an increase in GDP for both parties involved.[9] At the time of its conclusion, the FTA was hailed as 'the most ambitious free trade agreement ever negotiated by the EU',[10] and it is considered to be 'the second most significant bilateral trade agreement in trade terms after the North American Free Trade Agreement'.[11] Whilst some sources predict that the 'overall economic effects of the [FTA] are likely to be modest', one report highlights that 'there are further opportunities for intra-industry specialisation, scale effects, pro-competitive effects and induced investment and innovation effects . . . which tend to enhance productivity and stimulate innovation'.[12]

Moreover, the FTA also has a broader significance, because it is the first FTA to be concluded by the EU, since the adoption of the Global Europe policy in 2006.[13] As such, it could be influential on future agreements, and it is highly possible that the FTA could 'serve as a model for future FTA negotiations by the EU'.[14] Indeed, it can already be seen to have influenced the outcomes of the FTA negotiations with Colombia and Peru, which

---

[7] Ibid.

[8] Ibid.

[9] Y. Decreux, C. Milner and N. Péridy, *The Economic Impact of the Free Trade Agreement between the European Union and Korea*, Report prepared for the European Commission, May 2010, p. 4. According to the European Union: 'it is estimated that the FTA will create new trade in goods and services worth €19.1 billion for the EU and €12.8 billion for Korea', see European Commission, *The EU–Korea Free Trade Agreement in Practice* (Luxembourg: Publications Office of the European Union, 2011), p. 4, www.trade.ec.europa.eu/doclib/doc s/2010/may/tradoc_146174.pdf.

[10] See the comments of Karel De Gucht, European Commissioner for Trade, in European Commission, *The EU–Korea Free Trade Agreement in Practice*, p. 1.

[11] C. Brown, 'The European Union and Regional Trade Agreements: A Case Study of the EU–Korea FTA', in C. Hermann and J. P. Terhechte (eds), *European Yearbook of International Economic Law 2011* (Heidelberg: Springer-Verlag, 2011), p. 297.

[12] IBM Belgium in association with DMI, TAC & TICON, *Trade Sustainability Impact Assessment of the EU–Korea FTA: Final Report*, Report prepared for the European Commission, June 2008, p. 18, www.trade.ec.europa.eu/doclib/docs/2008/december/tradoc_141660.pdf.

[13] See Brown, 'The European Union and Regional Trade Agreements: A Case Study of the EU–Korea FTA', pp. 297–8.

[14] European Commission, Conference Report and Conclusions from Workshops, Conference on the implementation of the EU–South Korea Free Trade Agreement held on 27 October 2011, organised by Directorate-General Trade, Brussels, www.trade.ec.europa.eu/doclib/do cs/2011/november/tradoc_148383.pdf (accessed 2 August 2012); Dukgeun Ahn, 'Legal and Institutional Issues of Korea–EU FTA: New Model for Post-NAFTA FTAs?', Policy Brief, October 2010, p. 2. For the current status of on-going EU negotiations, see www.ec.europa. eu/trade/creating-opportunities/bilateral-relations/ (accessed 24 April 2012). For an overview of Korea's on-going negotiations, see www.mofat.go.kr/ENG/policy/fta/status/overview/inde x.jsp?menu=m_20_80_10 (accessed 24 April 2012).

were initialled in April 2011.[15] For this reason, the EU–Korea FTA, and its interpretation and application, becomes an important focus for study and analysis.

2 SCOPE AND CONTENT OF THE FREE TRADE AGREEMENT

The FTA is divided into fifteen chapters, plus an additional fourteen annexes. At the core of any FTA are the commitments to remove barriers to trade in goods and services. In this respect, the EU–Korea FTA offers significant benefits, including the removal of virtually all tariffs, after a transition period,[16] and substantial market access commitments across a broad range of service sectors.

In addition to these traditional aspects of trade liberalisation, the FTA also contains provisions which go beyond existing multilateral rules. So-called 'World Trade Organisation plus', or 'WTO plus', provisions can also be found in various chapters of the FTA. Boris Rigod highlights a number of innovative aspects of the FTA provisions on trade in goods, in Chapter 5 of this volume.

Another prominent example concerns the rules on intellectual property protection found in Chapter 10 of the Agreement, which not only commits the parties to respect existing obligations under the WTO Agreement on Trade-Related Aspects of Intellectual Property Rights (TRIPS Agreement), but also specifies new obligations, in relation to the types of intellectual property rights which must be protected and in relation to the enforcement of intellectual property rights. As a result, the conclusion of the FTA has led to extensive reform of intellectual property laws within Korea.[17] This extension of obligations is not only significant for the parties to the FTA, but, as noted by Ahn:

> WTO plus elements for intellectual property rights are actually subject to the most-favoured nation treatment (MFN) principle under the TRIPS Agreement that does not permit FTA exceptions . . . in other words, the intellectual property protection has been gradually strengthened through FTAs in Korea.[18]

The FTA also contains WTO-plus provisions, in relation to government procurement. As parties to the (optional) WTO Agreement on Government

---

[15] See www.ec.europa.eu/trade/creating-opportunities/bilateral-relations/regions/andean/ (accessed 7 June 2012).

[16] For a discussion of the provisions on tariff reduction, see Chapter 5 of this volume.

[17] J. J. Lee, 'Enactment of Korea–EU Free Trade Agreement triggers amendments to IP laws', *Intellectual Asset Management Blog*, 11 January 2012, www.iam-magazine.com/reports/Detail.aspx?g=faa96d6e-e406-4c5c-b630-a1ded7246248 (accessed 20 April 2012).

[18] Ahn, 'Legal and Institutional Issues of Korea–EU FTA', p. 8; see, also, B. Mercurio, 'TRIPS-Plus Provisions in FTAs: Recent Trends', in L. Bartels and F. Ortino (eds), *Regional Trade Agreements and the WTO Legal System* (Oxford: Oxford University Press, 2006), p. 223.

Procurement, both the EU and Korea are already committed to non-discriminatory tendering practices and national treatment in relation to procurement covered by the Agreement.[19] Article 9.1 of the FTA reaffirms their commitments under the Agreement on Government Procurement and their shared interest in seeking further liberalisation of this issue at the multilateral level. At the same time, they agree to apply the provisionally agreed, revised text of the Government Procurement Agreement between themselves, which extends their commitments to a broader scope of public works.[20] The significance of the chapter is lessened by the fact that the parties to the Government Procurement Agreement agreed to adopt the revised text at the eighth WTO Ministerial Conference in December 2011,[21] and a protocol amending Agreement on Government Procurement was formally adopted by the WTO Committee on Government Procurement on 30 March 2012.[22] Thus, these extended provisions will come into force for all parties to the Agreement on Government Procurement, once the ratification procedures have been completed. Nevertheless, Chapter 9 of the EU–Korea FTA provides an interesting example of the way in which bilateralism can be used as a stop-gap for multilateral efforts.

The FTA also, notably, addresses a number of issues that have been dropped from WTO negotiations, because of a lack of consensus.[23] Competition[24] and investment[25] are both covered by the FTA, extending the reach of the rule of law to these two economic issues, which have not been addressed at the multilateral level.[26] From this perspective, the FTA can be seen as a 'testing ground for new multilateral trade policy disciplines and regulations'.[27]

There are three protocols, which sit alongside the EU–Korea FTA, dealing with related subjects. First, there is a Protocol on Mutual Administrative

---

[19] Agreement on Government Procurement, Articles III and VII.

[20] EU–Korea FTA, Article 9.2.

[21] See WTO Press Release, 'Historic Deal reached on Government Procurement', 15 December 2011, www.wto.org/english/news_e/news11_e/gpro_15dec11_e.htm (accessed 24 April 2012).

[22] See Decision on the Outcomes of the Negotiations under Article XXIV: 7 of the Agreement on Government Procurement, Document GPA/113, 30 March 2012.

[23] See Decision adopted by the WTO General Council on 1 August 2004, Document WT/L/279, paragraph 1(g).

[24] See the discussion in Chapter 6.

[25] See Chapter 7 for more information.

[26] See, for example, D. -C. Horng, 'Reshaping the EU's FTA Policy in a Globalizing Economy: The Case of the EU–Korea FTA', *Journal of World Trade*, vol. 46 (2012), pp. 315–7. Horng also suggests that: 'the WTO-plus sectors must, indeed, be deemed necessary if the EU's [Common Commercial Policy] and foreign policy are to be lawfully pursued. From a jurisprudence angle, the failure to adopt these sectors in the new generation FTA would [compromise] the legality of EU actions because compliance with the specific objectives of Articles 3 and 207 TFEU and Article 21 TEU would no longer be guaranteed'; Ibid. p. 315.

[27] Ibid. p. 322.

Assistance in Customs Matters, which obliges the parties to provide relevant information to the other party, in order to enable the other party to ensure that its customs legislation is correctly applied.[28] The Protocol governs the procedures for such assistance,[29] and it guarantees the confidentiality of the information that is communicated under the Protocol.[30] The Customs Protocol overlaps, to a large extent, with the existing Agreement on Cooperation and Mutual Administrative Assistance in Customs Matters, which was concluded in 1997.[31] The Protocol does not affect the obligations under existing treaties, so the 1997 Agreement will continue to apply, between the EU and Korea.[32] However, the Protocol is broader in scope than the 1997 Agreement, in that it formally extends obligations to cooperate on customs matters to the EU Member States,[33] and it also introduces a third-party dispute settlement mechanism, unlike the 1997 Agreement.[34]

Second, there is a Protocol on Cultural Cooperation, which sets a framework for cooperation, in order to facilitate exchanges regarding cultural activities, goods and services, building upon the UNESCO Convention on the Protection and Promotion of the Diversity of Cultural Expressions, to which both the EU and Korea are parties.[35]

Finally, there is a Protocol concerning the definition of 'originating products' and methods of administrative cooperation. This is an important instrument, which sets the rules of origin for products which are to be covered by the FTA provisions on trade in goods.[36] It also contains a special provision, which allows a Committee on Outward Processing Zones on the Korean Peninsula to identify geographic areas that may be designated as outward processing zones.[37] The purpose of this provision is to facilitate

---

[28] Protocol on Mutual Administrative in Customs Matters, Article 3(1).

[29] Ibid. Articles 6–8.

[30] Ibid. Article 10.

[31] Agreement between the European Community and the Republic of Korea on cooperation and mutual administrative assistance in customs matters [1997] OJ L121/14, 13 May 1997.

[32] Protocol on Mutual Administrative in Customs Matters, Article 14(1).

[33] The 1997 Agreement was exclusively concluded by the European Community (as it was then), whereas the new Protocol is a mixed agreement, and it, therefore, binds both the EU and its Member States within their respective competences. Some EU Member States may have entered into individual agreements on mutual assistance with Korea. If so, the Protocol provides that it will: 'take precedence . . . insofar as the provisions of [individual agreements concluded by EU Member States] are incompatible with those of this Protocol'; Ibid. Article 14(2).

[34] EU–Korea FTA, Article 15.13.

[35] See www.portal.unesco.org/en/ev.php-URL_ID=31038&URL_DO=DO_TOPIC&URL_SECTION=201.html (accessed 24 April 2012).

[36] For more detail, see Chapter 5.

[37] Protocol concerning the definition of 'originating products' and methods of administrative cooperation, Article 12(3) and Annex IV. See Ahn, 'Legal and Institutional Issues of Korea–EU FTA', pp. 10–2.

the possibility for products manufactured in special industrial zones in North Korea (for example, Gaesung Industrial Complex), and subsequently imported into South Korea, to benefit from the protection of the FTA.

3 DISPUTE SETTLEMENT UNDER THE FREE TRADE AGREEMENT

One particular aspect of the FTA that is worthy of attention is the commitment to dispute settlement through third party mechanisms. In this regard, the FTA follows in the footsteps of the WTO regime, by confirming that it is appropriate to subject economic rules to oversight by judicial organs. Chapter 14 of the FTA is dedicated to dispute settlement. Prior to seizing the compulsory dispute settlement mechanism, the parties are required to resort to consultations, with the aim of reaching a mutually agreed solution.[38] Otherwise, the parties may have recourse to an *ad hoc* arbitration process.

The arbitration procedure is closely modelled upon the WTO system, although there are some key differences, which will be highlighted below. Generally speaking, a panel of three arbitrators is constituted to settle the dispute. Panels must make a decision within 120 days of their establishment,[39] and it is notable that this period is significantly shorter than the equivalent period under WTO dispute settlement proceedings, which normally take a total of nine months. Thus, where there is an overlap between the FTA and WTO rules, there is an incentive to use the dispute settlement procedures under the FTA, as they offer a quicker remedy. If a complaint is successful, the losing party has 30 days to indicate how long it needs to comply. If the winning party does not accept the timeframe proposed by the losing party, the issue can be submitted to the original arbitration panel, which will determine the length of a reasonable period of time for compliance.[40] There is also a mechanism to test the compatibility of any measure which has been taken to comply with the ruling of the panel.[41]

If the losing party fails to comply with the ruling of a panel, the winning party is permitted to temporarily suspend its own obligations in order to induce com-

[38] EU–Korea FTA, Article 14.3.
[39] EU–Korea FTA, Article 14.7(1). It is possible that a panel may take longer, although this provision unequivocally states that: 'under no circumstances should the ruling be issued later than 150 days after the date of the establishment of the panel'. It should be noted that this is hortatory language, which suggests that there may be circumstances, in which a panel may have no choice but to take longer than 150 days, and this will not prejudice the binding nature of the panel's decision. In this situation, the parties may be expected to extend the time limits by mutual agreement, using their power under Article 14.20(2).
[40] EU–Korea FTA, Article 14.9(2). This mechanism is equivalent to Article 21(3)(c) of the WTO Dispute Settlement Understanding.
[41] EU–Korea FTA, Article 14.10. This mechanism is equivalent to Article 21(5) of the WTO Dispute Settlement Understanding.

pliance.[42] Unlike the WTO Dispute Settlement Understanding, which requires a WTO Member to suspend concessions in the same sector as the sector in which the violation has taken place, unless it can be shown to be impractical or ineffective,[43] the FTA does not explicitly address cross-retaliation and it would appear that a party has a free choice as to the nature of the suspension.[44] Nor would the agreement seem to prohibit so-called 'carousel' or 'rotating' sanctions, even though the EU has complained against this practice in the WTO.[45] However, where the losing party considers that the suspension is not equivalent to the nullification or impairment caused by the violation, it may, again, send the issue to the original arbitration panel for a decision.[46]

Unlike the WTO system, awards of an arbitral panel under the FTA are immediately final and binding, from the time of their issue;[47] there is no possibility for appeal, and there would appear to be no requirement for the parties to adopt the award before it becomes binding.

These dispute settlement provisions apply to all disputes under the Agreement and its Annexes, Protocols and Notes,[48] unless expressly provided otherwise,[49] thus demonstrating a commitment by the parties in relation to the rule of law in their trade and economic relations. Indeed, the FTA extends the dispute settlement provisions to a number of areas which have not been subject to third party oversight at the multilateral level, for example, in relation to trade facilitation.[50] In some areas, specialist dispute settlement procedures are introduced, in order to take into account special needs or requirements. For example, in the case of disputes under the Protocol on Cultural Cooperation, the composition of the arbitration tribunal is modified to include individuals 'having necessary knowledge and experience on the subject matters of [the] Protocol'.[51] Other areas, which are

---

[42] EU–Korea FTA, Article 14.11(2), (3) and (6). This mechanism is equivalent to Article 22 of the WTO Dispute Settlement Understanding.

[43] Dispute Settlement Understanding, Article 22(3).

[44] This interpretation is supported by the reference to the suspension of 'obligations arising from *any* provision referred to in Article 14.2', EU–Korea FTA, Article 14.11(2) (emphasis added).

[45] See, for example, 'US delays "Carousel" Sanctions in EU Beef Controversy', Bridges Weekly Trade News Digest, vol. 13, no. 15 (29 April 2009), www.ictsd.org/i/news/bridgesweekly/45765/ (accessed 24 April 2012).

[46] EU–Korea FTA, Article 14.11(3). This mechanism is equivalent to Article 22(6) of the WTO Dispute Settlement Understanding.

[47] EU–Korea FTA, Article 14.17(2): 'any ruling of the arbitration panel shall be binding on the Parties . . .'.

[48] See EU–Korea FTA, Article 15.13.

[49] Ibid. Article 14.2. See, for example, the exception in Section A of Chapter 11 of the FTA, as discussed in Chapter 6 of this volume.

[50] See the discussion on trade facilitation by Rigod, in Chapter 5 of this volume.

[51] Protocol on Cultural Cooperation, Article 3bis. There is also the special procedure for disputes arising under the Chapter on Trade and Sustainable Development; for more information on this, please see the discussion in Chapter 8 of this volume.

less well developed, are excluded from the dispute settlement completely, although these are in the minority.[52]

Special provisions are put in place, so as to ensure that the parties do not abuse their legal rights when they have a choice of remedy, either under the FTA or under overlapping provisions under the WTO agreements. To this end, Article 14.9(2) provides that:

> a Party shall not seek redress of an obligation which is identical under this Agreement and under the WTO Agreement in the two forums. In such case, once a dispute settlement proceeding has been initiated, the Party shall not bring a claim seeking redress of the identical obligation under the other Agreement to the other forum, unless the forum selected fails for procedural or jurisdictional reasons to make findings on the claim seeking redress of that obligation.

It should be stressed that this provision only applies to *identical* obligations, and it, therefore, mirrors the litispendence principle.[53] Yet, the provision differs significantly from other FTAs, which seek to prohibit completely parallel proceedings under the FTA and the WTO, even where the obligations are not identical.[54] Whilst the EU–Korea FTA does not contain a clause which binds a party to its initial choice of procedure,[55] it does prevent the *simultaneous* pursuit of parallel remedies. In this regard, it provides that:

> where a Party has, with regard to a particular measure, initiated a dispute settlement proceeding, either under this Chapter or under the WTO Agreement, it may not institute proceedings regarding the same measure in the other forum until the first proceeding has been concluded.[56]

---

[52] See, for example, EU–Korea FTA, Article 11.8.

[53] See, for example, *Case Concerning Certain German Interests in Polish Upper Silesia* (1925) PCIJ Reports, Ser. A, No. 6, pp. 19–20. For a discussion of litispendence in international litigation, see Y. Shany, *The Competing Jurisdictions of International Courts and Tribunals* (Oxford: Oxford University Press, 2003), pp. 239–45; C. McLachlan, *Lis Pendens in International Litigation* (The Hague: Martinus Nijhoff, 2009).

[54] See, for example, North American Free Trade Agreement (NAFTA), Article 2005(6), which provides that: 'once dispute settlement procedures have been initiated under Article 2007 or dispute settlement proceedings have been initiated under the GATT, the forum selected shall be used to the exclusion of the other . . .'. This provision applies to 'disputes regarding any matter arising under both [the NAFTA] and [the GATT]'; Ibid. Article 2005(1). A very similar provision is found in Article 22.6 of the Korea–US FTA. On this issue, see, generally, K. Kwak and G. Marceau, 'Overlaps and Conflicts of Jurisdiction between the World Trade Organization and Regional Trade Agreements', in L. Bartels and F. Ortino (eds), *Regional Trade Agreements and the WTO Legal System* (Oxford: Oxford University Press, 2006), pp. 465–85.

[55] This is sometimes known as an *electa una via provision*; see Shany, *The Competing Jurisdictions of International Courts and Tribunals*, pp. 213–17.

[56] EU–Korea FTA, Article 14.19(2). See comments in Ahn, 'Legal and Institutional Issues of Korea–EU FTA', p. 19.

For the purposes of this provision, proceedings are deemed to be instituted, when a request for a panel is made in the WTO or under the FTA, which means that consultations may run in parallel, under both agreements.

4 INSTITUTIONAL FRAMEWORK AND IMPLEMENTATION

To complement the framework for the judicial settlement of disputes, the Agreement also establishes political institutions to oversee its implementation, notably the Trade Committee, whose role is to 'ensure that [the] Agreement operates properly'.[57] To this end, the Trade Committee has the power to make binding decisions, in respect of all matters covered by the Agreement.[58] It is assisted by a variety of specialist sub-committees and working groups, created under specific chapters of the FTA and the Protocols.[59] These provisions ensure that the FTA will be a living instrument, and the parties will be able to respond to challenges and opportunities that may arise in their economic relations, in a dynamic manner.[60] In this respect, the institutions established under the FTA offer a means through which the parties can further increase their economic cooperation and integration over time.

---

[57] EU–Korea FTA, Article 15.1(3)(a).
[58] Ibid. Article 15.4. The Trade Committee is expressly authorised to interpret the FTA (Article 15.1(4)(d)), to consider amendments to the FTA (Article 15.1(4)(c)) and to adopt amendments to the Annexes, Appendices, Protocols or Notes (Article 15.5(2)).
[59] Ibid. Articles 15.2 and 15.3. How the FTA and its Protocols relate to the other instruments and institutions, which form part of the EU–Korea common institutional framework, is carefully considered by Young Lo Ko in Chapter 10 of this volume.
[60] See, in particular, the comments on possible future developments in both Chapter 5 and Chapter 7 of this volume.

5

Trade in Goods under the EU–Korea FTA: Market Access and Regulatory Measures

Boris Rigod

1 INTRODUCTION

The EU ranks as Korea's fourth largest import and export partner, right after China, Japan and the United States. Trade with the EU accounts for approximately 10 per cent of Korea's external commerce. In 2010, Korea exported 38 billion euros worth of goods to the EU, more than 90 per cent of which was manufactured products – the bulk of them consisting of machineries and transport equipment. Korea, for its part, is the EU's ninth largest trading partner, accounting for about 2.3 per cent of EU external commerce. In 2010, the majority of exports to Korea were, likewise, manufactured goods, representing almost 90 per cent of the goods that were traded.[1] Thus, trade in industrial products dominates commerce between the parties. The 'gains from trade' under this setting arise primarily from the broader variety that is available to consumers and the opportunity of scale economies for producers.[2]

The rules in the EU–Korea Free Trade Agreement (FTA) are broadly based on the signatories' World Trade Organisation (WTO) obligations. Many substantive rules either resemble or incorporate the relevant WTO provisions. For this reason, and to avoid conflicting interpretations, Article 14.16 of the FTA stipulates that:

> Where an obligation under this Agreement is identical to an obligation under the WTO Agreement, the arbitration panel shall adopt an interpretation which is consistent with any relevant interpretation established in rulings of the WTO Dispute Settlement Body (hereinafter referred to as the 'DSB').

Thus, WTO case law might be useful to interpret and understand the provisions of the EU–Korea FTA, given that the treaty was set up with a view of ensuring consistency between the parties' multilateral obligations and those

---

[1] All figures are taken from the European Commission, DG Trade official trade statistics with Korea, www.trade.ec.europa.eu/doclib/docs/2006/september/tradoc_113448.pdf (accessed 10 April 2012).

[2] P. Krugman, 'Increasing Returns, Monopolistic Competition and International Trade', *Journal of International Economics*, vol. 9 (1979), pp. 469–79.

originating in the bilateral treaty.[3] At the same time, the FTA goes beyond the parties' multilateral market access commitments, and it introduces some innovations into the provisions on trade in goods.

This chapter, therefore, is organised, as follows. First, the rules on market access, that is, the provisions related to import measures applicable at the border, will be delineated and analysed. Subsequently, aspects of one of the most innovative parts of the agreement will be examined in detail: the section containing rules on domestic regulation, in particular, on technical regulations and standards.

2 MARKET ACCESS

2.1 Customs duties

The establishment of a free trade area between Korea and the EU requires, first and foremost, the abolition of the most obvious trade obstacles: customs duties. Before the FTA came into force, most-favoured nation tariffs applied to trade between the parties. In the EU, the customs duties applicable to imports from Korea were bound, on average, at levels of 5.2 per cent and 14.8 per cent for agricultural products. The tariff levels which EU products were facing at the Korean border were higher, averaging 6.8 per cent and 48 per cent on agricultural products.[4] The FTA, thus, brings about substantial relaxation, in the field of fiscal market access barriers.

In spite of the fact that the Agreement's ultimate aim is the free movement of goods, customs duties are not abolished at once. While the majority of duties were eliminated with the entry into force of the treaty, the FTA provides for a 'phase-in' period, during which the tariffs that were exempted from immediate liberalisation are gradually reduced, until they are fully removed.[5] To this end, the parties set out so-called 'base rates' – that is, rates of customs duties applicable at the moment of entry into force of the Agreement[6] – and they stipulate annual steps of reduction, until the applicable rates are sitting at zero. The annual percentages of reduction, however, vary, according to the respective category of the product. Whereas trade in some products is liberalised immediately, the full abolition of duties on highly sensitive goods – in particular, on agricultural products – may last up

---

[3] See EU–Korea FTA, Preamble and Article 1(2)(2)(a) and (b).

[4] Directorate-General for External Policies, 'An Assessment of the EU–Korea FTA', Report prepared for the European Parliament, July 2010, p. 78, www.europarl.europa.eu/committ ees/en/inta/studiesdownload.html?languageDocument=EN&file=32051 (accessed 2 August 2012).

[5] EU–Korea FTA, Article 2(5)(1).

[6] If a party should unilaterally reduce its MFN-tariff, after the entry into force of an agreement, that rate shall apply as the base rate. Ibid. Article 2(5)(3).

Figure 5.1 *Customs duties on Fuji Variety apples under the EU–Korea FTA.*

to twenty years.[7] Determining the actual duty applicable and the amount of time scheduled until full liberalisation takes place requires, first, an examination of the base rate, followed by the identification of the category that the respective product is listed in. The product category determines the period of time that has to elapse, until the product in question can freely enter the market. For example, the base rate on imports of apples of the Fuji Variety, to Korea, is 45 per cent.[8] The product is listed under Category 20. In year one of the FTA, importers thus have to pay the tariff rate of 45 per cent. Subsequently, duties on the apples will be cut in equal stages, over a period of twenty years – that is, an annual cut of 2.25 per cent. Hence, after the first year, the applicable duty will be 42.25 per cent, after the second year, 40 per cent and so forth, until the customs duties are abolished altogether, after twenty years.

The rationale for different phase-in periods is to grant the sectors concerned enough time for structural adjustments, so as to mitigate the social costs, resulting from liberalisation. In other words, slower liberalisation may allow limiting labour market adjustments. In the EU, this concerns, in particular, the automotive sector, while, in Korea, some parts of the agri-food sector are primarily considered to be particularly sensitive.[9]

The FTA provides for a stand-still clause on new tariffs, complementing the elimination of existing tariffs. According to the proviso, neither party may increase existing duties, nor may they enact any new duties.[10] Read in conjunction, these two mechanisms ensure the permanent abolition of tariff barriers between Korea and the EU; existing tariffs must be abolished, and the introduction of new duties is prohibited.

[7]   Ibid. Annex 2-A, paragraph 1(a) and (l).

[8]   EU–Korea FTA, Annex 2-A Tariff Schedule of Korea, HS Korea 2007: 0808100000.

[9]   European Commission, *Trade Sustainability Impact Assessment of the Free Trade Agreement between the EU and the Republic of Korea: Position Paper* (Brussels: European Commission, 2010), p. 5, www.trade.ec.europa.eu/doclib/docs/2010/july/tradoc_146324.pdf (accessed 17 August 2012).

[10] EU–Korea FTA, Article 2(6).

These rules ensure the consistency of the FTA with WTO obligations, given that WTO law explicitly requires the elimination of customs duties, between the parties to a free trade agreement.[11] In order to comply with the requirements set out in Article XXIV of the GATT 1994, 'substantially all the trade' must be liberalised between the parties.[12] Although the precise meaning of the term is contested,[13] the liberalisation of 90 per cent of trade between the parties is generally considered to satisfy the requirement.[14] After the entry into force of the FTA, parties are granted a ten-year period to comply with this requirement.[15] With regards to tariff liberalisation, there is, thus, little doubt that the EU–Korea FTA is consistent with the requirements set forth by WTO rules.

2.2 Rules relating to the imposition of customs duties

2.2.1 Overview

Customs duties are easy to detect. Whether a collected duty is equivalent to a party's market access commitment, as provided for in the party's tariff schedule, is just a question of calculation. Nevertheless, there are other intricate questions, which arise in respect of the imposition of tariffs. Indeed, several different determinations may need to be made, in the process of applying tariffs to a particular product. These comprise, in particular, customs classifications, customs valuations and the determination of a product's origin.

2.2.2 Customs classification

In contrast to most previous EU FTAs, the EU–Korea FTA addresses the question of customs classification – that is, the proper classification of a good, under a specific tariff line. The relevant provision reads:[16]

> The classification of goods in trade between the Parties shall be that set out in each Party's respective tariff nomenclature interpreted in conformity with the Harmonised System of the *International Convention on the Harmonised Commodity Description and Coding System*, done at Brussels on 14 June 1983.

---

[11] GATT 1994, Article XXIV(8)(b).

[12] GATT 1994, Article XXIV(8)(a)(i).

[13] For an overview on the different positions, see WTO Committee on Regional Trade Agreements, 'Annotated Checklist of Systemic Issues', Document WT/REG/W/16, 26 May 1997.

[14] For the calculation method, see Understanding on the Interpretation of Article XXIV of the General Agreement on Tariffs and Trade 1994, paragraph 2. See, also, P. Hilpold, 'Regional Integration According to GATT Article XXIV – Between Law and Politics', *Max Planck Yearbook of United Nations Law*, vol. 7 (2003), p. 235, with further references.

[15] Understanding on the Interpretation of Article XXIV GATT, paragraph 3.

[16] EU–Korea FTA, Article 2(4) (italics in the original).

The Annex to the International Convention on the Harmonised Commodity Description and Coding System,[17] invoked for interpretative purposes, consists of the General Rules for the Interpretation of the Harmonised System, which sets out specific instructions in cases of doubt. For example, when goods are potentially classifiable under two or more tariff lines, the tariff line that provides the most specific description shall be preferred to headings providing more general descriptions.[18]

The WTO Agreements, as well as previous EU FTAs, lack sufficient reference to the Convention on the Harmonised System. Since most EU FTA partners, as well as most WTO Member States, are parties to the Convention on the Harmonised System, the most-favoured nation obligations under WTO law nonetheless ensure uniform application of customs classification procedures.[19] Hence, the reference to the Convention on the Harmonised System is a clarification, but not an extension, of the already existing rights and obligations under WTO law.

2.2.3 Customs valuation

In order to calculate the applicable customs duty for *ad valorem* duties,[20] customs authorities have to determine the value of the imported goods. The EU–Korea FTA provides for the incorporation of the relevant WTO rule, in this regard, but rules out the possibility of special and differential treatment for developing countries, which would allow them to delay the implementation of the Customs Valuation Agreement.[21] The respective provision states:[22]

> The Agreement on Implementation of Article VII of GATT 1994 contained in Annex 1A to the WTO Agreement (hereinafter referred to as the 'Customs Valuation Agreement'), is incorporated into and made part of this Agreement, mutatis mutandis. The reservations and options provided for in Article 20 and paragraphs 2 through 4 of Annex III of the Customs Valuation Agreement shall not be applicable.

Customs valuations, thus, must be conducted pursuant to Article VII of the GATT 1994 and the Customs Valuation Agreement. The clarification

---

17 International Convention on the Harmonised Commodity Description and Coding System (Convention on the Harmonised System) (14 June 1983) 1503 UNTS 168.
18 Annex to the Convention on the Harmonized System, 'General Rules for the Interpretation of the Harmonised System', 2012 edition, Rule 3(a).
19 To this effect, see *Spain – Tariff Treatment of Unroasted Coffee* L/5135, GATT Panel Report, 7 November 1989, BISD 36S/202, paragraph 4.4.
20 Tariffs are commonly collected either on the basis of an imported good's value (*ad valorem*), per unit (specific) or a combination of the two (compound). For more information, see R. Carbaugh, *International Economics* (Mason, OH: South-Western Cengage Learning, 2011), p.113.
21 Agreement on Implementation of Article VII of the General Agreement on Tariffs and Trade 1994 (Customs Valuation Agreement), Article 20 and Annex III.
22 EU–Korea FTA, Articles 2.12 and 6.12.

is directed at Korea, which has claimed 'developing country' status in the WTO on various occasions.[23] This was possible, because, under WTO law, there are no specific rules defining what a 'developing country' must be. Members announce for themselves whether they fall under this category. This is a clear indication that Korea is not counted as a developing country, for the purposes of the EU–Korea FTA.

According to Article VII:2(a) of the GATT 1994:

> The value for customs purposes of imported merchandise should be based on the actual value of the imported merchandise on which duty is assessed, or of like merchandise, and should not be based on the value of merchandise of national origin or on arbitrary or fictitious values.

This proviso is further specified in Article 1.1 of the Customs Valuation Agreement, which states that calculations shall be based on the transaction value – that is, the price actually paid or payable for the goods, when sold for export to the country of importation. Only if the value cannot be determined through this approach may customs authorities resort to other methods of valuation, as they are set out in Articles 2, 3 and 5–7 of the Agreement.[24]

2.2.4 Rules of origin

The proper functioning of a free trade area requires the determination of an imported good's nationality, in order to ascertain whether it benefits from preferential treatment under the Agreement. This is to counter the problem of so-called 'trade deflection' or 'trans-shipment'. These denote the exploitation of tariff differences between countries forming a free trade area, with products from non-participating countries destined for one of the FTA parties (the one with the higher external tariff) being redirected through FTA partners (the one with the lower external tariff), in order to avoid the higher duty. To address this problem, parties to FTAs establish so-called rules of origin. These rules determine under which conditions a 'good' qualifies, as originating in one of the parties' territories.[25]

Under the EU–Korea FTA, goods, in principle, benefit from preferential originating status, when they satisfy one of two alternative requirements.

---

[23] See, for example, *Korea – Measures Affecting Imports of Fresh, Chilled and Frozen Beef*, Appellate Body Report WT/DS160, 169/AB/R, 10 January 2001, paragraphs 110–11.

[24] These other methods include: 'transaction value of identical goods' (Article 2); 'transaction value of similar goods' (Article 3); 'deductive method' (Article 5); 'computed value' (Article 6) and; 'fall-back method' (Article 7). For a full account on the Customs Valuation Agreement, see S. Rosenow and B. O'Shea, *A Handbook on the WTO Customs Valuation Agreement* (Cambridge: Cambridge University Press, 2010).

[25] This is the economic rationale underlying rules of origin. Of course, rules of origin also serve administrative purposes, such as controlling quotas, embargos, tariff-rate quotas, administering anti-dumping and countervailing duties procedures, and so on.

Table 5.1 Types of rules, relating to the 'sufficient work or processing' requirement.

Rule	Sample position and product	Working or processing requirement I	Working or processing requirement II
1. Only wholly obtained products can be used	Chapter 3: Fish and crustaceans, molluscs and other aquatic invertebrates	Manufacture, in which all the materials of Chapter 3 used are wholly obtained	
2. Non-originating materials from certain positions can be used in, or are excluded from, the working or processing	1302 19: Vegetable saps and extracts, other	Manufacture from materials of any heading, except those of sub-heading 1211 20	
3. A specific working or processing operation must be carried out	2525 20: Mica Powder	Grinding of mica or mica waste	
4. A certain percentage of value is added or cannot be exceeded in the production process	Ex 3507: Prepared enzymes not elsewhere specified or included	Manufacture, in which the value of all the materials used does not exceed 50% of the ex-works price of the product	
5. A combination of different rules	4871: Envelopes, letter cards, plain postcards and correspondence cards of paper or paperboard; boxes, pouches, wallets and writing compendiums of paper or paperboard, containing an assortment of paper stationery	Manufacture: – from materials of any heading, except that of the product; and – in which the value of all the materials used does not exceed 50 % of the ex-works price of the product	

6. A choice between different rules	8542 8542 8542 31 to 33 and 39: Monolithic integrated circuits	Manufacture from materials of any heading, except that of the product; or the operation of diffusion, in which integrated circuits are formed on a semi-conductor substrate, by the selective introduction of an appropriate dopant, whether or not assembled and/or tested in a non-party	Manufacture, in which the value of all the materials used does not exceed 45% of the ex-works price of the product

Source: The Free Trade Agreement between the European Union and its Member States of the one part and the Republic of Korea of the other part.

Either the imported good must be (1) 'wholly obtained' in the exporting party; or (2) it must have undergone 'sufficient working or processing' in the exporting party.[26] The 'wholly obtained' rule is mainly applicable to agricultural and fishery products, as well as to raw materials, and, thus, comprises primarily untreated products, which do not contain any intermediate inputs. The 'sufficient working or processing' rule, on the other hand, concerns products containing intermediate materials, which do not originate in the exporting party. Such goods qualify as 'originating', only when certain working or processing requirements have been carried out on the non-originating products.[27] The respective working and processing requirements are set out in a list annexed to the respective agreements. This list of working or processing requirements is based on the Harmonised System and contains, for each position,[28] the necessary conditions that must be met. In total, there are six different rules, under which a product may obtain originating status.

In order to encourage the full exploitation of the advantages of trade liberalisation, the EU–Korea FTA provides for preferential rules of origin, on the use of intermediate components originating in the free trade area ('cumulation'). According to these provisions:

> products shall be considered as originating in a Party if such products are obtained there, incorporating materials originating in the other Party, provided that the working or processing carried out goes beyond [certain minimum requirements].[29]

By contrast, in relation to the use of non-originating materials, 'originating' status, under the rules of cumulation, is granted, without the requirement of 'sufficient work or processing'. The economic effect of this rule is that it shields suppliers of intermediate inputs inside the free trade area from competition with producers located in non-member countries. In order to qualify their final products as products originating in the territory of a FTA party, producers have an incentive to buy from suppliers within the area, even if these are not the most efficient (cheapest) ones, as long as the advantage of 'originating status' (zero tariff) outweighs the higher price of the intermediate input.[30]

---

[26] Protocol concerning the definition of 'originating products and methods of administrative co-operation' (hereby referred to as the Protocol on Originating Products), Article 2.

[27] Protocol on Originating Products, Article 5.

[28] A position can be all products of a chapter, a heading or a group of headings or just a specific selection of these products (so-called 'ex' position).

[29] The minimum requirements are set out in the FTA and comprise minor working acts, such as peeling, washing and so on. For more information, see the Protocol on Originating Products, Article 6.

[30] K. Krishna and A. Kruger, 'Implementing Free Trade Areas: Rules of Origin and Hidden Protection', in A. Deardorff, J. Levinsohn and R. Stern (eds), *New Directions in Trade Theory* (Ann Arbor, MI: University of Michigan Press, 1995), pp. 149–87.

2.3 Fees and other charges

Fiscal market access barriers also arise from 'fees and other charges on imports'.[31] These are import-related financial charges, which are not ordinary customs duties. Given this definition, in principle, there should not be an overlap with customs duties. This is important, considering that tariffs are bound to a certain ceiling or even abolished, whereas fees and other charges are permitted, provided that they satisfy certain conditions. Unfortunately, there is no clear defined legal concept of 'fees and other charges'. WTO case law, however, gives better guidance on how to interpret this expression, through examples such as security deposits, due on the importation of the product,[32] statistical taxes to finance the collection of statistical information[33] and financial charges, imposed for the processing of imported goods by the customs authorities, also known as customs fees.[34]

The EU–Korea FTA largely follows Article VIII: 1(a) of the GATT 1994, in addressing the problem of 'fees and other charges'. The relevant provision states that:[35]

> Each Party shall ensure that all fees and charges of whatever character (other than customs duties and the items that are excluded from the definition of a customs duty under [the respective provision defining 'customs duties']) imposed on, or in connection with, importation are limited in amount to the approximate cost of services rendered, are not calculated on an *ad valorem* basis, and do not represent an indirect protection to domestic goods or taxation of imports for fiscal purposes.

Hence, fees and other charges are not generally prohibited, but they have to satisfy the one positive and three negative requirements set out in the provision. The positive requirement is that such charges must be limited in amount to the cost of services rendered.[36] The three negative conditions imply that the charges should not be calculated on an *ad valorem* basis, should not be protectionist and should not constitute taxation for fiscal purposes.

Explicitly prohibiting the calculation of fees and other charges on an *ad valorem* basis distinguishes the EU–Korea FTA from the wording of Article

---

[31] GATT 1994 Article VIII:1

[32] *EEC – Programme of Minimum Import Prices, Licences and Security Deposits for Certain Processed Fruits and Vegetables*, GATT Panel Report, 18 October 1978, BISD 25S/68; *EEC – Animal Feed Proteins*, GATT Panel Report, 14 March 1978, BISD 25S/49.

[33] *Argentina – Measures Affecting Imports of Footwear, Textiles, Apparel and other Items*, Appellate Body Report, 22 April 1998, WT/DS56/AB/R.

[34] *United States – Customs User Fee*, GATT Panel Report, 2 February 1988, BISD 35S/245.

[35] EU–Korea FTA, Article 2.10 (italics in the original).

[36] For an interpretation of the term 'services rendered', see *United States – Customs User Fee*, paragraph 77.

VIII:1(a) of the GATT 1994, although this modification reflects the relevant GATT case law.[37]

Finally, the EU–Korea FTA addresses transparency problems, arising in respect of fees and other charges. Unlike tariffs, their amount is not fixed, and parties may, thus, wish to implement new measures, which would result in uncertainty for trade. To mitigate this effect, the FTA stipulates that fees and charges shall be published via an officially designated medium and, preferably, the internet. New or amended fees and charges cannot be imposed, until such information is made readily available.[38]

2.4 *Quantitative restrictions*

Quantitative restrictions are measures that limit the quantity of a product that may be imported or exported. Not limited to a specific kind of measure, the term encompasses many different types of import restrictions.[39] Whereas previous EU FTAs resembled, more or less accurately, the wording of Article XI of the GATT,[40] the EU–Korea FTA incorporates the relevant WTO disciplines directly. The relevant provision states:[41]

> Neither Party may adopt or maintain any prohibition or restriction other than duties, taxes or other charges on the importation of any good of the other Party or on the exportation or sale for export of any good destined for the territory of the other Party, in accordance with Article XI of GATT 1994 and its interpretative notes. To this end, Article XI of GATT 1994 and its interpretative notes are incorporated into and made part of this Agreement, *mutatis mutandis*.

Both panels and the Appellate Body have identified, *inter alia*, the following measures, as being prohibited under Article XI of the GATT 1994: discriminatory product bans,[42] minimum import prices,[43] import monopolies[44] and non-automatic import licensing systems.[45] Notably, the broad wording of the provision covers not only laws and regulations, but also non-mandatory

---

[37] *Argentina – Measures Affecting Imports of Footwear, Textiles Apparel and other Items*, Panel Report, 22 April 1998, WT/DS56/R, paragraph 6.75.

[38] EU–Korea FTA, Article 6.9(e)–(f).

[39] See the illustrative list in the Annex of the WTO Council for Trade in Goods, 'Decision on Notification Procedure for Quantitative Restrictions', G/L/59, 10 January 1996.

[40] See EU–Chile Association Agreement, Article 76.

[41] EU–Korea FTA, Article 2.9.

[42] *US – Import Prohibition on Certain Shrimp and Shrimp Product*, Panel Report, 6 November 1998, WT/DS58/R, paragraphs 7.17 and 8.1.

[43] *EEC – Minimum Import Prices*, paragraph 4.14.

[44] *Japan – Restriction on Imports of Certain Agricultural Products*, GATT Panel Report, 2 February 1988, BISD 34S/83, paragraph 5.2.2.2.

[45] *India – Quantitative Restrictions on Imports of Agricultural, Textile and Industrial Products*, Panel Report, 22 September 1999, WT/DS90/R, paragraph 5.130.

measures, when they result in a restriction,[46] and impediments of a *de facto* nature.[47]

2.5 Customs and trade facilitation

Having achieved major gains in the progressive elimination of tariffs, the attention of trade negotiators has also turned to others aspects of international trade, including the efficacy of importing goods and the related costs of trade. Questions of customs and trade facilitation are high on the agenda in multilateral, as well as in bilateral, trade relations. The actual costs of cumbersome customs proceedings can have significant welfare-reducing effects. The OECD calculated that each per cent of worldwide reduction in trade-related transaction costs is worth $40 billion.[48] The same study estimates that trade transaction costs lie between 2 per cent and 15 per cent of the value of an imported good.[49] Hence, the completion of customs clearance inflicts considerable costs on traders and may even deter economic operators from trading altogether, thus compromising the goals of trade liberalisation.[50]

The EU–Korea FTA addresses the question of customs and trade facilitation quite comprehensively in its sixth chapter. The text is based on the 1999 International Convention on the Simplification and Harmonisation of Customs Procedures.[51] It provides for detailed rules on many technical aspects of customs clearance procedures, such as the rules on the release of goods, risk management, transparency, advance rulings, appeal procedures, confidentiality and cooperation between the respective customs

---

[46] *Japan – Trade in Semi-Conductors*, GATT Panel Report, 4 May 1988, BISD 35S/116, paragraph 104 *et. seq.*

[47] *Argentina – Measures Affecting the Export of Bovine Hides and the Import of Finished Leather*, Panel Report, 16 February 2001, WT/DS115/R, paragraph 11.17.

[48] OECD, 'Quantitative Assessment of the Benefits of Trade Facilitation', Working Party of the Trade Committee, TD/TC/WP (2003)/Final, Paris, 2003, p. 21.

[49] Ibid. p. 6. A World Bank Study concluded that the costs of shipping a standard cargo container are about 6 per cent of the average shipment value for importers and 5 per cent for exporters; for more information, see A. Portugal-Perez and J. Wilson, 'Export Performance and Trade Facilitation – Hard and Soft Infrastructure', World Bank Policy Research Working Paper No. 5261 (2010).

[50] The red-tape character of many border control measures is formidably shown by a UNCTAD study, which indicated that an average transaction involves twenty-seven to thirty parties (brokers, vendors, carriers, freight forwards, and so on). It needs at least forty documents, for both government authorities and related businesses. Typically, over 200 data elements are requested, of which 60 per cent to 70 per cent are rekeyed at least once, while 15 per cent are retyped up to thirty times. See UNCTAD, 'Fact Sheet 5' (1994), presented at the United Nations International Symposium on Trade Efficiency, organised by the United Nations Conference on Trade and Development, 17–21 October 1994, Columbus, OH. See, also, A. Grainger, *Journal of World Trade*, vol. 45 (1994), p. 58, fn. 58.

[51] International Convention on the Simplification and Harmonisation of Customs Procedures (revised Kyoto Convention) [2003] OJ L86/23 (3 April 2003).

authorities.[52] These very detailed procedural provisions bind the parties, in the organisation of their customs procedure schemes and ensure, to a certain extent, the predictability of import and export procedures for traders.

In addition to the regulation of import control measures, the EU–Korea FTA provides for a quasi-proportionality test, concerning border transaction procedures. The relevant provision states that the adoption and application of 'import, export and transit requirements and procedures shall be no more administratively burdensome or trade restrictive than necessary to achieve legitimate objectives'.[53] Accordingly, any measure qualifying as an import, export or transit requirement must satisfy, at least, a two-pronged test.

First, the measure must pursue a legitimate objective and be suitable to attain this objective. One problem with this prong of the test is that the FTA does not set forth a description detailing what 'legitimate objectives' might be. In view of the essential purpose of customs procedures, one can, at least, identify the prevention of customs circumvention and deceptive practices, as well as risk-avoidance and measures concerning national security as legitimate goals.

Second, the measure must not be more administratively burdensome or trade restrictive than necessary, in order to attain the objective. To identify the meaning of 'necessary', in the context of the FTA, it seems sensible to resort to established WTO case law. Pursuant to established WTO practice, once it is determined that a measure is trade restrictive, it must be demonstrated that the measure in question is the least trade restrictive among all reasonably available measures that are equally effective.[54] In WTO case law, the least restrictive means test amounts to a form of 'crude cost-benefit balancing, highly attenuate to error costs and uncertainty'.[55] That is to say, when highly important goals are at stake, WTO adjudicators would rather abstain from accepting alternative measures as equally effective, but less restrictive, and, in turn, they will not consider the costs of an equally effective measure, if the goal pursued by the national regulator is considered less vital.[56] Whether arbitration panels, established under Chapter 14 of the FTA, would adopt the same approach remains to be seen. Formally speaking, they would not be required to do so, given that the provision is not 'identical' to an obligation under the WTO Agreements.[57]

---

[52] EU–Korea FTA, Article 6.2–6.8 and 6.13.

[53] EU–Korea FTA, Article 6.1(a)(ii).

[54] *Thailand – Restrictions on the Importation of and Internal Taxes on Cigarettes*, GATT Panel Report, 7 November 1990, BISD 37S/200, paragraph 75.

[55] A. Sykes, 'The Least Restrictive Means', *University of Chicago Law Review*, vol. 70, no. 1 (2003), p. 415.

[56] Ibid. pp. 416–19. See, also, *United States – Measures Affecting the Cross-Border Supply of Gambling and Betting Services*, Appellate Body Report, 20 April 2005, WT/DS285/AB/R, paragraph 143.

[57] EU–Korea FTA, Article 14.16.

2.6 Interim conclusion on market access

In line with relevant WTO law, the FTA will eliminate all tariffs between the EU and Korea. Moreover, the FTA also tackles many other barriers to market access. The provisions on market access in the EU–Korea FTA are broadly based on the relevant GATT rules. Only the chapter on customs and trade facilitation goes substantially beyond the existing body of WTO law. The extension of the FTA to these issues gives an indication of where, in today's world, the principal obstacles to trade are located. Given that GATT rules on customs duties are already generally effective, there was no need to elaborate too much on the existing GATT framework on border measures, apart from adding some quite detailed supplements. On the other hand, the chapter on customs and trade facilitation reflects the ever-growing concerns, regarding red tape and other non-tariff barriers and the need for a legal framework to tackle these issues, in particular, by strengthening the obligations' enforceability. It is noteworthy that the revised Kyoto Convention – the template for the chapter – provides solely for a rather 'soft' form of dispute settlement, on the basis of recommendations from the contracting parties.[58] The FTA, by contrast, subjects the matter to binding third-party adjudication.[59]

3 MARKET REGULATION

3.1 Introduction

Non-tariff barriers were among the main concerns identified in the Commission's Global Europe communication, which initiated the shift towards bilateralism and identified Korea as a priority FTA partner.[60] The communication states, in relevant parts, that:[61]

> Reducing tariffs remains important to opening markets to Europe's industrial and agricultural exports. But as tariffs fall, non-tariff barriers, such as unnecessarily trade-restricting regulations and procedures become the main obstacles. These are often less visible, more complex and can be more sensitive because they touch directly on domestic regulation. Regulating trade is necessary, but it must be

---

[58] Revised Kyoto Convention, Article 14.

[59] EU–Korea FTA, Article 14.2.

[60] European Commission, *Communication on Global Europe: Competing in the World. A Contribution to the EU's Growth and Job Strategy* (Global Europe Strategy), Document COM(2006)567 final, Brussels, 4 October 2006, endorsed by the Council, 'Conclusions on Global Europe – Competing in the World' (14799/06) 13 November 2006. On the 'Global Europe' strategy and its legal implications, see B. Rigod, 'Global Europe: The EU's New Trade Policy in its Legal Context', *Columbia Journal of European Law*, vol. 18 (2012, forthcoming).

[61] European Commission, *Global Europe Strategy*, pp. 5–6.

done in a transparent and non-discriminatory manner, with the least restriction on trade consistent with achieving other legitimate policy objectives. Addressing non-tariff barriers is complicated, resource-intensive and is not fully covered in the WTO system. Instruments such as mutual recognition agreements, international standardisation and regulatory dialogues, as well as technical assistance to third countries, will play an increasingly important role in promoting trade and preventing distorting rules and standards.

In line with this statement, the provisions on domestic regulatory measures in the EU–Korea FTA are considered to be the Agreement's main innovation, in terms of rule development in the field of trade in goods.[62] While the FTA incorporates Article III of the GATT 1994[63] on national treatment and reaffirms the signatories' rights and obligations under the Agreement on Technical Barriers to Trade (TBT Agreement)[64] and the Agreement on Sanitary and Phytosanitary (SPS Agreement),[65] it goes well beyond the WTO obligations of the parties. The reason for the presence of additional provisions on TBT and, to some extent, SPS, is that national treatment may solve the problem of overtly discriminatory and, thus, protectionist regulation, but the discipline is ill-equipped to address two specific difficulties.

First, non-discrimination does not tackle the problem of good faith market fragmentation. Many regulatory measures are put in place to pursue legitimate policy objectives, such as addressing information asymmetries, negative externalities and so forth, without any protectionist motivation. Although legitimate, these measures may have the effect of increasing transaction costs and, thus, ban products *de facto* from the market. This is especially the case, when producers are faced with the costs of two conformity assessment procedures: one in their home country and one in the export market. To overcome this problem, there are three basic alternatives. States may opt for some weak form of policed decentralisation, primarily based on transparency, notification requirements and the like; states may opt for the harmonisation of their standards or; states may choose the mutual recognition of their respective domestic regulations.[66]

Secondly, to ascertain the regulatory intent behind a measure is often difficult in practice, but it is key to determining whether the measure should be allowed or condemned under international trade law. Despite the fact that non-protectionist regulation may also have the effect of excluding foreign

---

[62] C. Brown, 'The European Union and Regional Trade Agreements: A Case Study of the EU–Korea FTA', in C. Hermann and J. P. Terhechte (eds), *European Yearbook of International Economic Law 2011* (Heidelberg: Springer-Verlag, 2011), p. 301.

[63] EU–Korea FTA, Article 2.8.

[64] Ibid. Article 4.1.

[65] EU–Korea FTA, Article 5.4.

[66] A. Sykes, 'The (Limited) Role of Regulatory Harmonization in International Goods and Services Markets', *Journal of International Economic Law*, vol. 2 (1999), p. 50.

products from domestic markets, this is acceptable, because it is globally efficient, as long as the measure's purpose is not protectionist. In other words,
regulatory measures should be allowed, as long as they are not enacted 'so as
to afford protection' to domestic producers.[67] Any regulation of standards
must, thus, strike a balance between inhibiting such protectionist measures
and not interfering with states' regulatory autonomy to adopt necessary and
legitimate domestic measures.

The additional disciplines in the EU–Korea FTA should be understood
against this background. On the one hand, they are 'proxies' to ascertain
regulatory intent, serving to distinguish protectionist motivated regulation
from measures that were promulgated in good faith and pursuing legitimate
goals. On the other hand, they address the problem of *bona fide* market
fragmentation, by reducing transaction costs for exporters through different
mechanisms, such as the recognition of foreign standards and conformity
assessments and the alignment of regulations on the basis of international
standards.

3.2 Technical barriers to trade

Technical barriers to trade may result from mandatory technical regulations
or voluntary standards specifying product characteristics, as well as from
conformity assessment requirements, which certify a product's compliance
with the relevant regulatory scheme.[68] The truly innovative part about the
FTA is its sector-specific rules on TBT measures. In contrast to the EU's
previous FTAs, annexes to the agreement with Korea contain detailed rules
on regulatory measures in the four following sectors: consumer electronics, motor vehicles and parts, chemicals and pharmaceutical products. The
approaches towards the four sectors differ, ranging from harmonisation,
on the basis of international standards, to mutual recognition, to enhanced
transparency requirements.

In the case of consumer electronics, the parties principally agreed
to base their domestic regulation on international standards established by the International Organisation for Standardisation (ISO), the
International Electrotechnical Commission (IEC) and the International
Telecommunication Union (ITU).[69] Except for instances where no relevant
international standards exist or one of the parties decides to deviate from the
international standard for legitimate reasons, such as safety or other public
interest requirements,[70] domestic regulation in the EU and Korea should,

---

[67] G. Grossmann, H. Horn and P. Mavroidis (eds), *Principles of World Trade: National
   Treatment* (Cambridge: Cambridge University Press, forthcoming), Section 3.2.
[68] The respective terms are legally defined in Annex 1 (1), (2) and (3) of the TBT Agreement.
[69] EU–Korea FTA, Annex 2-B, Article 2(2).
[70] Ibid. Annex 2-B, Footnote 2.

after implementation of these rules, be very similar and, thus, no longer be an obstacle to cross-border trade. In addition to this, Korea committed to accept suppliers' declarations of conformity for the majority of products,[71] after a transitional period,[72] instead of requiring third-party certification.[73] This exempts EU producers from conducting conformity assessments in Korea and should, thus, further reduce the costs of exporting to Korea.

Regulatory obstacles to trade in automotive products are tackled through partial alignment of standards,[74] as well as through partial recognition of the other parties' standards.[75] Korea and the EU explicitly spelled out which specific standards they would recognise as equivalent to their domestic regulation,[76] as well as which specific United Nations Economic Commission for Europe (UNECE) standards would form the basis of the harmonisation of regulation.[77] Manufacturers will not have to adapt their products to the individual markets anymore and can, therefore, fully exploit the resulting economies of scale. With respect to internal taxation and emission regulations, either party is obliged to extend any advantage that is granted to a third party to the FTA partner.[78] The aim of this provision is to prevent the erosion of market access concessions, through the conclusion of subsequent and more favourable FTAs with third parties. Finally, the Annex is subject to special dispute settlement rules. Disputes concerning motor vehicles and parts thereof shall always be considered as a matter of urgency, and time periods, concerning consultations, panel proceedings and compliance with rulings, are shortened accordingly, in comparison to ordinary dispute settlement proceedings.[79]

With regards to pharmaceutical products and medical devices, the FTA focuses on two specific issues. First, for cases in which reimbursement is determined by government agencies, the FTA provides for rules, ensuring that pricing and reimbursement is 'fair, transparent and non-discriminatory'.[80] In particular, manufacturers shall have the opportunity to apply for 'price adjustments'[81] – that is to say, they will have a right to demand higher prices, and they shall have the right to be heard, before any *ex officio* price adjustment by the competent authority.[82] Second, the Annex

---

[71] For the details, see European Commission, *The EU–Korea Free Trade Agreement in Practice* (Luxembourg: Publications Office at the European Union, 2011), pp. 8–10.

[72] EU–Korea FTA, Annex 2-B, Articles 3 and 4.

[73] In emergency cases, either party may still require third party certification; for more information, see Ibid. Annex 2-B, Article 6.

[74] Ibid. Annex 2-C, Article 3(a)(iii).

[75] Ibid. Annex 2-C, Article 3(a)(i)(ii).

[76] Ibid. Appendices 2-C-2 and 2-C-3, Table 1.

[77] Ibid. Appendices 2-C-2 and 2-C-3, Table 2.

[78] Ibid. Annex 2-C, Article 5.

[79] EU–Korea FTA, Annex 2-C, Article 10.

[80] Ibid. Annex 2-D, Article 2(a).

[81] Ibid. Annex 2-D, Article 2(b)(i)–(iv).

[82] Ibid. Annex 2-D, Article 2(b)(v).

contains specific transparency requirements for domestic measures, which affect reimbursement or pricing.[83] However, these provisions have little bite, given that all of them are formulated in a best-endeavour language, such as 'to the extent possible'. The least ambitious rules are those concerning chemicals. The relevant Annex contains little more than a list of several duties to strive for cooperation.[84]

Various sector-specific working groups and committees established under the FTA aim at further eliminating barriers to trade, through cooperation and consultations.[8584] Working groups are set up for all four sectors and not only promote common rule development, but also prevent trade conflicts, before they arise. To that end, the parties are committed to inform each other about any measure that affects trade and to consult on such matters, with a view to come to mutually satisfactory outcomes.[86]

The sector-specific rules in the EU–Korea FTA raise interesting questions, in relation to WTO law. Given that mutual recognition under the Agreement is limited to the FTA parties, the relevant FTA provisions may run afoul of the parties' most-favoured nation obligation under WTO law, which prohibits any differentiation between products on the basis of origin.[87] While it is true that the TBT Agreement encourages mutual recognition,[88] it is not clear whether WTO law allows limiting recognition to only some WTO members, without extending it to others, where the same conditions prevail.[89]

It is doubtful whether the provisions could pass muster under Article XXIV GATT necessity-test, as established by the Appellate Body in *Turkey – Textiles*.[90] Under this test, stipulations in a preferential trade agreement, running afoul of Members' GATT obligations, can be justified, if they are 'necessary' to form the preferential arrangement. Whether without the

---

[83] Ibid. Annex 2-D, Article 3.

[84] Ibid. Annex 2-E.

[85] For a general account, see D. Steger, 'Institutions for Regulatory Cooperation in "New Generation" Economic and Trade Agreements', *Legal Issues of Economic Integration*, vol. 39 (2012), pp.109–26.

[86] For instance, EU–Korea FTA, Annex 2-C, Article 9. The mechanism appears to work quite well. For example, after consultations with the EU, Korea adopted adjustments to a regulation on CO_2 emissions and fuel efficiency; for more information, see www.trade.ec.europa.eu/doclib/press/index.cfm?id=677 (accessed 10 April 2012).

[87] GATT 1994, Article I.

[88] TBT Agreement, Article 2(7).

[89] J. Trachtman, 'The Limits of PTAs – WTO Legal Restrictions on the Use of WTO-Plus Standards Regulations in PTAs', in K. Bagwell and P. Mavroidis (eds), *Preferential Trade Agreements – A Law and Economics Analysis* (Cambridge: Cambridge University Press, 2011), pp. 115–49; L. Bartels, 'The Legality of the EC Mutual Recognition Clause under WTO Law', *Journal of International Economic Law*, vol. 8 (2005), pp. 691–720.

[90] *Turkey – Restrictions on Imports of Textiles and Clothing Products*, Appellate Body Report, 19 November 1999, WT/DS34/AB/R, paragraph 58.

special TBT rules the parties would inevitably be prevented from establishing the FTA is, at the very least, questionable.

Finally, the TBT chapter provides for an interesting mechanism, aimed at diminishing the trade restrictiveness of technical barriers on the side of the EU. Upon notifying Korea that a EU Member State's measure is not in compliance with the Treaty on the Functioning of the EU,[91] the EU authorities 'will make its best endeavours to address the issue in a timely manner'.[92] This proviso is geared to its Member States, and it reflects Korea's worries, concerning variations in Member States' legislation, which would, potentially, result in obstacles to trade. Therefore, the EU–Korea FTA extends Korea's rights to a certain extent, in that it allows it to not only claim non-compliance with the FTA, but also non-consistency of domestic legislation with the TFEU. The underlying assumption is that a measure that is not hindering trade between EU Member States does not impede trade between the EU and Korea, either. This is sensible, given the broad definition of a 'measure having an equivalent effect to a quantitative restriction', pursuant to Article 34 of the TFEU,[93] which goes well beyond the requirements set out in the FTA. It is hardly imaginable, but, of course, possible, that a measure that would not be considered as a trade hindrance in intra-EU trade could present an obstacle to EU–Korea commerce.

3.3 SPS measures

Roughly speaking, a SPS measure refers to any measure adopted for the protection of humans or animals from food-borne health risks or for the protection of humans, animals and plants from pests and diseases.[94] The products covered include mainly agricultural goods and processed foodstuffs, given the characteristics described in the definition.

The FTA does not provide for any substantive obligations, going beyond the parties' WTO obligations under the GATT or SPS Agreement. However, it encourages cooperation on subject matters, such as harmonisation, on the basis of international standards, rule development[95] and animal welfare.[96] To that end, a committee on SPS is established under the FTA.[97]

---

[91] Consolidated Version of the Treaty on the European Union (TEU) [2010] OJ C83/13, 30 March 2010.

[92] EU–Korea FTA, Article 4.4(3).

[93] *Dassonville*, ECJ Case 8/74 [1974] ECR 837, paragraph 5. See, for a detailed account, J. Weiler, 'The Constitution of the Common Market Place: Text and Context in the Evolution of the Free Movement of Goods', in P. Craig and G. De Búrca (eds), *The Evolution of EU Law* (Oxford: Oxford University Press, 1999), pp. 349–76.

[94] EU–Korea FTA, Article 5(3), in conjunction with Annex 1(1) of the SPS Agreement.

[95] Ibid. Article 5.6.

[96] Ibid. Article 5.9.

[97] Ibid. Article 5.10.

3.4 Interim conclusion on market regulation

Despite the fact that the EU–Korea FTA contains very detailed rules on certain subject matters, the realm of domestic regulatory measures is still only partially governed by the Agreement. The vast majority of potentially trade-hindering measures are not directly addressed by the FTA, given that the sector-specific rules only apply to certain product categories. In order to tackle those other potential trade obstacles, or at least mitigate their negative effects on trade, the FTA provides, instead, for various means of cooperation in different committees and sector-specific working groups. Apart from the four sector-specific working groups and some other working groups,[98] the FTA establishes a Committee on Trade in Goods,[99] a Committee on Sanitary and Phytosanitary Measures,[100] and the parties agreed to nominate TBT-coordinators, whose role is to ensure the proper implementation of the TBT chapters of the Agreement.[101]

From an economic point of view, this approach is very sensible. In terms of negotiating costs, it would simply be too expensive to regulate all domestic instruments that have an impact on international trade, because any such instrument may potentially affect trade between the parties.[102] However, it is inefficient to provide for detailed rules on every form of domestic regulation. This is because the returns from bargaining over individual instruments are diminishing in the course of negotiations. While the benefits of negotiating market access for, say, motor vehicles may outweigh the associated costs, this might not be the case for, say, toys. The rising costs of negotiating rules for the regulation of all market sectors are prohibitively high, the consequence of which, is that taking the costs of contracting into account, optimal trade agreements are necessarily endogenously incomplete contracts.[103] That is to say, in contrast to tariffs, it would be too costly, relative to the gains, and, thus, inefficient, to 'bind' all domestic instruments *ex ante*. Indeed, even if one would decide to bargain over all imaginable domestic measures at the time of negotiations, one would still have to find a solution that is sufficiently flexible to cater for technological or scientific changes. This is the reason why the EU–Korea FTA provides for so many institutional arrangements, namely, so as to complete the contract *ex post*. In simple terms, currently, less urgent problems should be solved at the point when they actually become pressing.

---

[98] EU–Korea FTA, Article 15.3(1).

[99] Ibid. Article 2.16.

[100] Ibid. Article 5.10.

[101] Ibid. Article 4.10.

[102] R. Hudec, *The GATT Legal System and World Trade Diplomacy* (New York: Praeger, 1990), p. 24.

[103] H. Horn, G. Maggi and R. Staiger, 'Trade Agreements as Endogenously Incomplete Contracts', *American Economic Review*, vol. 100 (2010), pp. 394–419.

4 CONCLUSION

This chapter has shown two sides of the EU–Korea FTA. On the one hand, it is a very traditional trade agreement, largely based on existing WTO provisions. This is particularly the case in those parts of the agreement concerning border measures. On the other hand, in particular, concerning the sector-specific rules on technical barriers to trade, the agreement is quite innovative and breaks new grounds, with respect to the regulation of domestic instruments.

It has also been established that the Agreement is, to a large extent, a 'living instrument'. Many of the remaining lacunae in the field of domestic regulation must be dealt with in the future, through cooperation and consultations within the different committees and working groups. This is the Agreement's approach to tackle its endogenous incompleteness, which is inherent in any trade agreement. From this angle, the EU–Korea FTA may not only be understood as a static body of rules, but also as a framework for collaboration that helps to find prompt and appropriate responses to changes in real-world conditions, thus facilitating trade relations between the parties in the long run. In other words, the various committees and working groups are an in-built mechanism to improve the incomplete contract in a relatively inexpensive manner. Only time will tell, if the agreement will live up to this expectation.

6

Some Reflections on Competition and Subsidies under the EU–Korea FTA

Jae Ho Sung

1 INTRODUCTION

The Organisation for Economic Co-operation and Development (OECD) Member States have agreed that further efforts towards international cooperation for standardisation of competition policies, based on comity, are necessary.[1] Five types of international cooperation were suggested by the OECD Secretariat: voluntary acceptance, based on OECD recommendations; bilateral agreement, relevant to competition; a competition chapter in bilateral or regional Free Trade Agreements (FTAs); a multi-party agreement, among more than three states and; multilateral agreements, concluded under the auspices of an international organisation, such as the World Trade Organization (WTO). In addition, the creation of a new global body responsible for the adoption of global competition standards has been suggested.[2]

At present, the WTO agreements do not directly address competition issues. In 2001, 'the interaction between trade and competition policy' was selected as a topic for discussion on the Doha Development Agenda (DDA) of the WTO,[3] but it proved impossible to overcome the differences amongst nations, and the July 2004 Package nominally excluded competition from the DDA.[4] This setback suggests that movement on a multilateral agreement on competition is unlikely in the near future.

Given the lack of progress in the WTO, FTAs are potentially an important means of addressing competition law and policy at the international level. If competition policy is included in FTAs, the country with a more

[1] Meekyung Yoon, Jongkun Kim and Youngsuk Ra, *OECD Discussion on Trade and Competition Policies and their Implications on the South Korean Economy* (Seoul: Korea Institute of International Economic Policy, 1999), p. 21.

[2] W. Sugden, 'Global Antitrust and the Evolution of an International Standard', *Vanderbilt Journal of Transnational Law*, vol. 35 (2002), p. 1001.

[3] World Trade Organization, *Ministerial Declaration*, Document WT/MIN(01)/DEC/1, paragraph 25: '. . . further work in the Working Group on the Interaction between Trade and Competition Policy will focus on the clarification of: core principles, including transparency, non-discrimination and procedural fairness, and provisions on hardcore cartels; modalities for voluntary cooperation; and support for progressive reinforcement of competition institutions in developing countries through capacity building'.

[4] WTO General Council Decision of 1 August 2004, Document WT/L/579, paragraph 1(g).

advanced legal system can help the other country develop or improve its competition law. As a result, international cooperation is strengthened with regard to economic policies and competition laws. Furthermore, incorporating competition into FTAs means that contracting parties also take a step towards mutual recognition on competition.[5] Thus, competition laws among the parties to an FTA are becoming increasingly similar.

The EU–Korea FTA is one of an increasing number of FTAs, which deals with competition in an independent chapter of the agreement.[6] Chapter 11 of the FTA is dedicated to 'competition'. Section A deals with certain aspects of competition law, whereas Section B contains provisions on subsidies. The Ministry of Foreign Affairs and Trade of Korea explains that the definition of the subsidy, and related contents mentioned in the competition chapter of the FTA, are identical to those of the WTO Agreement on Subsidies, and, therefore, Korea will not take on any additional obligations.[7] Yet, others have suggested that the EU–Korea FTA stipulates the issue of subsidies more systematically and in a more detailed way.[8] This is an important discussion, particularly as subsidies have been an issue that has spurred several trade disputes between the EU and Korea.[9]

This paper will examine the arguments for addressing competition issues within FTAs and the scope of the competition provisions in the EU–Korea FTA. It will also explore the reason why subsidy provisions are included in Chapter 11 of the EU–Korea FTA.

2 THE INCLUSION OF COMPETITION IN FREE TRADE AGREEMENTS

2.1 The objectives of competition law and policy

At a national level, governments often intervene in the market in order to promote fair competition, which is the basis of competition policy.

---

[5] See Chunsoo Yang, 'The Competition in Global Competition Laws', *Korea International Economic Law Journal*, vol. 8 (2010), pp. 86–7.

[6] As for the FTAs that Korea has concluded, only the one with the Association of Southeast Asian Nations (ASEAN) does not deal with competition. FTAs concluded by the EU also tend to include a competition chapter.

[7] Ministry of Foreign Affairs and Trade, *EU–Korea FTA Commentary* (Seoul: Republic of Korea Ministry of Foreign Affairs and Trade, 2009), p. 145

[8] A. Jarosz-Friis, N. Pesaresi and C. Kerle, 'EU–Korea FTA: A Stepping Stone towards Better Subsidies Control at the International Level', *Competition Policy Newsletter*, vol. 1 (2010), p. 80, www.ec.europa.eu/competition/publications/cpn/2010_1_19.pdf (accessed 1 May 2011).

[9] Three disputes concerning subsidies have been litigated in the WTO; see *Korea – Measures affecting Trade in Commercial Vessels*, WTO Panel Report, 11 April 2005, Document WT/DS273/R; *EC – Measures affecting Trade in Commercial Vessels*, WTO Panel Report, 20 June 2005, Document WT/DS301/R; *EC – Countervailing Measures on Dynamic Random Access Memory Chips from Korea*, WTO Panel Report, 3 August 2005, Document WT/DS299/R.

Competition in the market is secured, either by regulating or limiting monopolies or by restricting the excessive use of a company's dominant power in the market. Measures that are taken by way of competition policy aim not only at free and fair competition, but also at the protection of the process of competition. The validity of competition policy can be explained by the 'Theory of Second Best', which argues that the government's intervention may supplement the instability of the market.[10]

In this sense, the objective of competition law can be differentiated from other areas of trade policy, particularly anti-dumping law. While the former focuses on securing fair competition and protecting the competition process itself, even though profits may be curtailed, the latter protects the interests of the domestic producers, even though efficient competition is constrained.[11] Although they both regulate price discrimination in some way, they are different, in that anti-dumping law is applied when price discrimination injures the domestic industries, while competition law is applied, when price discrimination injures the consumers by impeding competition.[12] *Matsushita Electric Industrial Co., LTD* v. *Zenith Radio Corp.* is a typical case, in which price discrimination was at issue.[13] In this case, the US Supreme Court applied competition law in favour of the defendant, Matsushita.

The two types of law are also different from each other, in that competition takes on an *ex-ante* regulation, and anti-dumping provides an *ex-post* remedy.[14]

These differences have led to arguments that competition law should replace anti-dumping laws in agreements that aim to minimise trade barriers. For instance, the anti-dumping duties imposed on Korean colour TVs by the United States in the 1980s triggered the argument for some WTO Member States, such as Japan and Korea, that WTO rules, related to trade remedies having anti-competition factors should be reviewed from the competition perspective.[15]

2.2 Problems arising from including competition within FTAs

It is partly for the reason described above that many FTAs do not rely solely on anti-dumping provisions between the parties, rather they apply competition

---

[10] M. Taylor, *International Competition Law: A New Dimension for the WTO?* (Cambridge: Cambridge University Press, 2006), pp. 14–16.

[11] Ibid. p. 272.

[12] Meekyung Yoon, Jongkun Kim and Youngsuk Ra, *OECD Discussion on Trade and Competition Policies and Their Implications on the South Korean Economy*, 99–24 OECD Research Series (Seoul: Korea Institute of International Economic Policy, 1999), p. 34.

[13] *Matsushita Elec. Industrial Co.* v. *Zenith Radio*, 475 U.S. 574 (1986).

[14] JaeHo Sung and Eunsun Chae, 'A Review of the Terms of Subsidies in the EU–Korea FTA', *Korean Journal of International Law*, vol. 56 (2011), p. 77.

[15] Meekyung Yoon, Jongkun Kim and Youngsuk Ra, *OECD Discussion on Trade and Competition Policies and their Implications on the South Korean Economy*, p. 37.

clauses. In other words, since the FTA narrows the price difference,[16] the contracting parties of the FTA tried to promote an economic efficiency through competition, rather than through anti-dumping regulation.[17] Yet, there are problems with regulating competition at the international level.

Competition policy reveals not only the correlation between complete competition and efficiency, but also fairness. Yet, the definition of fairness is different from country to country, by virtue of their social values, norms and customs. For instance, the United States focuses more on protecting consumers in its competition policy,[18] whereas Japan focuses on protecting producers. For its part, Korea aims at promoting creative business activities, protecting consumers and pursuing the balanced development of the national economy.[19] The EU also has its own approach to competition, which will be explained below.

It follows that the goal of competition chapters in FTAs are formulated in slightly different ways. For example, some FTAs stipulate that competition is for the 'promotion of economic efficiency and consumer welfare'.[20] Meanwhile, another FTA provision reads that the competition is included in the FTA, in order to 'contribute to the protection of free trade and strengthen the cooperation and mediation between the two countries'.[21] Some FTAs admit more directly that anti-competitive activities may damage the objectives of the FTA.[22] Nevertheless, these provisions are largely concerned with setting general objectives, rather than delimiting the actual content of the competition provisions.

2.3 The approach to competition in FTAs

Rather than setting norms concerning competition, competition chapters in FTAs tend to establish certain principles, which should guide the parties in

---

[16] Taylor, *International Competition Law: A New Dimension for the WTO?*, p. 279.

[17] Ibid. p. 280.

[18] The first competition laws – the Sherman Act and Clayton Act of the United States – both of which are anti-monopoly laws, contain clauses exclusively intended for protecting the consumers, mainly with the support and assistance of the small states that have no monopoly company at the national level. Thus, it can be safely said that the Sherman Act and Clayton Act originally intended to deal with the Federal Government's fiscal and redistribution policies, with regard to the state governments, and that competition policies were established and implemented by the Federal Government, because political and economic integration was required at the national level, after the Civil War, for which reason, the Sherman Act and Clayton Act were promulgated as competition laws. See Aditi Bagchi, 'The Political Economy of Merger Regulation', *American Journal of Comparative Law*, vol. 53 (2005), p. 3.

[19] Taylor, *International Competition Law: A New Dimension for the WTO?*, p. 26.

[20] EU–Korea FTA, Article 11.1(1); Korea–US FTA, Article 16.1(1).

[21] Korea–India FTA, Article 11.1.

[22] Korea–EFTA FTA, Article 5.1(1); Mexico–EFTA FTA, Article 51; US–Singapore FTA, Article 12.1.

developing their own competition laws. Such principles can be said to have taken a major step forward, in that the FTAs include some provisions on competition, whereas no multilateral treaty standards on the issue of competition currently exist.

Yet, it must be admitted that the actual contents of FTA chapters on competition tend to be limited. Rather than setting substantive competition rules, they merely confirm the goal of competition policy and stress the need for cooperation toward these goals. Competition chapters under FTAs also stipulate the responsibility that each party has to establish a competition law, in accordance with the goals set by the FTA. Thus, if a state did not have a competition law before the conclusion of the FTA, they are now obliged to introduce one.[23] Furthermore, FTAs tend to prescribe that the domestic law regarding competition should be applied in a non-discriminatory manner.[24]

Generally, the competition policy targets not only market dominance power, but the concerted behaviour and mergers among the participants in the market.[25] As will be seen below, this pattern is largely followed by the EU–Korea FTA, although there are some important differences, particularly when it comes to subsidies.

3 COMPETITION IN THE EU–KOREA FREE TRADE AGREEMENT

Section A of Chapter 11 of the EU–Korea FTA deals with the principles related to the enactment and enforcement of competition laws, cooperation between the competent authorities and the duties applicable to public corporations and state monopolies.

The EU–Korea FTA defines activities that restrict competition, as follows:[26]

The Parties agree that the following activities restricting competition are incompatible with the proper functioning of this Agreement, in so far as they may affect trade between them:

(a) agreements between enterprises, decisions by associations of enterprises and concerted practices, which have as their object or effect the prevention, restriction or distortion of competition in the territory of either Party as a whole or in a substantial part thereof;

(b) any abuse by one or more enterprises of a dominant position in the territory of either Party as a whole or in a substantial part thereof; or

(c) concentrations between enterprises, which significantly impede effective

---

[23] See, for example, US–Singapore FTA, Article 12.2(1). A footnote to this provision says that: 'Singapore shall enact general competition legislation by January 2005, and shall not exclude enterprises from that legislation on the basis of their status as government enterprises'.

[24] Korea–US FTA, Article 16.1(2).

[25] Taylor, *International Competition Law: A New Dimension for the WTO?*, p. 16.

[26] EU–Korea FTA, Article 11.1(3).

competition, in particular as a result of the creation or strengthening of a dominant position in the territory of either Party as a whole or in a substantial part
thereof.

On the basis of this understanding, the parties agree to 'maintain in their
respective territories comprehensive competitions laws'.[27] Following many
other FTAs, the EU–Korea FTA specifies that competition laws shall be
applied in a 'transparent, timely and non-discriminatory manner'.[28]

With respect to public enterprises and enterprises entrusted with special
rights or exclusive rights, the FTA also provides that:[29]

> (a) neither Party shall adopt or maintain any measure contrary to the principles
> contained in Article 11.1; and
> (b) the Parties shall ensure that such enterprises are subject to the competition
> laws set out in Article 11.2, in so far as the application of these principles and
> competition laws does not obstruct the performance, in law or in fact, of the
> particular tasks assigned to them.

Thus, the FTA stipulates that the competition law can be applied to public
companies and corporations that are granted special rights by the government. However, this provision does not 'prevent a Party from establishing
or maintaining a public enterprise, entrusting enterprises with special or
exclusive rights or maintaining such rights'.[30] In connection with public
companies that receive a variety of assistance, according to specific industry
regulations, these provisions could serve as a legal battleground. It is possible, however, that competition law cannot be applied to a public company,
when such application of the competition law legally influences or hampers
the implementation of its duties.[31] Indeed, while the state's monopoly of a
commercial character should be 'adjusted',[32] the regulations do not, in principle, prohibit a state's monopoly in any industry.[33]

As well as addressing substantive aspects of competition law, the
parties also agree to 'maintain an authority or authorities responsible for,
and appropriately equipped for, the implementation of [its] competition
laws'.[34] In the EU, this task is carried out by the European Commission,
whereas it is the responsibility of the Korean Fair Trade Commission in
Korea.

---

[27] Ibid. Article 11.1(2).
[28] Ibid. Article 11.3(2).
[29] Ibid. Article 11.4(1) –(2).
[30] EU–Korea FTA, Article 11.4(1)–(2).
[31] Bongchul Kim, 'The Legal Challenges in the FTA between South Korea and the European
Union, and the Field of Competition', *Korea Journal of International Trade Law*, vol. 18
(2009), p. 89.
[32] EU–Korea FTA, Article 11.5(1).
[33] Ibid. Article 11.5(2).
[34] Ibid. Article 11.3(1).

Both Parties recognise the importance of cooperation and coordination between their respective competition authorities to further enhance effective competition law enforcement and to fulfill the objectives of this Agreement, through the promotion of competition and the curtailment of anti-competitive business conduct or anti-competitive transactions.[35]

Such cooperation is explicitly authorised by Article 36 (International Cooperation of Fair Trade Commission) of the Monopoly Regulation and Fair Trade Act of Korea,[36] which stipulates that:

> (a) The Government may conclude treaties with foreign governments within the scope of not violating Acts and not infringing on interests of the Republic of Korea in order to enforce this Act.
> (b) The Fair Trade Commission may assist foreign governments in enforcing Acts according to the treaties concluded pursuant to paragraph (1).

The FTA is not the first instrument to regulate cooperation on competition issues between the EU and Korea. In 2009, Korea and EU concluded the Agreement between the Government of the Republic of Korea and the European Community concerning Cooperation on Anti-competitive Activities,[37] through which they agreed on cooperation in the application of their respective competition laws. The agreement is still effective, even after the entry into force of the EU–Korea FTA.[38]

The 2009 Competition Agreement contains duties of notification,[39] assistance[40] and coordination.[41] Perhaps most significantly for present purposes, the Agreement requires that the parties 'give careful consideration to the important interests of the other party throughout all phases of its enforcement activities'.[42] Furthermore, if a Party believes that anti-competitive activities, carried out in the territory of the other Party, adversely affect its own important interests, it may 'request that the competition authority

---

[35] Ibid. Article 11.6.

[36] The Monopoly Regulation and Fair Trade Act was enacted as a general competition law in December 1980. The Fair Trade Commission governs a total of 11 acts, including the Consumer Fundamental Act, the Control Act on General Clauses, the Installment Transaction Act, the Door-to-Door Sales Act and the Fair Trade Act. It is estimated that Korea has almost completed the competition act system, which is as good as those in other countries. Bongeu Lee, 'Competition as an Orderly-Policy Challenge: Past and Future', *Korean Journal of Competition Law*, vol. 23 (2011), pp. 196–7.

[37] Agreement concerning Cooperation on Anti-Competitive Practices (Competition Agreement) [2009] OJ L202/36, 4 August 2009. The Competition Agreement entered into force on 1 July 2009.

[38] EU–Korea FTA, Article 11.6(2).

[39] Competition Agreement, Article 2.

[40] Ibid. Article 3.

[41] Ibid. Article 4.

[42] Ibid. Article 5(1).

of the other Party initiate appropriate enforcement activities'.[43] Neither of these duties restricts the absolute discretion of the parties, in deciding when to initiate competition investigations or enforcement action.[44] Yet they do require the parties to take into account the interests of the other party in their decision-making process.

If the arrangements in the Agreement are to work, they will require the competition authorities to work together closely and build up a relationship of mutual trust and respect. To further this end, there is a requirement that the competition authorities meet at least once a year, in order to exchange information and discuss general policy issues of mutual interest.[45]

The 2009 Agreement is the first treaty on competition that Korea has concluded in the form of an individual agreement. However, the contents of the Competition Agreement, which was separated from the FTA, are considerably similar to those of the FTA between Korea and Singapore. It is believed that the Agreement will help to enhance the predictability of the competition policies and law enforcement between the two countries and will also help prevent anti-competition behaviour.[46] Indeed, the Agreement must be read alongside the FTA, and it can be argued that it forms part of the common institutional framework for EU–Korea bilateral relations.[47]

Although the FTA, alongside the Competition Agreement, introduces some interesting new provisions, which go beyond existing multilateral disciplines, it must be noted that the competition provisions in Section A of Chapter 11 are not subject to arbitration under the dispute settlement chapter of the FTA.[48] Rather, the cooperative mechanisms set up under the FTA and the 2009 Agreement provide the only forum for settling disputes. The FTA clarifies that the Parties may carry out consultations on general issues of competition law and policy, and, in addition to this, a Party may request consultations on 'specific matters that arise under [Section A]'.[49] It follows, then, that disputes must be settled through negotiation, rather than litigation.

[43] Ibid. Article 6(1).

[44] Ibid. Articles 5(2) and 6(4).

[45] Ibid. Article 8(2); see, also, the Memorandum of Understanding between the Fair Trade Commission of the Republic of Korea and the Competition Directorate-General of the European Commission, www. ec.europa.eu/competition/international/legislation/korea.pdf (accessed 7 June 2012).

[46] Bongchul Kim, 'The Legal Challenges in the FTA between South Korea and the European Union, and the Field of Competition', p. 89.

[47] For a discussion of the common institutional framework, see Chapter 10 of this volume.

[48] EU–Korea FTA, Article 11.8.

[49] EU–Korea FTA, Article 11.7(1). See, also, S. Baier, 'The Korea–EU FTA: Implications for the Enforcement of Korean and European Competition Law', *Yonsei Law Journal*, vol. 2 (2011), pp. 45–6.

4 COMPETITION AND SUBSIDIES

4.1 The link between competition and subsidies

The EU–Korea FTA differs from many other FTAs, in that it deals with subsidies within the chapter on competition. This approach mirrors the Treaty on the Functioning of the EU, which clearly classifies 'state aid' as a part of competition law.[50] Thus, the competition chapter in the EU–Korea FTA seems to reflect the existing example of the TFEU, even though the Monopoly Regulation and Fair Trade Act in Korea does not address subsidies.

Clearly, there are many types of state measures, such as spending decisions, decisions to subsidise or the granting of aid[51] – all of which may distort competition between producers. By way of distorting the competitive relationship between those who received the aid and those who did not, subsidies (state aid) have been dealt as an important subject in the discourse of competition.[52] If a subsidy aims at distorting competition or helping manufacturers who produce inefficient and poor quality products, that subsidy may reduce the overall welfare.[53] Generally, an efficient manufacturer produces goods at the point where marginal returns and marginal cost are met. If a subsidy gives an advantage to one of the two elements discussed above, then competition becomes distorted.[54]

Some scholars have analysed that the EU's inclusion of subsidy in the competition chapters of its FTAs and the different stance on subsidy between EU and WTO come not only from the objectives of subsidy control within WTO and EU, but also from the objectives of both organisations. Therefore, it is necessary to understand the EU's stance on subsidies, since Korea has traditionally defined subsidies, as a question of trade remedies.

4.2 Guaranteeing competition and regulating subsidies in the EU

From the outset, competition has been included in the treaties underpinning the EU. A competition-related clause was already incorporated in the European Coal and Steel Community (ECSC) Treaty in 1951. The drafters decided to include basic competition provisions in the ECSC Treaty,

---

[50] Consolidated Version of the Treaty for the Functioning of the European Union (TFEU) [2010] OJ C83/47, 30 March 2010, Article 107.

[51] OECD, *Competition Policy in Subsidies and State Aid*, Document DAFFE/CLP (2001)24, 12 November 2001, p. 81.

[52] Luca Rubini, *The Definition of Subsidy and State Aid* (Oxford: Oxford University Press, 2009), p. 382.

[53] OECD, *Competition Policy in Subsidies and State Aid*, p. 8.

[54] Rubini, *The Definition of Subsidy and State Aid*, pp. 382–3.

because they were worried ECSC could be seen as a cartel in Europe.[55] This practice was significantly developed under the EEC Treaty and subsequent agreements.

The reason that the EU included state aid in the category of competition might come from the perspective of creating a common market. Within a common market, like the EU, competition restriction may occur, by both the private person and the states themselves.[56] Thus, the EU regarded state-aid as a part of competition, based on their principle that neither a state nor a private person may distort competition.[57] According to the Spaak Report, drafted by the Spaak Committee in 1956, the aim of the European common market was to create a large region, in which people's living standards would be properly improved and a harmonious relationship would be developed among the Member States, based on common economic policies.[58] The Spaak Report, which played a pivotal role in the negotiation of the treaties establishing the European Economic Community and the European Atomic Energy Community in 1957, already included state aid in the category of competition. The White Paper on the competition of the internal market (14 June 1985), which demanded that the single common market be completed by the year 1992, stressed that the partition of the market, due to state aid or restrictive practices by companies, must not be allowed and that they should be guaranteed, through strong and consistent economic policies.[59]

The main goals of the EU economic policies, which were adopted through the aforementioned processes, are as follows. First, the unity of the single market should be maintained through competition policies, so that anti-competition agreements, such as monopolies and market partitions among businesses, should be prohibited. Second, distorted competition, due to the establishment of a market-dominating position, through the association of companies enjoying market-dominating positions in the single market, should be prohibited. Third, subsidy policies and aid to state-owned companies or private companies by each Member State, which could lead to competition distortion and restriction, should also be prohibited.[60] The third aim dealt with subsidies, which cannot be found in the domestic laws of the other countries.

Any types of aid offered by EU Member States or through national resources, which benefit certain undertakings or production of certain goods

[55] Marie-Laure Djelic, 'From Local Legislation to Global Structuring Frame: The Story of Antitrust', *Global Social Policy*, vol. 5 (2005), p. 160.

[56] Sung and Chae, 'A Review of the Terms of Subsidies in the Korea–EU FTA', p. 79.

[57] TFEU, Article 107 (ex-Treaty on the European Community, Article 87).

[58] The Spaak Report is available at www.aei.pitt.edu/995/ (21 March 2012).

[59] European Commission, *White Paper on Completing the Internal Market*, Document COM (85) 310 final, Brussels, 14 June 1985.

[60] Junsung Hwang, 'Characteristics and Implications of the European Union Economic Policies: Legal and Institutional Analyses', *Journal on the EU*, vol. 8 (2003), p. 43.

and affect trade among EU members, are considered not in accord with the internal market of EU.[61]

The relation between subsidy and competition can be approached either from the relation between subsidy and market access or from the viewpoint of competition and welfare. The first approach explains the relation between subsidy and market access in the following way: state-aid can directly abolish or reduce tariffs.[62] Exported goods that receive state-aid can hinder goods from another country from advancing into the domestic market of the importing country. Also, it can encroach on the value of the concession. Such explanations can be applied to the argument that state-aid infringes the functions of EU's internal market. The state-aid offered by EU Member States toward its domestic industry is regulated by the EU, which reflects the awareness that not only is it necessary to protect trade and prevent the distortion of competition in the internal market, but it is also necessary to protect community interest.

The second viewpoint – the relation between competition and welfare – considers that state-aid causes inefficiency in various aspects and that there exists a close causality between inefficiency and distortion. Based on such logic, the competitive impact, due to state-aid, determines the relation between state-aid and inefficiency, as well as the distortion of competition.

What has become apparent as a problem related to EU's competition policies is that they have political goals, rather than economic goals – a problem involving a conflict between the terms of the EU's competition policies, including subsidies, and those of its Member States, amongst others.[63] In particular, as for subsidies, the EU divides state aid into two categories: subsidies in accord with the common market and subsidies not in accord with the common market. It should be pointed out, however, that the aim of fairness of the competition conditions within the EU veers away from the single market's goal. The reason for this is that the exception to the granting of state aid, according to Article 107 of TFEU, 'as long as it does not have an adverse effect on the trade terms that can negatively influence the common interest', is ambiguous. This provides the European Commission with greater leverage, and some people thus indicate that competition can be more severely distorted, when it can lead to conflicts among interest groups, due to industrial aid.[64] The fact that the EU has been using competition policies as a means to curb foreign companies, instead of tariff and non-tariff barriers, has already been pointed out as a problem. It is widely perceived that the competition policies intended for maintaining the market order

---

[61] TFEU, Article 107.1 (ex-Article 87 TEC).

[62] Rubini, *The Definition of Subsidy and State Aid*, p. 39.

[63] Junsung Hwang, 'Characteristics and Implications of the European Union Economic Policies: Legal and Institutional Analyses', p. 54.

[64] Ibid.

within EU are being used as a tool to undermine the competitiveness of non-European companies.[65]

The EU's regulations on state aid seem to be more rigid than WTO rules on subsidies found in GATT and the Agreement on Subsidies and Countervailing Measures. The cases of commercial vessels with Korea[66] and of civil aircraft with the United States[67] show that the way that the EU sees the granting of state aid, as a means to secure a competitive edge in its common market, can have an adverse effect on the markets outside the EU. Some believe, more fundamentally, that it would be difficult to apply WTO subsidy rules to the civil-aircraft dispute, from the standpoint that a civil airline requires a tremendous amount of capital and that a government needs to provide subsidies, when a new airliner tries to enter the existing market. The civil aircraft dispute between the US and the EU can therefore be seen as a collision between industrial policies and competition policies. The industrial policy is defined as a series of strategic policy mixes that lead the state's industry structure towards the intended direction, through the government's advancement into a specific industrial activity or market and its effective distribution of the country's resources to fix the market's failure or to secure a dynamic comparative advantage. While the industrial policies can be seen as being against competition policies, in light of the aforementioned definition, the legitimacy of industrial policies is judged, based on the competition policies of the competition laws, when a dispute takes place between states, since the competition policies are designed to invigorate the market as a whole.

The EU requires its Member States to report their state aids to the European Commission in advance. Considering its industrial policies, however, the EU allows state aids for small and medium-sized enterprises, research and development, environmental protection and employment and training, as well as regional subsidies (in accordance with the European Commission's guidelines), to be exempted from such rule. The EU Council is supposed to set general exception groups and the European Commission must rule, unconditionally, that all state aid grants falling under such categories are in harmony with the common market and should not be subjected to advanced notice.[68] The EU Council will decide on the exemption list,

---

[65] Ibid. p. 57.

[66] *Korea – Measures Affecting Trade in Commercial Vessels*, WTO Panel Report, 7 March 2005, WT/DS273/R; *European Communities – Measures Affecting Trade in Commercial Vessels*, WTO Panel Report, 22 April 2005, WT/DS301/R; Request for Consultations by Korea, *European Communities – Aid for Commercial Vessels*, Document WT/DS307/1, G/L/671, G/SCM/D58/1, 19 February 2004.

[67] *European Communities – Measures Affecting Trade in Large Civil Aircraft*, WTO Appellate Body Report, 18 May 2011, WT/DS316/AB/R.

[68] Council Regulation (EC) No. 994/98, 7 May 1998, on the application of Article 92 and 93 of the Treaty establishing the European Community to certain categories of horizontal state aid, Article 1(1). As the Council's Regulation No. 994/98 granted the Commission authority

after consultation with the European Parliament, according to the European Commission's proposal.[69]

4.3 Subsidies and competition in the EU–Korea FTA

Section B of Chapter 11 of the EU–Korea FTA deals with subsidies. The provisions of Section B apply to subsidies for goods, with the exception of fisheries subsidies, subsidies related to products covered by Annex 1 of the Agreement on Agriculture and other subsidies covered by the Agreement on Agriculture. These issues are, therefore, only regulated by WTO rules, where they exist.[70]

The basic principle in Section B of Chapter 11 of the EU–Korea FTA is that:

> the Parties agree to use their best endeavors to remedy or remove through the application of their competition laws or otherwise, distortions of competition caused by subsidies in so far as they affect international trade, and to prevent the occurrence of such situations.[71]

This principle, therefore, classifies subsidies as falling within the realm of competition law, although it also permits the parties to use other means to remedy or remove distortion of competition that has been caused by subsidies, in so far as they affect international trade.

According to the EU–Korea FTA, both parties' right to take trade remedy measures under the WTO agreements is still guaranteed, as the FTA maintains the rights and responsibilities under WTO law, regarding subsidies and countervailing measures.[72] This means that countervailing measures can still be taken, in response to trade distorting subsidies. The FTA also uses the

---

to rule that the general exception groups are in harmony with the common market under specific conditions, the Commission adopted a number of regulations. On 6 August 2008, it adopted Commission Regulation (EC) No. 800/2008, declaring certain categories of aid compatible with the common market, in the application of Article 87 and 88 of the Treaty (General Block Exemption Regulation) (text with EEA relevance), replacing the numerous existing regulations. Commission Regulation No. 800/2008 consists of two chapters, 'Common Provisions' (Chapter 1) and 'Specific Provisions for the Different Categories of Aid' (Chapter 2), and it also contains three annexes. For state aid to be acknowledged as a general exception, it should meet all the requirements defined by the first chapter and should be in line with all the regulations defined by the second chapter; Commission Regulation No. 800/2008, Article 3(1). See, also, Sung and Chae, 'A Review of the Terms of Subsidies in the Korea–EU FTA', p. 83.

[69] TFEU, Article 109.

[70] The clarification and improvement of rules relating to fisheries subsidies is currently on the agenda of the on-going round of WTO trade negotiations; see Doha Ministerial Declaration, Document WT/MIN(01)/DEC/1, 14 November 2001, paragraph 28.

[71] EU–Korea FTA, Article 11.9.

[72] Ibid. Article 11.13.

WTO Agreement on Subsidies and Countervailing Measures as a reference point to define a subsidy.[73]

The subsidies provisions of the EU–Korea FTA, however, also potentially go beyond the provisions of the WTO Agreement on Subsidies and Countervailing Measures. Article 11.11 of the FTA specifies that the two following types of subsidy shall be prohibited, insofar as they adversely affect international trade:[74]

> (a) subsidies granted under any legal arrangement whereby a government or any public body is responsible for covering debts or liabilities of certain enterprises within the meaning of Article 2.1 of the (WTO Subsidies Agreement) without any limitation, in law or fact, as to the amount of those debts and liabilities or the duration of such responsibility;
>
> (b) subsidies to insolvent or ailing enterprises, without a credible restructuring plan based on realistic assumptions with a view to ensuring the return of the insolvent or ailing enterprise within a reasonable period of time to long-term viability and without the enterprise significantly contributing itself to the costs of restructuring.

Thus, the EU–Korea FTA prohibits subsidies that have a negative effect on international trade, which would otherwise correspond to actionable subsidies under the WTO Agreement on Subsidies and Countervailing Measures. If one party does not prohibit the subsidies identified in this provision, the matter cannot be settled through the WTO dispute settlement procedure, because it does not violate the WTO rules against subsidies.[75] Thus, the matters related to this rule must be handled by the EU–Korea FTA dispute settlement procedures.[76]

In order to oversee the implementation of these restrictions on subsidies that may distort international trade, both parties take the responsibility to report, each year, relevant information – for example, the objective, type, amount or budget of subsidy granted by the government or public institutions – and, if possible, information on the receiver.[77] The Parties shall keep under constant review the matters to which reference is made in Section B. In the case of problems, each Party may refer such matters to the Trade Committee.[78]

The Parties agree to review progress, in implementing Section B every two years after the entry into force of this Agreement, unless both Parties agree

---

[73] Ibid. Article 11.10.

[74] It continues that this does not apply to subsidies granted as compensation for carrying out public service obligations or to the coal industry.

[75] Sung and Chae, 'A Review of the Terms of Subsidies in the Korea–EU FTA', pp. 84–6.

[76] For more information on the FTA dispute settlement procedures, see Chapter 4 of this volume.

[77] EU–Korea FTA, Article 11.12.

[78] EU–Korea FTA, Article 11.14.

otherwise.[79] The Parties have also agreed to use their best endeavours to develop rules applicable to subsidies to services, taking into account developments at the multilateral level,[80] and to exchange information upon the request of either Party.[81] Thus, the regulation of subsidies and competition law between the EU and Korea is likely to develop over time, as they gain experience from implementing Chapter 11 of the FTA.

---

[79] Ibid.

[80] See the General Agreement on Trade in Services, Article XV: 'Members recognize that, in certain circumstances, subsidies may have distortive effects on trade in services. Members shall enter into negotiations with a view to developing the necessary multilateral disciplines to avoid such trade-distortive effects'. These negotiations are on-going.

[81] Ibid. Article 11.15(2).

7

The Legal Framework for Investment Protection between the European Union and Korea: Towards a Level Playing Field for Investors?

James Harrison

1 INTRODUCTION

Investment has traditionally been regulated at the international level, through bilateral investment treaties (BITs). Each of these instruments contained its own set of rules and dispute settlement procedures relating to investment protection. Such treaties commonly contained provisions relating to the fair and equitable treatment of investments, as well as other substantive standards of protection. Even though there were similarities in these BITs that had been concluded by states, there was no uniform practice.

The purpose of this chapter is to demonstrate the diversity in the standards of protection offered by existing BITs, concluded between EU Member States and Korea, and to consider the opportunities and challenges involved in concluding a comprehensive EU–Korea investment agreement, in order to establish a level playing field for investors.

The first part of the paper compares and contrasts the content of existing BITs, concluded between EU Member States and Korea. This part will show that although almost all of the BITs contain some similar standards of protection, there are important divergences, in both the scope of protection and the mechanisms for dispute settlement. Thus, under the existing legal framework, the degree of protection enjoyed by an investor depends, to some extent, on the terms of the applicable treaty involved, if, indeed, there is one. It follows that a level playing field can only be established by action taken at the EU level.

The need for a common investment policy has been expressly recognised by the EU. Recent amendments to the Treaty on the Functioning of the European Union[1] have included foreign direct investment in the common commercial policy for the first time, meaning that the EU is now competent to enter into treaties on this subject matter. This chapter will show that some tentative steps towards a common legal framework for investment protection

---

[1] Consolidated Version of the Treaty for the Functioning of the European Union (TFEU) [2010] OJ C83/47, 30 March 2010.

have been taken with the conclusion of the EU–Korea Free Trade Agreement (FTA), but that this instrument falls short of harmonising the substantive standards of protection, which have been traditionally addressed by BITs. Therefore, the chapter will consider the additional steps that may be taken in order to conclude a new comprehensive EU–Korea investment agreement. The objective of such an agreement would be to establish a level playing field for European and Korean investors, by ensuring that they all enjoy the same standards of protection. Firstly, the paper examines the nature and scope of the new competence conferred upon the EU, in relation to foreign direct investment, asking whether a new agreement should be concluded by the EU alone or as a 'mixed agreement', involving both the EU and the Member States. The paper then considers some of the substantive and procedural issues that should be addressed in an EU investment agreement with Korea.

2 BILATERAL INVESTMENT TREATIES BETWEEN EU MEMBER STATES AND KOREA

2.1 Similarities and differences in bilateral investment treaties

For the past half-century, BITs have been the principal instruments used by Member States to promote and protect overseas investments by their nationals. European states have been at the forefront of this treaty-making activity, from the 1960s onwards.[2] Over that time, EU Member States have collectively entered into more than 2,000 BITs.[3] For its part, Korea has also been active in negotiating BITs, and it now has 'agreements with most major countries responsible for FDI outflows and inflows'.[4] Twenty-one of the EU Member States already have a BIT with Korea.[5]

Although each of the existing BITs have been negotiated separately, there are many similarities, in practice, between the BITs concluded by EU

---

[2] The first modern BIT was famously concluded between Germany and Pakistan in 1959.

[3] European Commission, *Communication, Towards a Comprehensive European International Investment Policy*, Document COM (2010)343 final, Brussels, 7 July 2010, p. 11. See, also, the table of European BITs presented in J. Chaisse, 'Promises and Pitfalls of the European Union Policy on Foreign Investment – How will the New EU Competence on FDI Affect the Emerging Global Regime', *Journal of International Economic Law*, vol. 15 (2012), p. 53.

[4] J. Kim, 'The Evolution of Korea's Modern Investment Treaties and Investor–State Dispute Settlement Provisions', in V. Bath and L. Nottage (eds), *Foreign Investment and Dispute Resolution Law and Practice in Asia* (Abingdon: Routledge, 2011), p. 220.

[5] Korea has concluded twenty BITs with the following twenty-one EU Member States: Germany (1967), Netherlands (1974), Belgo–Luxembourg Economic Union (1974), United Kingdom (1976), France (1977), Denmark (1988), Hungary (1989), Poland (1989), Italy (1989), Romania (1990), Austria (1991), Czech Republic (1992), Lithuania (1993), Finland (1993), Spain (1994), Sweden (1995), Portugal (1995), Greece (1995), Latvia (1996), Slovak Republic (2005). See www.unctad.org/sections/dite_pcbb/docs/bits_korea_republic.pdf (accessed 16 February 2012).

Member States and Korea. Indeed, in general, states tend to follow very similar patterns and structures in their investment agreements.[6]

All the existing BITs between EU Member States and Korea provide for the core standards of protection that are common in international investment law, namely, most-favoured nation treatment, national treatment, fair and equitable treatment, repatriation of investments and returns, and compensation in the case of the direct or indirect expropriation of an investment. Even though the text of these BIT provisions is not identical, tribunals often adopt interpretations which effectively minimise the differences in wording.[7]

The interpretation of the fair and equitable treatment standard provides a good example of this trend. This standard is found in all of the BITs between Korea and Member States, albeit in different formulations. For instance, the Korea–Italy BIT refers not to 'fair and equitable treatment', but, rather, to 'reasonable and equitable treatment'.[8] Nevertheless, arbitrators have tended to ignore such differences and adopted a single standard. Thus, in the case of *Parkerings* v. *Lithuania*, the tribunal refused to interpret a provision calling for 'equitable and reasonable treatment' in a different manner to the standard 'fair and equitable treatment'.[9] A similar approach can be observed in *AWG and others* v. *Argentina*, where claims were brought by the partners in a consortium under three separate BITs which had been concluded by European states with Argentina. Whereas the UK–Argentina BIT and the Spain–Argentina BIT both referred to 'fair and equitable treatment', the France–Argentina BIT referred to 'just and equitable treatment, in accordance with the principles of international law'.[10] Despite the obvious difference in wording, the tribunal decided that all three provisions, in essence, 'mean the same thing'.[11]

Yet, it is, arguably, inappropriate to talk of a single international regime.[12] Indeed, there are significant divergences, which arise for a number of reasons. First, tribunals are alert to the possibility that the drafters of BITs may have intended to set a different standard, by choosing particular wording which was different from other BITs. This point was stressed by the arbitral tribunal, in the case of *AES* v. *Argentina*, when it said that: 'each BIT has its own identity; its [sic] very terms should consequently be carefully analyzed

[6] See S. Schill, *The Multilateralization of International Investment Law* (Cambridge: Cambridge University Press, 2009), Chapter 3.

[7] Ibid. Chapter 7.

[8] Italy–Korea BIT, Article 1.

[9] *Parkerings* v. *Lithuania*, ICSID Case No ARB/05/08, Award of 11 September 2007, paragraphs 277–8.

[10] For the text of these provisions, see *AWG and others* v. *Argentina*, UNCITRAL Arbitration, Decision on Liability of 30 July 2010, paragraphs 180-182.

[11] *AWG and others* v. *Argentina*, paragraph 183.

[12] Contra J. W. Salacuse, 'The Emerging Global Regime for Investment', *Harvard International Law Journal*, vol. 51 (2010), p. 444.

for determining the exact scope of consent expressed by its two Parties'.[13] Indeed, even if two BITs contain identical wording, it cannot necessarily be assumed that they should be interpreted in precisely the same manner. As was stressed by the International Tribunal for the Law of the Sea in the *Mox Plant Case*, 'the application of international law rules on interpretation of treaties to identical or similar provisions of different treaties may not yield the same results, having regard to, inter alia, differences in the respective contexts, objects and purposes, subsequent practice of the parties and travaux préparatoires'.[14]

Second, it is wrong to assume that BITs always contain all of the same standards. Indeed, there are several important issues on which BITs have taken a remarkably different approach. One important example of diversity in BIT practice is the use of the so-called umbrella clause – a provision which requires states to observe any obligations that they have entered into with an investor. Of all the BITs concluded between Korea and the Member States, only seven contain an umbrella clause.[15] Moreover, there are significant differences of wording between these seven umbrella clauses, which probably could not be overcome through interpretation. The majority of the umbrella clauses require contracting parties to observe 'any obligation it may have entered into with regard to the investments of the investors of the other contracting party'.[16] This is a broad umbrella clause, which would generally be interpreted to cover all different types of obligations.[17] On the other hand, the umbrella clause in one of the BITs is much more restrictive in its scope, only referring to the observance of 'contractual obligations'.[18] The difference in wording is significant, as it clearly limits the types of obligations that fall within the scope of the umbrella clause.

Dispute settlement is another area where there are significant differences between the BITs concluded between the EU Member States and Korea. It is common, today, for BITs to contain provisions for an investor to bring a claim directly against a state. Indeed, this mechanism is considered to be one of the principal advantages of modern international investment law.[19] Yet,

---

[13] AES v. *Argentina*, ICSID Case No ARB/02/17, Decision on Jurisdiction of 26 April 2005, paragraphs 24–5.

[14] *The MOX Plant Case (Provisional Measures)*, Order of 3 December 2001, paragraph 51.

[15] UK–Korea BIT; Portugal–Korea BIT; Latvia–Korea BIT; Greece–Korea BIT; Austria–Korea BIT; Germany–Korea BIT; and Denmark–Korea BIT.

[16] UK–Korea BIT, Article 2(2); Portugal–Korea BIT, Article 10(2); Latvia–Korea BIT, Article 2(4); Greece–Korea BIT, Article 10(2); Germany–Korea BIT, Article 7; Denmark–Korea BIT, Article 2(3).

[17] See, for example, *LG & E* v. *Argentina*, ICSID Case ARB/02/1, Award of 3 October 2006, paragraphs 169–75. See, also, OECD, *International Investment Law: Understanding Concepts and Tracking Innovations* (Paris: OECD Publishing, 2008), pp. 111–12.

[18] Austria–Korea BIT, Article 7(2).

[19] See, for example, M. Sornarajah, *The International Law of Foreign Investment* (3rd edn) (Cambridge: Cambridge University Press, 2010), p. 216.

not all of the BITs concluded by Korea and the EU Member States contain investor–state dispute settlement provisions. For instance, there is no provision for investor–state dispute settlement in the Germany–Korea BIT, only a provision on state-to-state arbitration.[20] Similarly, the France–Korea BIT has no general provision for investor–state dispute settlement.[21] Given the importance of having a remedy to protect the rights that are contained in BITs, the lack of an investor–state dispute settlement clause would seem to present significant disadvantages to the investors covered by these treaties.

Even where there is provision for investor–state dispute settlement in BITs, there are differences in the procedures that are to be applied. Some differences relate to the forum to which a dispute may be submitted. Whilst most of the BITs between the EU Member States and Korea allow recourse to the International Centre for the Settlement of Disputes (ICSID), some BITs allow a different choice of forum. Thus, the BIT between Korea and the Slovak Republic offers a choice between ICSID arbitration and arbitration under the rules of the United Nations Commission on International Trade Law (UNCITRAL).[22] This gives an advantage to these particular investors, who may select the forum which is most favourable to them in their particular circumstances. Other differences arise, in relation to the details of the procedure to be observed. For instance, the waiting period before proceedings can be initiated varies, from six months,[23] to three months,[24] to none at all.[25] In the case of the Netherlands–Korea BIT, investors must exhaust all internal administrative and juridical remedies, before they can bring a case to ICSID.[26] There are also differences in the scope of jurisdiction. The Hungary–Korea BIT contains a particularly narrow dispute settlement clause, as it only allows for disputes concerning expropriation or nationalisation to be unilaterally referred to ICSID, whereas other disputes may only be referred to arbitration with the consent of both parties.[27]

From this analysis, it would seem that some significant differences have

---

[20] Germany–Korea BIT, Article 11.

[21] France–Korea BIT, Article 4 provides that: 'Investments made under a special agreement by one of the Contracting Parties in enterprises belonging to nationals or companies of the other Party shall be governed by the provisions of this Agreement and the said special agreement. Should investors so request, each of the Contracting Parties shall agree to insert in the said special agreement a provision providing for recourse, in the event of a dispute, to the International Centre for Settlement of Investment Disputes (ICSID)'.

[22] Slovak Republic–Korea BIT, Article 8(3); see, also, Spain–Korea BIT, Article 9(2); Czech Republic–Korea BIT, Article 8(2).

[23] Sweden–Korea BIT; Spain–Korea BIT; Romania–Korea BIT; Portugal–Korea BIT; Lithuania–Korea BIT; Latvia–Korea BIT; Italy–Korea BIT; Greece–Korea BIT; Finland–Korea BIT; Hungary–Korea BIT; Slovak Republic–Korea BIT.

[24] UK–Korea BIT; Austria–Korea BIT; Czech Republic–Korea BIT; Denmark–Korea BIT.

[25] Belgo–Luxemburg Economic Union–Korea BIT.

[26] Netherlands–Korea BIT, Article 6.

[27] Hungary–Korea BIT, Article 10.

arisen, in practice, between the EU Member States, in the types of provisions that they include in their BITs with third states, and, notably, with Korea. However, before turning to focus on the steps that could be taken to conclude an EU–Korea comprehensive investment agreement, we must first ask whether there are mechanisms within international investment law which might effectively diminish the existing differences.

2.2 Harmonisation of investment protection through the Most-Favoured Nation Clause

Where there are differences between the specific standards found in the treaties, such as those described above, it may still be possible to achieve a common standard of protection, through the application of the Most-Favoured Nation (MFN) clause, which is found in most treaties.[28] The MFN clause has been used by claimants in past cases to rely on substantive standards found in other treaties concluded by the relevant contracting party. For instance, in *Bayindir v. Pakistan*, the tribunal accepted that the MFN clause in the Pakistan–Turkey BIT could be used in order to rely upon the fair and equitable treatment standard found in another treaty concluded by Pakistan.[29] Presumably, the MFN clause could be used in this manner to harmonise the substantive standards of protection that can be expected by Korean or European investors.

However, there may be limits in using the MFN clause to achieve harmonisation. First, it must be noted that 'the most-favoured nation clause can only attract matters belonging to the same category of subjects to which the clause relates'.[30] In other words, the MFN clause may, itself, limit the type of protection that may be incorporated. Thus, in *Paushok v. Mongolia*, the tribunal held that: '[the] investor cannot use that MFN clause to introduce into the Treaty completely new substantive rights, such as those granted under the umbrella clause', because the MFN clause was limited to claims relating to fair and equitable treatment.[31]

Second, it is not entirely clear to what extent the MFN clause may be used to overcome differences in the dispute settlement provisions of BITs. This is a highly controversial area of international investment law, and one tribunal recently concluded that: 'a jurisprudence constante of general applicability is

---

[28] See, generally, Schill, *The Multilateralization of International Investment Law*, Chapter 4.

[29] *Bayindir v. Pakistan*, ICSID Case No. ARB/03/29, Decision on Jurisdiction of 14 November 2005, paragraphs 230–2. See, also, *MTD v. Chile*, ICSID Case No. ARB/01/7, Award of 25 May 2004, paragraphs 100–4; *Paushok v. Mongolia*, UNCITRAL Arbitration, Award on Jurisdiction and Liability of 28 April 2011, paragraphs 571–2.

[30] *Ambatielos Claim (Greece v. United Kingdom)*, Reports of International Arbitral Awards, vol. 12 (1963), p. 107.

[31] *Paushok v. Mongolia*, paragraph 570.

not yet firmly established'.[32] There are instances where tribunals have used the MFN clause, so as to avoid the application of strict waiting times in a treaty. For instance, in *Suez and others* v. *Argentina*, the tribunal used the MFN clause to harmonise the waiting period in BITs, which were being invoked in that case.[33] However, their approach can be contrasted with that of the tribunal in *Plama* v. *Bulgaria*, where the tribunal held that the MFN clause did not apply to procedural aspects of dispute settlement.[34] Even more controversial is whether or not the MFN clause can be used to circumvent substantive restrictions on jurisdiction, like those found in the Hungary–Korea BIT. Different positions have been taken on this point, as evidenced in the case law to-date.[35] Often, the answer to this question will depend upon the actual wording of the MFN provision, which may itself vary from BIT to BIT.

From this analysis, it follows that the level of investment protection will vary, depending on the applicable BIT. Inevitably, there will be substantive differences between the level of protection that Korean and European investors may enjoy under the existing legal framework. Indeed, sometimes there may be no protection available at all, because several EU Member States do not have a BIT with Korea.[36] It is this situation that the European Commission has described as 'an uneven playing field for EU companies investing abroad',[37] and it has been suggested that 'the uneven distribution of BITs among [Member States] could . . . distort investment flows within the single market'.[38] This is one reason why EU Member States have started to deal with investment at the EU level, rather than through individual BITs. Indeed, with the entry into force of the Lisbon Treaty on 1 December 2009, the common commercial policy was expanded to expressly include 'foreign direct investment', meaning that this issue now falls within the

---

[32] *Renta 4* v. *Russian Federation*, Arbitration Institute of Stockholm Chamber of Commerce, Award on Preliminary Objections of 20 March 2009, paragraph 94.

[33] *Suez and others* v. *Argentina*, ICSID Case No ARB/03/19, Decision on Jurisdiction of 3 August 2006, paragraph 55.

[34] *Plama* v. *Bulgaria*, ICSID Case No. ARB/03/24, Decision on Jurisdiction of 8 February 2005, paragraph 224.

[35] Contrast *RosInvest Co UK Ltd* v. *Russian Federation* (Award on Jurisdiction of October 2007) SCC Arbitration Case No V/079/2005, with *Wintershall* v. *Argentina*, ICSID Case No. ARB/04/14, Award of 8 December 2008. See, also, A. Reinisch, 'How Narrow are Narrow Dispute Settlement Clauses in Investment Treaties?', *Journal of International Dispute Settlement*, vol. 2 (2011), pp. 115–74; Z. Douglas, 'The MFN Clause in Investment Arbitration: Treaty Interpretation off the Rails', *Journal of International Dispute Settlement*, vol. 2 (2011), pp. 97–113.

[36] Notably, Ireland, Estonia, Bulgaria, Cyprus, Malta and Slovenia.

[37] Commission Communication, *Towards a Comprehensive European International Investment Policy*, p. 5.

[38] Commission Communication, *Towards a Comprehensive European International Investment Policy*, p. 10. See, also, M. Burgstaller, 'The Future of Bilateral Investment Treaties of EU Member States', in M. Bungenberg, J. Griebel, and S. Hindelang (eds), *International Investment Law and the EU* (Berlin: Springer-Verlag, 2011), pp. 69–70.

exclusive competence of the EU.[39] One of the main rationales for transferring competence for foreign direct investment to the EU is to 're-establish equality amongst European investment in the long-run'.[40] We must now, therefore, consider to what extent investment has been dealt with in existing instruments between the EU and Korea, and what are the opportunities and challenges for concluding further agreements on this topic.

3 INVESTMENT PROVISIONS IN THE EU–KOREA FTA

3.1 Overview

The recent negotiation of the EU–Korea FTA clearly offered an opportunity for the two parties to address some of the discrepancies that have been identified above. Indeed, it has been suggested that 'the EU–Korea FTA includes, as it currently stands, the most comprehensive investment provisions when compared to the other EU external trade agreements'.[41] Nevertheless, as will be seen below, the FTA does not reconcile all of the differences in the investment practices of individual EU Member States in their BITs with Korea.

3.2 Commitments on establishment

The main provisions on investment in the FTA are found in Section C of Chapter 7, dealing with 'establishment', which is defined as 'the constitution, acquisition or maintenance of a juridical person or the creation or maintenance of a branch or representative office within the territory of a Party for the purpose of performing an economic activity'.[42] This definition includes both the provision of services through commercial presence, but also other types of foreign direct investment, including mining or manufacturing.

Section C of Chapter 7 largely deals with the liberalisation of market access restrictions for foreign direct investments. As a matter of principle, it covers all sectors, apart from those specifically excluded.[43] In addition to this, Chapter 7 does not affect government procurement, subsidies or measures affecting natural persons seeking access to the employment market of a party.[44]

---

[39] TFEU, Article 207.
[40] European Parliament Directorate-General for External Policies, *The EU Approach to International Investment Policy after the Lisbon Treaty*, Document EXPO/B/INTA/FWC/2009-01/Lot7/07-08-09, October 2010, p. 14.
[41] C.-H. Wu, 'Foreign Direct Investment as Common Commercial Policy: EU External Economic Competence After Lisbon', in J. Cardwell (ed.), *EU Relations Law and Policy in the Post-Lisbon Era* (The Hague: TM Asser Press, 2012), p. 395.
[42] EU–Korea FTA, Article 7.9.
[43] For a list of exceptions, see EU–Korea FTA, Article 7.10.
[44] Ibid. Article 7.1.

One of the main obligations found in Section C is the requirement for MFN treatment in Article 7.14(1), which provides that:

> with respect to any measures covered by this Section affecting establishment, unless otherwise provided for in this Article, each Party shall accord to establishments and investors of the other Party treatment no less favourable than that it accords to like establishments and investors of any third country in the context of an economic integration agreement signed after the entry into force of this Agreement.

Ordinarily, the MFN principle is an important way of guaranteeing non-discriminatory treatment for investors of one country, compared to investors of another country. Yet, the wording of this provision limits the scope of MFN treatment, in a number of ways.

First, it only applies to measures 'affecting' establishment. In accordance with the definition of establishment that is cited above, this provision would seem to apply only to measures affecting 'the constitution, acquisition or maintenance of a juridical person', rather than the treatment of an investment more generally. Thus, it has a different scope than the MFN standard found in most BITs, which apply to the treatment of investments once they have already been made.[45]

Second, this provision restricts MFN treatment to treatment arising from other regional economic integration agreements (REIAs).[46] Thus, it will not cover treatment provided outwith the context of a REIA – for example, through national legislative or administrative measures. This is a serious limitation on the scope of the MFN clause. Moreover, it only applies to treatment arising from a REIA that is *signed* after the entry into force of the EU–Korea FTA. In other words, it will not capture existing agreements concluded by EU or Korea, such as the Korea–US FTA or the EU–CARIFORUM EPA, regardless of when they enter into force.

An additional limitation of this provision is found in Article 7.14(2), which exempts treatment arising from a REIA, if that treatment is granted under sectoral or horizontal commitments, for which the REIA stipulates a significantly higher level of obligation than those undertaken between Korea and the EU. The purpose of this condition would seem to be to prevent an investor that was covered by the EU–Korea FTA from claiming more favourable treatment under another FTA that goes significantly beyond the rights granted in the EU–Korea FTA. Annex 7-B clarifies that in order to qualify as being significantly higher, obligations in other REIAs must either create

---

[45] See Section 2.2 of this chapter.
[46] For the purposes of the FTA, an economic integration agreement is defined as 'an agreement substantially liberalising trade in services and established pursuant to the WTO Agreement, in particular Articles V and V of GATS', EU–Korea FTA, Article 17.2(g). Note that there is no requirement for an economic integration agreement to substantially liberalise establishment.

an internal market on services and establishment or encompass both the right of establishment and the approximation of legislation. This provision thus introduces a degree of conditionality into the MFN standard, and it is a departure from the more common MFN practice of states in recent years.[47]

Despite the fact that the MFN standard is already quite narrow, Article 7.14(3) of the FTA also allows the parties to list specific exemptions to MFN treatment in Annex 7-C. This possibility allows a party to exempt entire sectors from the MFN standard, if it so wishes. For example, both the EU and Korea have exempted the fisheries sector from MFN treatment under the FTA.[48]

Finally, the MFN treatment obligation does not apply to the mutual recognition of qualifications, licences or prudential measures, in accordance with Article VII of GATS or its Annex on Financial Services or to treatment granted under an international taxation agreement.[49]

In consideration of other provisions in Chapter 7, Section C deals with market access and national treatment. In this regard, the FTA generally follows a positive list approach to liberalising establishment, similar to the approach applied to services under the General Agreement on Trade in Services in the World Trade Organisation (WTO).[50] In other words, the provisions on market access and national treatment only apply to those sectors for which the parties have specifically undertaken commitments. Specific commitments made by the parties are listed in annexes to the FTA, which include a list of sectors in which commitments have been made, as well as accompanying conditions attached thereto. As existing BITs concluded by EU Member States with Korea do not deal with entry and establishment rights of investors, these provisions of the FTA create new commitments for the parties in the field of investment law.[51]

3.3 *Payments and capital movements*

Further provisions on investment are found in Chapter 8 of the FTA. In particular, Article 8.2 provides that:

---

[47] Conditional MFN treatment was largely phased out during the twentieth century, when states moved to unconditional MFN treatment; see International Law Commission, *Report of the Working Group on Most Favoured Nation Treatment*, Document A/CN.4/L.719, 20 July 2007, Annex, paragraph 7.

[48] EU–Korea FTA, Annex 7-C.

[49] Ibid. Article 7.14(3).

[50] See, generally, R. Dolzer and C. Schreuer, *Principles of International Investment Law* (Oxford: Oxford University Press, 2008), p. 81.

[51] Where the parties have granted a right of national treatment to a particular sector under the FTA, there may be an overlap with the right to national treatment granted by a BIT. To this extent, there is potential for the harmonisation of protection for European investors, in relation to the national treatment standard. It is also worth observing, however, that the Schedules allow reservations to be made by individual EU Member States, so this harmonising effect does not necessarily extend to Korean investors in the EU.

the Parties undertake to impose no restrictions on the free movement of capital relating to direct investments made in accordance with the laws of the host country, to investments and other transactions liberalised in accordance with Chapter Seven and to the liquidation and repatriation of such invested capital and of any profit generated therefrom.

However, this is not an absolute obligation. The FTA makes it abundantly clear that restrictions may be imposed, if they are necessary to protect public security and public morals or to maintain public order or if they are necessary in order to secure compliance with laws or regulations which are not inconsistent with the provisions of the Chapter, provided that such restrictions are not imposed in a manner which would constitute a means of arbitrary or unjustifiable discrimination or a disguised restriction on capital movements.[52] In other words, such restrictions must be imposed in good faith.[53]

Another exception exists for restrictions on payments and capital movements, which may cause, or threaten to cause, serious difficulties for the operation of monetary policy or exchange rate policy. These sorts of measures may be taken in times of financial crisis, such as those recently witnessed in many countries. Safeguard measures are also subject to limitations; they must not last more than six months, and they may only be taken when *strictly* necessary. This latter test would seem to impose a severe burden on states wishing to take safeguard measures, and they must be introduced in such a way, so as to minimise the obvious burden placed on investors.[54] In order to ensure that the conditions on safeguard measures are met, they should be notified to the Trade Committee, along with a timeframe for their removal. Disputes concerning compliance with the limitations set out in the FTA may also be submitted to dispute settlement, under Chapter 22 of the FTA.[55]

It is on this issue of payments and capital movements that the FTA comes closest to the provisions that have already been adopted by Member States in BITs. As noted in section 2, most BITs contain their own provisions on the repatriation of investment and returns. However, the FTA does not replace those pre-existing provisions. The FTA makes clear that it does not affect the application of other treaties relating to investment, to which one of the EU Member States and Korea are a party.[56] Thus, whilst the FTA extends this type of protection to all investors that are covered by the Agreement, it falls short of creating a uniform regime, in relation to payments and capital movements.

---

[52] EU–Korea FTA, Article 8.3.
[53] The WTO Appellate Body interpreted similar language in the GATT in *US – Shrimp*, WTO Appellate Body Report, WT/DS58/AB/R, adopted 12 October 1998, paragraph 158.
[54] See Footnote 2, Article 8.4, EU–Korea FTA.
[55] The dispute settlement system of the FTA is described and analysed in Chapter 4.
[56] EU–Korea FTA, Article 7.15.

3.4 Review of the investment regime

It is clear from the above analysis that it does not address the types of investment protection commonly found in BITs, such as fair and equitable treatment and protection from expropriation. However, the FTA does recognise that it may be desirable to conclude a further agreement on investment protection in the future. In this regard, Article 17.6 provides that:

> with a view to progressively liberalising investments, the Parties shall review the investment legal framework, the investment environment and the flow of investment between them consistently with their commitments in international agreements no later than three years after the entry into force of this Agreement and at regular intervals thereafter.

The FTA goes on to say that this review shall include the possibility of opening negotiations on 'general principles of investment protection'.[57] This is a clear indication that a review will not be limited to assessing the effectiveness of the existing provisions, but that the scope of the investment provisions may be extended to including the types of standards of protection that are currently found in BITs, such as fair and equitable treatment and the regulation of expropriation. Indeed, as noted above, it is only through the negotiation of such provisions that a level playing field can be achieved.

Another factor which may drive the conclusion of a comprehensive investment agreement between the EU and Korea is the desire of the EU to achieve 'full parity' with FTAs already concluded by competitor nations.[58] Given that FTAs concluded by Korea with other states already contain standards of investment protection,[59] it is likely that EU investors would want to achieve similar protection, from which they can all benefit.[60]

It is not only investors that are calling for the EU to exercise its new competence in the field of foreign direct investment. The European Parliament has called for the Commission to 'take the necessary steps towards a progressive replacement of all existing bilateral agreements on investment of Member States with new EU-wide agreements'.[61] The following sections will

---

[57] EU–Korea FTA, Article 7.16(2).

[58] European Commission, *Communication on Global Europe: Competing in the World. A Contribution to the EU's Growth and Job Strategy (Global Europe Strategy)*, Document COM(2006)567 final, Brussels, 4 October 2006, endorsed by the Council, 'Conclusions on Global Europe – Competing in the World' (14799/06) 13 November 2006.

[59] See, for example, FTAs concluded with the US, Chapter 11; Chile, Chapter 10; Singapore, Chapter 10; Peru, Chapter 9.

[60] See, for example, Business Europe Position Paper, 'Priorities for External Competitiveness 2010–2014: Building on Global Europe', February 2010, p. 5: 'the EU should seek a robust outward- looking investment policy, securing the highest level of protection for its investors in key markets'.

[61] *Position of the European Parliament adopted at first reading on 10 May 2011*, Document EP-PE_TC1-COD(2010)0197.

consider some of the issues that may arise in the negotiation process of a comprehensive EU–Korea investment agreement.

4 TOWARDS A COMPREHENSIVE INVESTMENT AGREEMENT

4.1 *What form should a new investment agreement take?*

The first issue that must be decided upon is the form of a new investment agreement between the EU and Korea. There are a number of ways in which the parties may want to address this issue. Either the parties could decide to add a new chapter to the current EU–Korea FTA or they could conclude a free-standing treaty, specifically dealing with investment protection.[62]

Amendments to the FTA must first be considered by the Trade Committee.[63] Once adopted by the parties, they will then enter into force 'after the Parties exchange written notifications certifying that they have completed their respective applicable legal requirements and procedures'.[64] The advantage of adopting new investment provisions as an amendment to the FTA is that it keeps all of the investment-related provisions grouped together in a single instrument.

On the other hand, the parties may want to avoid opening up the re-negotiation of the FTA at such an early stage in its existence, as this may trigger calls for changes in other areas. They may, therefore, favour concluding a new comprehensive EU–Korea investment agreement. If so, it must be considered whether it should be concluded by the EU alone or as a mixed agreement.

Although foreign direct investment is now expressly included within the EU's common commercial policy,[65] debates continue over the precise scope of exclusive competence in relation to investment. For its part, the Commission takes the view that the conclusion of investment treaties comes under the 'exclusive Union competence'.[66] However, there are at least two arguments for a narrower reading of the new EU competence.

First, some commentators have argued that the new competence only pertains to the liberalisation of investment.[67] This view stresses the wording

---

[62] Such a treaty would likely form part of the common institutional framework created by the Framework Agreement; Ko discusses the parameters of the common institutional framework in Chapter 10.

[63] EU–Korea FTA, Article 15.1(4)(c).

[64] Ibid. Article 15.5(1).

[65] TFEU, Article 207.

[66] European Commission, *Proposal for a Regulation Establishing Transitional Arrangements for Bilateral Investment Agreements between Member States and Third Countries*, Document COM(2010) 344, Brussels, 7 July 2010, Recital 3.

[67] J. Ceyssens, 'Towards a Common Investment Policy', *Legal Issues of Economic Integration*, vol. 32 (2005), p. 281.

of Article 206 of the TFEU, which says that 'the Union shall contribute to the . . . the progressive abolition of restrictions on international trade and on foreign direct investment'. According to this point of view, the external competence mirrors that of the internal competence.[68] In contrast, other commentators argue that investment liberalisation and protection cannot be separated.[69] Indeed, it has been pointed out that post-establishment restrictions are just as important as pre-establishment restrictions.[70] Therefore, it is more convincing to interpret the new competence, as including the power to agree on standards of investment protection.

A more difficult issue pertains to whether the new EU competence covers all the types of investment traditionally regulated by BITs. In this regard, several scholars have argued that the new competence of the EU only applies to foreign *direct* investment, and it, therefore, excludes some forms of indirect investments, such as portfolio investments.[71] In other words, the EU alone can negotiate agreements that relate to investments, which involve 'a strategic long-term relationship with the direct investment enterprise to ensure a significant degree of influence by the direct investor in the management of the direct investment enterprise'.[72] As a consequence, these scholars conclude that the common commercial policy 'only partially covers conventional BITs and other comprehensive bilateral or multilateral investment instruments protecting and promoting both direct and indirect foreign investments'.[73] It follows that a comprehensive EU–Korea investment agreement, covering the same scope as BITs, would have to be concluded as a 'mixed agreement', involving both the EU and its Member States.[74] This removes some of the advantages of conferring exclusive competence on the EU. In particular, it means that the consent of each and every EU Member State is needed for the launch of negotiations.[75] Moreover, mixed agreements

---

[68] Ibid.
[69] W. Shan and S. Zhang, 'The Treaty of Lisbon: Half Way Toward a Common Investment Policy', *European Journal of International Law*, vol. 21 (2010), p. 1061; J. Karl, 'The Competence for Foreign Direct Investment: New Powers for the European Union?', *Journal of World Investment & Trade*, vol. 5 (2004), pp. 421–2.
[70] J. A. Bischoff, 'Just a little BIT of "Mixity"? The EU's Role in the Field of International Investment Protection Law', *Common Market Law Review*, vol. 48 (2011), p. 1540.
[71] Burgstaller, 'The Future of Bilateral Investment Treaties of EU Member States', p. 66; Shan and Zhang, 'The Treaty of Lisbon', p. 1059; Bischoff, 'Just a little BIT of "Mixity"?', p. 1534.
[72] *OECD Benchmark Definition of Foreign Direct Investment* (4th edn) (2008), paragraph 11. It continues: 'The "lasting interest" is evidenced when the direct investor owns at least 10% of the voting power of the direct investment enterprise'.
[73] Shan and Zhang, 'The Treaty of Lisbon', p. 1059.
[74] European Parliament Directorate-General for External Policies, *The EU Approach to International Investment Policy after the Lisbon Treaty*, p. 6; see, also, Bischoff, 'Just a little BIT of "Mixity"?', p. 1546; Chaisse, 'Promises and Pitfalls of the European Union Policy on Foreign Investment', pp. 60–1.
[75] It should be noted that the TFEU also provides, in Article 207(4), that: 'For the negotiation and conclusion of agreements in the fields of . . . foreign direct investment, the Council shall

must pass through the national ratification procedures of all the EU Member States before they enter into force, which can be a lengthy process.[76]

As has been discussed, the choice of form for a future instrument is complex, and it is clear that there remains a lot of uncertainty surrounding the new scope of the EU's competence, particularly in relation to investment. There is a very real danger that this uncertainty could delay the negotiation of an EU–Korea investment agreement, until a clearer picture emerges.

4.2 What should a comprehensive investment agreement contain?

A key goal of a comprehensive EU–Korea investment agreement would be to harmonise standards relating to investment protection, thereby overcoming the fragmentation that currently exists. Whilst this diversity is the catalyst for an EU–Korea agreement in the first place, it is also, potentially, a stumbling block, as the parties involved would have to agree on what to include in the agreement.

It is unlikely that there will be a problem in agreeing on those standards which are already common to the EU Member States' BITs with Korea. Thus, the Council of the European Union has already suggested that fair and equitable treatment, non-discrimination, full protection and security, protection against expropriation and the free transfer of funds of capital and payments should form the 'main pillars of future investment agreements'.[77]

It may be more problematic, however, where current BIT practice is at its most diverse. One approach to overcome this is to adopt the highest possible standards that are currently on offer. To this end, the Commission has stated that: 'the Union should follow the available best practices to ensure that no EU investor would be worse off than they would be under Member States' BITs'.[78] Yet, it is not clear that this approach will be endorsed by all of the Member States.

---

act unanimously where such agreements include provisions for which unanimity is required for the adoption of internal rules'.

[76] In some cases, such obstacles may be overcome by permitting the provisional application of the agreement, pending its entry into force. The EU–Korea FTA itself contains a provisional application clause in Article 15.10(5). Moreover, this technique has been used in other investment agreements, permitting investors to bring claims prior to the formal entry into force of the agreement, see, for example, M. H. Arsanjani and W. M. Reisman, 'Provisional Application of Treaties in International Law: The Energy Charter Treaty Awards', in E. Carnnizzaro (ed.), *The Law of Treaties Beyond the Vienna Convention* (Oxford: Oxford University Press, 2011).

[77] Council of the European Union, *Conclusions on a Comprehensive European International Investment Policy*, adopted at the 3041st Foreign Affairs Council Meeting, 25 October 2010, paragraph 14.

[78] European Commission, *Communication: Towards a Comprehensive European International Investment Policy*, p. 11.

The umbrella clause is one example where differences of opinion exist. The position of the EU Council on the umbrella clause appears to be ambivalent, suggesting that there is no clear consensus on this issue between the Member States.[79] Moreover, it should be noted that it is not just the Commission and the Member States which will be involved in deciding these issues, but also the European Parliament, which has a greater role in treaty-making under the Lisbon Treaty.[80] In this context, the European Parliament, whilst approving the inclusion of some standards, has shown some skepticism with regards to particular standards, notably, the umbrella clause.[81] These differences of opinion between the EU institutions will make agreement on a future EU investment policy particularly challenging, and there is no guarantee that the highest possible standards of protection will be maintained.[82]

Another issue that arises for the EU is how to coordinate its investment policies with other policy objectives contained in the EU treaties. Article 7 of the TFEU provides that: 'The Union shall ensure consistency between its policies and activities, taking all of its objectives into account . . .', and Article 3(5) of the TEU provides the general objectives for the pursuit of relations with third states:

> In its relations with the wider world, the Union shall uphold and promote its values and interests and contribute to the protection of its citizens. It shall contribute to peace, security, the sustainable development of the Earth, solidarity and mutual respect among peoples, free and fair trade, eradication of poverty and the protection of human rights, in particular the rights of the child, as well as to the strict observance and the development of international law, including respect for the principles of the United Nations Charter.[83]

This provision reflects a range of values beyond economic interests, which must be taken into account in the negotiation of an investment agreement.[84]

---

[79] Council of the European Union, *Conclusions on a Comprehensive European International Investment Policy*, paragraph 14.

[80] TFEU, Article 218. The EU decision-making procedures are explained in more detail in Chapter 2.

[81] European Parliament resolution of 6 April 2011 on the future of European international investment policy, paragraph 20.

[82] See M. Maes, 'While the EU Member States Insist on the Status Quo, the European Parliament Calls for a Reformed European Investment Policy', Investment Treaty News, 1 July 2011, www.iisd.org/itn/2011/07/01/while-the-eu-member-states-insist-on-the-status-quo-the-european-parliament-calls-for-a-reformed-european-investment-policy/ (accessed 28 February 2012); A. Dimopoulos, 'Creating an EU Investment Policy', in J. Cardwell (ed.), *EU Relations Law and Policy in the Post-Lisbon Era* (The Hague: TM Asser Press, 2012), p. 414.

[83] See, also, Consolidated Version of the Treaty on the European Union (TEU) [2010] OJ C83/13, 30 March 2010, Article 21.

[84] See, also, TFEU, Article 207(1): 'The common commercial policy shall be conducted in the context of the principles and objectives of the Union's external action'.

It must also be remembered that any EU–Korea investment agreement will be negotiated against the backdrop of the Framework Agreement, which places sustainable development at the heart of the strategic partnership.[85]

The FTA already contains some provisions, which regulate these issues pertaining to sustainability. Although its title only refers to *trade* and sustainable development, Chapter 13 of the FTA also briefly touches on the relationship between investment and environmental/labour protection, providing that:

> A Party shall not fail to effectively enforce its environmental and labour laws, through a sustained or recurring course of action or inaction, in a manner affecting trade or *investment* between the Parties. A Party shall not weaken or reduce the environmental or labour protections afforded in its laws to encourage trade or *investment*, by waiving or otherwise derogating from, or offering to waive or otherwise derogate from, its laws, regulations or standards, in a manner affecting trade or investment between the Parties.[86]

Moreover, many of the other existing FTA provisions dealing with environmental and labour standards will also operate, so as to ensure that the investment regime, as well as the trade regime, does not undermine the protection of these values.[87] However, there may be other questions concerning how to balance investment protection with the pursuit of other values, and whether it is necessary to include public policy exceptions in an investment agreement.[88] The EU Council has said that: 'the European investment policy must continue to allow the EU and the Member States to adopt and enforce measures necessary to pursue public policy objectives'.[89] Such a balance is needed not only to promote these values, but it is also necessary if EU industries are going to remain competitive in a global market.[90] At the same time, there is the danger that the incorporation of non-economic values into an investment agreement may lead to 'a politicisation of investment protection, promotion and liberalisation'.[91] The negotiators of an instrument must, therefore, carefully balance these objectives.

Another vital issue that must be addressed in an investment agreement

---

[85] Framework Agreement, Article 3(1). A similar, albeit softer, provision is included, amongst the objectives of the FTA in Article 1.1(2)(h).

[86] EU–Korea FTA, Article 13.7 (emphasis added).

[87] See further discussion in Chapter 9 by Marín-Durán.

[88] Dimopoulos, 'Creating an EU Investment Policy', p. 412.

[89] Council of the European Union, *Conclusions on a Comprehensive European International Investment Policy*, paragraph 14.

[90] See, for example, Opinion of the European Economic and Social Committee on a Comprehensive European International Investment Policy, Document CESE 1184/2011, paragraphs 5.4 and 5.5.

[91] European Parliament Directorate-General for External Policies, *The EU Approach to International Investment Policy after the Lisbon Treaty*, p. 14.

is how disputes should be settled. From the EU perspective, investor–state dispute settlement is supported both by the Commission[92] and the Council.[93] Yet, an issue that is commonly faced by negotiators is the level of detail that is to be included in investor–state dispute settlement procedures. Whereas the provisions of the existing BITs between EU Member States and Korea simply tend to establish consent to arbitration, without specifying the details of the procedure, it is common for dispute settlement clauses in modern BITs to be much more extensive in their provision. Many modern investment agreements specify rules concerning the initiation of the procedure, the constitution of the tribunal and the procedure to be followed by the tribunal, including issues such as transparency and the participation of other non-disputing parties.[94] The Commission has identified these issues as important priorities for a future investment policy, but as there is no 'best practice' amongst the Member States, it will be necessary for the EU to construct a new policy entirely from scratch. Indeed, the EU may also need to overcome apparent differences between the EU institutions in this area, with the European Parliament suggesting the inclusion of an exhaustion of local remedies rule in EU investment treaties, which is contrary to the practice of most EU Members States on this issue.[95]

There are further complications concerning the development of dispute settlement procedures, which arise because of the peculiar status of the EU as an international actor. First, given that the EU is not able to become a party to the ICSID Convention, because it is not a state,[96] any dispute settlement mechanism must make reference to alternative procedures or try to get around this impediment in a creative manner.[97] Second, if an investment instrument is concluded as a mixed agreement, the parties must also deal

---

[92] European Commission, *Communication: Towards a Comprehensive European International Investment Policy*, p. 10.

[93] Council of the European Union, *Conclusions on a Comprehensive European International Investment Policy*, paragraph 18.

[94] UNCTAD, *International Investment Rule-Making: Stocktaking, Challenges and the Way Forward* (Geneva: UNCTAD Series on International Investment Policies for Development, 2008), pp. 43–4.

[95] See European Parliament Resolution of 6 April 2011 on the Future European International Investment Policy (2010/2203(INI)), paragraph 31; see, also, M. Sattorova, 'Return to the Local Remedies Rule in European BITs? Power (Inequalities), Dispute Settlement, and Change in Investment Treaty Law', *Legal Issues of Economic Integration*, vol. 39 (2012), pp. 223–47.

[96] Convention on the Settlement of Investment Disputes between States and Nationals of other States (ICSID Convention), Article 67.

[97] For a discussion of the various possibilities, see Bischoff, 'Just a Little BIT of "Mixity"?', pp. 1566–8; see, also, M. Burgstaller, 'Investor–State Arbitration in EU International Investment Agreements with Third States', *Legal Issues of Economic Integration*, vol. 39 (2012), pp. 207–21. See, also, Council of the European Union, *Conclusions on a Comprehensive European International Investment Policy*, paragraph 18, which calls on the Commission to 'carry out a detailed study on the relevant issues concerning international arbitration systems . . .'.

with the allocation of responsibility between the EU and its Member States for violations of investment protection standards.[98]

The novelty of the issues raised in investment negotiations is, arguably, a significant challenge for the EU. Whilst the diversity in the current practice in relation to investment protection is one of the leading rationales for the adoption of a uniform investment policy at the EU level, this diversity also presents the greatest obstacle, as it requires the twenty-seven Member States and the EU institutions to uniformly agree on a common position in relation to many of the most controversial and difficult aspects of international investment law.

Whatever challenges are faced internally by the EU when developing an investment policy, it must also be remembered that any agreement will be the result of negotiations with Korea. The fact that Korea is an emerging economic power means that the EU will not simply be able to impose its will on Korea.[99] Indeed, Korea already has significant experience in the negotiation of modern and detailed investment protection provisions.[100] Yet, Korea may also have its own challenges in concluding an investment agreement with the EU, not least, popular dissatisfaction with investor–state dispute settlement, which came to the surface during the negotiations of the Korea–US FTA.[101] Whilst investor–state dispute settlement is today a common feature of investment agreements, it is not always referred to in investment treaties, and there are a number of recent investment agreements between developed states that have excluded investor–state dispute settlement.[102] These exemplars could provide a precedent for future negotiations, making the negotiations even more difficult than they stand at present.

4.3 Transition from BITS to an EU–Korea investment instrument

Although competence for foreign direct investment has been transferred to the EU under the TFEU, the transitional arrangements proposed by

---

[98] See Bischoff, 'Just a Little BIT of "Mixity"?', p. 1565, where he argues that: 'if the BIT provides for an explicit delimitation clause referring to the internal competences, only the entity enjoying the competence will be liable. If there is no such delimitation clause, this would be an argument in favour of joint liability of the EU and the Member States'.

[99] For a discussion on the status of Korea, see Chapter 1.

[100] See Kim, 'The Evolution of Korea's Modern Investment Treaties and Investor–State Dispute Settlement Provisions'.

[101] See the discussion of Kim in Chapter 3.

[102] See, for example, A. Capling and K. R. Nossal, 'Blowback: Investor–State Dispute Mechanisms in International Trade Agreements', *Governance*, vol. 19 (2006), p. 151. It has, however, been suggested that the failure to include investor–state dispute settlement provisions renders the protections irrelevant; W. S. Dodge, 'Investor-State Dispute Settlement between Developed Countries: Reflections on the Australia–United States Free Trade Agreement', *Vanderbilt Journal of Transnational Law*, vol. 39 (2006), p. 1; see, also, European Parliament Directorate-General for External Policies, *The EU Approach to International Investment Policy after the Lisbon Treaty*, p. 39.

the European Commission foresee that Member States will be permitted to maintain their BITs for the time being.[103] Yet, this is only a short-term solution. Thus, under the proposal, the Commission would have the power to, inter alia, require Member States to terminate BITs in a number of situations, including if the BIT overlaps with an agreement entered into by the EU or if it constitutes an obstacle to the development of any union policies relating to investment.[104] The Commission would undoubtedly request the termination of existing BITs with Korea, if an investment agreement was reached with the EU.

A problem that arises in this context is that the termination of a BIT does not necessarily put an end to the possibility of investors continuing to make claims under the treaty. Whereas termination of a treaty normally stops claims being brought under that treaty, most BITs contain a so-called survival clause, which allows investors to bring a claim in relation to an investment that was made whilst the BIT was in force. An example of a typical survival clause reads as follows:

> In respect of investments made prior to the date when the notice of termination of this Agreement becomes effective, the provisions of Articles 1 to 9 shall remain in force for a further period of ten years from that date.[105]

The effect of such a clause is to limit the ability of a party to unilaterally opt out of the treaty, so that 'even though a State may terminate a BIT, it will often still remain bound by its provisions vis-à-vis investments made prior to the treaty's termination'.[106] There has been little in-depth research of survival clauses, however, and several questions arise concerning their operation.[107]

Whilst a survival clause will apply when a party to the treaty unilaterally withdraws its consent, it is not clear whether a survival clause applies if the parties have terminated the treaty by mutual agreement. This may, in part, largely depend upon the wording of a particular survival clause. Nevertheless, it could be argued that a survival clause should not limit the ability of the contracting parties to terminate the treaty, using their inherent powers under the law of treaties. In this respect, Article 54 of the Vienna Convention on the Law of Treaties provides that:

---

[103] European Commission, *Proposal for a Regulation Establishing Transitional Arrangements for Bilateral Investment Agreements between Member States and Third Countries.*

[104] Ibid. Reg. 6.

[105] Denmark–Korea BIT, Article 10(3).

[106] UNCTAD, *Denunciation of the ICSID Convention and BITS: Impact on Investor–State Claims*, IIA Issues Note No. 2, December 2010, p. 3.

[107] See further, J. Harrison, 'The Life and Death of BITs: Legal Issues concerning Survival Clauses and the Termination of Investment Treaties', *Journal of World Investment and Trade*, vol. 13 (2012), pp. 928–50.

the termination of a treaty or the withdrawal of a party may take place: (a) in conformity with the provisions of the treaty; *or* (b) at any time by consent of all the parties after consultation with the other contracting States.

Thus, agreement between the parties is an alternative to using the specific procedures in a treaty, and it could be argued that mutual consent can override any conditions contained in the treaty.

At the same time, there is also an argument that this provision cannot be applied to investment treaties, because they establish substantive rights for investors, which cannot be withdrawn without the consent of the right holders.[108] Indeed, in this regard, the Vienna Convention on the Law of Treaties provides that:

> when a right has arisen for a third [party] in conformity with article 36, the right may not be revoked or modified by the parties if it is established that the right was intended not to be revocable or subject to modification without the consent of the third [party].[109]

This conclusion also appears to be supported by the object of purpose of investment treaties, which are designed to promote stability for investors.[110]

It follows that the survival clauses in existing BITs are capable of potentially presenting problems for the establishment of a level playing field for European and Korean investors in the short-term. The majority of the survival clauses in BITs between the EU Member States and Korea last five or ten years, but some go up to fifteen or twenty years. Indeed, the French–Korea BIT appears to apply indefinitely to investments made during the period when the BIT was in force.[111] The precise effects of survival clauses need further study, but it is clear that these provisions may pose an impediment to the achievement of a level playing field, at least in the short-term.

---

[108] This appears to be the position taken by the Court of Appeal of England and Wales in *Occidental* v. *Ecuador* [2005] EWCA Civ 1116, paragraph 37: '[The case] concerns a Treaty intended by its signatories to give rise to rights in favour of private investors capable of enforcement, to an extent specified by the Treaty wording, in consensual arbitration against one or other of its signatory States'. See, also, Z. Douglas, 'The Hybrid Foundation of Investment Treaty Arbitration', *British Yearbook of International Law*, vol. 74 (2003), pp. 181–4.

[109] 1969 Vienna Convention on the Law of Treaties, Article 37(2).

[110] This was a factor that was taken into account by the Court of Appeal of England and Wales in *Occidental* v. *Ecuador* [2007] EWCA Civ 656, paragraph 28; see, also, SGS v. *Philippines* (2004) 8 ICSID Reports 515, paragraph 116. One could also argue that this conclusion is supported by the *contra proferentum* principle, whereby a treaty must be interpreted for the benefit of third parties, who have relied on it.

[111] France–Korea BIT, Article 9(4) provides that: 'in the event of termination, the provisions of this Agreement shall continue to be applicable to the investments covered by its provisions and made during the period when it was in force'.

5 CONCLUSION

This chapter has presented an overview of the fragmented legal framework that currently governs investments between the EU and Korea, highlighting the diverse practice in relation to standards of protection for investors and dispute settlement procedures. It has also discussed some of the difficult challenges that may lie ahead, if the parties decide to go ahead and conclude a comprehensive agreement on investment in the future in order to promote a uniform legal framework. It is clear that these issues involve a complex interaction between international investment law, on the one hand, and EU external relations law, on the other hand. Whilst these challenges are surmountable, it is likely that the establishment of a level playing field for European and Korean investors will take a great deal of time, effort and imagination to achieve. Nevertheless, the negotiation of a new, comprehensive instrument on investment protection would benefit both European and Korean investors seeking to make the most of the market access rights and other protections that are offered by the FTA. Therefore, it can be argued that it should be a policy priority for both the EU and Korea, in the implementation of their strategic partnership.

8

Innovations and Implications of the Trade and Sustainable Development Chapter in the EU–Korea Free Trade Agreement

Gracia Marín Durán

1 INTRODUCTION

As previous contributions to this volume have illustrated, EU–Korea trade and economic relations have been significantly broadened and strengthened with the conclusion of the bilateral Free Trade Agreement (FTA)[1] in October 2010, which followed the launch of negotiations on new 'competitiveness-driven' FTAs and the designation of Korea as a 'priority partner' in the Global Europe Strategy adopted by the EU in November 2006.[2] In the words of the European Commission, the EU–Korea FTA is ground-breaking, as the first such trade deal to be concluded by the Union with an Asian country and containing the most comprehensive trade provisions outside the EU enlargement context.[3] The focus of this contribution is on Chapter 13 of the EU–Korea FTA, entitled 'Trade and Sustainable Development' (T&SD),

---

[1] Free Trade Agreement between the European Union and its Member States of the one part, and the Republic of Korea, of the other part (EU–Korea FTA) [2011] OJ L127/6 14 May 2001. It has been provisionally applied since 1 July 2011: 'Notice concerning the provisional application of the Free Trade Agreement between the European Union and its Member States, of the one part, and the Republic of Korea, of the other part' [2011] OJ L168/1.

[2] European Commission, *Communication on Global Europe: Competing in the World. A Contribution to the EU's Growth and Job Strategy (Global Europe Strategy)*, Document COM (2006) 567final, Brussels, 4 October 2006, endorsed by the Council, 'Conclusions on Global Europe – Competing in the World' (14799/06) 13 November 2006. See, for further discussion, Chapter 2 of this volume and S. J. Evenett, '"Global Europe": An Initial Assessment of the European Commission's New Trade Policy' (18 December 2006), www.imd.org/uupload /EvianGroup/PUBLICATIONS/1456.pdf (accessed 27 April 2012).

[3] European Commission, *The EU–Korea Free Trade Agreement in Practice* (Luxembourg: Publications Office of the European Union, 2011), p. 1, www.trade.ec.europa.eu/doclib/d ocs/2011/october/tradoc_148303.pdf (accessed 27 April 2012). Even before the provisional application of the FTA, in 2010, the EU was among Korea's major trading partners, ranked fourth in terms of imports (9.4 per cent of total, behind China, Japan and the US) and second in terms of exports (11.9 per cent of total, after China). In 2011, Korea was the EU's tenth trading partner in terms of imports (2.1 per cent of total) and 11th in terms of exports (2.1 per cent of total); see www.trade.ec.europa.eu/doclib/docs/2006/september/tradoc_113448.p df (accessed 27 April 2012).

which addresses the interface between trade policy, on the one hand, and environmental and labour protection objectives, on the other. As will be seen, the T&SD chapter can equally be considered as breaking new ground in its development of a regulatory approach to these issues at the bilateral/ regional level, which the EU, furthermore, wishes to replicate in its future FTA negotiations.[4]

The chapter begins by placing the T&SD chapter of the EU–Korea FTA into its broader regulatory context at both EU and international levels, as a backdrop for gauging the innovative elements that it has introduced to the regulation of trade–environment and trade–labour linkages. It then turns to analysing the substantive and institutional provisions of the T&SD chapter, highlighting differences and similarities in regulatory approaches vis-à-vis EU practice under other FTAs. In this comparative outlook, particular attention will be paid to the FTA concluded with Colombia and Peru (COPE) in March 2011,[5] in order to assess the extent to which the EU–Korea T&SD chapter has served as a model for other FTA negotiations, following the adoption of the Global Europe Strategy. Where relevant, comparisons will also be made with the environment and labour chapters of the Korea–US FTA, concluded in June 2007,[6] which may have been influential in shaping the substantive rules of the EU–Korea T&SD chapter, albeit the two agreements differ significantly in terms of enforcement mechanisms. Following this textual analysis, the chapter identifies and reflects on some critical legal and policy questions that are likely to arise, in relation to bilateral cooperation under the T&SD chapter in the years to come. In the final section, the T&SD chapter is assessed in terms of its potential to act as an alternative model for regulating trade–environment and trade–labour linkages in the framework of regional trade agreements, as well as its broader implications for multilateral processes on these issues.

[4] European Commission, *Global Europe Strategy*, p. 11. The priority trading partners, with which the EU will seek to conclude new-generation FTAs, are, in addition to Korea: the Association of South-East Asian Nations (ASEAN, comprising: Brunei Darussalam, Cambodia, Indonesia, Lao PDR, Malaysia, Myanmar (Burma), Philippines, Singapore, Thailand and Vietnam); the Gulf Cooperation Council countries (Bahrain, Kuwait, Oman, Qatar, Saudi Arabia and United Arab Emirates); India; MERCOSUR countries (Argentina, Brazil, Paraguay and Uruguay); and Russia.

[5] Free Trade Agreement between the EU and its Member States, on one side, and Colombia and Peru, on the other, initialled on 23 and 24 March 2011 (COPE FTA), www.trade.ec.eur opa.eu/doclib/press/index.cfm?id=691 (accessed 27 April 2012).

[6] United States – Korea Free Trade Agreement (Korea–US FTA), signed on 30 June 2007, Chapter 19 (Labour) and Chapter 20 (Environment), www.ustr.gov/trade-agreements/free-trade-agreements/korus-fta (accessed 27 April 2012).

2 INNOVATIONS OF THE T&SD CHAPTER

2.1 An insight into the broader context

The EU–Korea FTA is not, of course, the first agreement[7] to link trade and 'sustainable development' – a notion which was first conceived in the area of international environmental law[8] and more recently redefined at the 2002 World Summit on Sustainable Development (WSSD) held in Johannesburg. At the WSSD, the international community undertook to:

> advance and strengthen the interdependent and mutually reinforcing pillars of sustainable development: economic development, social development and environmental protection at the local, national, regional and global levels.[9]

Therefore, the common objective of sustainable development demands the integration of economic, social and environmental policies and laws in a non-hierarchical and balanced manner at all levels of decision-making, including in the context of regional trade agreements.

However, the exact implications of sustainable development for trade agreements – whether at the multilateral or the regional level – are far from clear. This is partly due to the normative uncertainty surrounding the concept of sustainable development, which has played out differently in varied contexts and is still subject to evolution.[10] Nonetheless, the Johannesburg Plan of Implementation[11] that was also adopted at the WSSD

---

[7] Notably, the objective of sustainable development is stated in the Preamble of the Marrakesh Agreement establishing the World Trade Organization, 15 April 1994.

[8] What is traditionally considered the first definition of sustainable development is that proposed by the World Commission on Environment and Development, *Our Common Future (Brundtland Report)* (Oxford: Oxford University Press, 1987), chapter 2, paragraph 1. This was further elaborated in the Rio Declaration on Environment and Development, Document UN Doc A/CONF.155/26 vol. 1 Annex 1, 12 August 1992 (Rio Declaration), particularly, Principles 1–3.

[9] Political Declaration of the World Summit on Sustainable Development, Document UN Doc A/CONF.199/20 Resolution 1, 4 September 2002 (WSSD Declaration), paragraph 5

[10] On the origins and normative evolution of the concept of sustainable development in public international law, see V. Barral, *Le Développement Durable en Droit International: Essai sur les Incidences Juridiques d'un Concept Évolutif* (Florence: European University Institute Doctoral Thesis, 2007); M.-C. Cordonier-Segger and A. Khalfan, *Sustainable Development Law – Principles, Practices and Prospects* (Oxford: Oxford University Press, 2004), pp. 15–31; V. Lowe 'Sustainable Development and Unsustainable Arguments', in A. Boyle and D. Freestone (eds), *International Law and Sustainable Development – Past Achievements and Future Prospects* (Oxford: Oxford University Press, 1999); Y. Matsui, 'The Road to Sustainable Development: Evolution of the Concept of Development in the UN', in K. Ginther, E. Denters and P. de Waart (eds), *Sustainable Development and Good Governance* (Dordrecht: Martinus Nijhoff, 1995). For an examination of its meaning in EU law, see G. Marín Durán and E. Morgera, *Environmental Integration in the EU's External Relations – Beyond Multilateral Dimensions* (Oxford: Hart Publishing, 2012), pp. 34–40.

[11] Johannesburg Plan of Implementation, Document UN Doc A/CONF.199/20 Resolution 2,

singles out a number of international legal instruments as the central tenets of the international sustainable development agenda. Of utmost relevance to our analysis, these international legal instruments include 11 key multilateral environmental agreements (MEAs) and the 1998 Declaration on Fundamental Principles and Rights at Work.[12] But how, exactly, should trade, environmental and labour regimes be integrated, so as to ensure a 'mutually supportive' relationship between the three components of sustainable development?

Regulatory linkages between trade and labour/environment have been a controversial issue in international trade relations, even before the endorsement of the global agenda on sustainable development, and they have been particularly divisive when standards of protection vary across countries, in light of their different stages of development. At the most basic level, these recurring debates reflect a profound disagreement over two key questions. First, do national differences in standards of labour or environmental protection have an impact on the international competitiveness of traded goods and services? And, if so, should lower standards be accepted as a 'legitimate' source of comparative advantage in world trade? Second, is it appropriate to use trade measures for environmental or social protection goals?[13]

Within the multilateral trading system, the relationship (and potential tension) between trade liberalisation commitments, on the one hand, and environmental and social protection objectives, on the other, has been traditionally addressed through general exceptions clauses, notably Article XX of the General Agreement on Tariffs and Trade (GATT).[14] Such

---

4 September 2002 (JPOI). For a commentary, see Cordonier-Segger and Khalfan, *Sustainable Development Law – Principles, Practices and Prospects*, pp. 31–43.

[12] International Labour Conference (86th Session), 'Declaration on Fundamental Principles and Rights at Work', 18 June 1998 (1998 ILO Declaration), www.ilo.org/declaration/thedecl aration/lang--en/index.htm (accessed 27 April 2012).

[13] This is not the place to elaborate further on these discussions. For an overview of the trade and environment debate, see H. Cameron, 'The Evolution of the Trade and Environment Debate at the WTO', in A. Najam, M. Halle and R. Meléndez-Ortiz (eds), *Trade and Environment – A Resource Book* (Geneva: ICTSD/IISD/The Ring, 2007), www.ictsd.org/i /environment/11235/ (accessed 27 April 2012) and, more generally, J. Wiers, *Trade and Environment in the EC and the WTO – A Legal Analysis* (Groningen: Europa Law Publishing, 2002). On the trade and labour debate, see C. McCrudden and A. Davies, 'A Perspective on Trade and Labour Rights', *Journal of International Economic Law*, vol. 3 (2000), pp. 43–62, and, more generally, C. Barry and S. G. Reddy, *International Trade and Labour Standards* (New York: Columbia University Press, 2008).

[14] Article XX GATT, entitled 'General Exceptions', recognises WTO members' right to adopt (or enforce) measures 'necessary to protect human, animal, or plant life or health' (paragraph b), 'relating the products of prison labour' (paragraph e) and 'related to the conservation of exhaustible natural resources' (paragraph g), subject to the requirement that such measures are not applied in a manner that would constitute 'a means of arbitrary or unjustifiable discrimination' or a 'disguised restriction' on trade between the parties (chapeau). See, also, Article XIV GATS. For an examination of relevant case law, see P. van den Bossche, *The*

clauses are *permissive* and conditional in nature; that is, they establish the conditions under which it is considered appropriate (from a World Trade Organization (WTO) law perspective) to allow WTO members to deviate from their obligations when adopting trade-related measures aimed at environmental or social protection (mainly health issues). Labour standards, as such, do not fall within the scope of these exception clauses, following the position adopted at the first WTO Ministerial Conference in Singapore in December 1996; namely, that labour issues are to be addressed through the International Labour Organisation (ILO) and kept out of the WTO and that 'the comparative advantage of countries, particularly low-wage developing countries, must in no way be put into question'.[15] Meanwhile, discussions are ongoing, under the Doha Round launched in November 2001, on the relationship between the WTO and MEAs, with a view to avoiding conflicts between the two regimes.[16] Yet, here too, it is generally recognised that each WTO member has the right to set its own environmental standards 'at the level it considers appropriate',[17] in line with the principle of common but differentiated responsibility,[18] and, arguably, it would be beyond the WTO mandate – not being an environmental agency – to require otherwise.

The regulatory approach to these issues in the context of regional trade agreements has gone significantly beyond that of the WTO and, particularly, when such agreements involve countries at different levels of development, with a well-known pioneering example being the North American Free Trade Agreement (NAFTA) and its Side Agreements on Environmental and Labour Cooperation.[19] Not only are labour matters also addressed at the regional level, but the scope of regulation is not confined to reconciling possible tensions between trade liberalisation commitments and labour/environmental protection norms. Unlike in the WTO, we find in the NAFTA Side Agreements and the other FTAs concluded thereafter by the

---

Law and Policy of the World Trade Organization (Cambridge: Cambridge University Press, 2008), pp. 616–64.

[15] Singapore Ministerial Declaration, Document WTO WTO/MIN (96)/DEC, 18 December 1996, paragraph 4; this was re-affirmed in the Doha Ministerial Declaration, Document WTO/MIN(01)/DEC/1, 14 November 2001 (Doha Declaration), paragraph 8.

[16] Doha Declaration, paragraph 31 (i) the relationship between existing WTO rules and specific trade obligations set out in multilateral environmental agreements. The negotiations shall be limited in scope to the applicability of such existing WTO rules as among parties to the MEA in question; and 31 (ii) procedures for regular information exchange between MEA Secretariats and the relevant WTO committees. For an overview of the negotiations, see V. Yu, 'Multilateral Environmental Agreements' in Najam, Halle and Meléndez-Ortiz (eds), *Trade and Environment – A Resource Book*.

[17] Doha Declaration, paragraph 6.

[18] Rio Declaration, Principles 7 and 11.

[19] North American Agreement on Environmental Cooperation and North American Agreement on Labour Cooperation, signed on 14 September 1993, www.ustr.gov/trade -agreements/free-trade-agreements/korus-fta (accessed 27 April 2012).

US,[20] a set of *prescriptive* provisions that establish what regional partners *should* and *should not* do in terms of environmental/labour protection standards.[21]

These provisions often respond to fears of a race to the bottom in environmental and labour regulations, which is primarily an issue for (developed) countries with more stringent standards of protection concerned with being undercut by foreign competitors, who are capable of producing goods or providing services at lower costs because of weaker environmental and labour protection regimes. In other words, they are aimed at preventing what has become known as social dumping and environmental dumping, and at ensuring a level playing field between regional partners as regards environmental and labour protection standards. In doing so, however, they clearly question the comparative advantage of (less developed) countries with lower standards of protection and constrain their capacity to use these as a means to encourage trade or investment.

For its part, the EU's approach to the regulation of trade and environmental/ labour issues under FTAs was, until the agreement with Korea, essentially permissive and limited to general exceptions clauses, usually modelled on Article 36 of the TFEU, which is considered more flexible than Article XX GATT in allowing countries to pursue environmental and social protection objectives.[22] Yet, a policy shift was announced in the renewed Sustainable Development Strategy adopted in June 2006, where the European Council gave a clear mandate for the integration of environmental and social concerns in bilateral and inter-regional trade and cooperation agreements, 'as a tool to achieve genuine global sustainable development'.[23] This was followed

[20] See, for instance, the United States–Singapore Free Trade Agreement (signed on 6 May 2003); the United States–Chile Free Trade Agreement (signed on 6 June 2003); the United States–Morocco Free Trade Agreement (signed on 15 June 2004); and the United States–Dominican Republic/Central America Free Trade Agreement (signed on 5 August 2004), all of which contain similar environment and labour chapters. These are available at www.ustr. gov/trade-agreements/free-trade-agreements/korus-fta (accessed 27 April 2012).

[21] On the difference between permissive and prescriptive regulatory approaches in the context of the trade and environment nexus, see G. Marín Durán, 'The Role of the EU in Shaping the Trade and Environment Nexus: Multilateral and Regional Approaches', in S. Blockmans, B. van Booren and J. Wouters (eds), *The Legal Dimension of Global Governance – What Role for the EU?* (Oxford: Oxford University Press, forthcoming 2013).

[22] Given that Article 36 of the TFEU allows for the adoption of measures that are more broadly justified on grounds of 'public policy', see A. Cosbey, S. Tay, H. Lim and M. Walls 'The Rush to Regionalism: Sustainable Development and Regional/Bilateral Approaches to Trade and Investment Liberalisation', *International Institute for Sustainable Development*, A Scoping Paper Prepared for the International Development Research Centre, Canada, November 2004, p. 12, www.iisd.org/publications/pub.aspx?id=670 (accessed 27 April 2012). For an overview of the trade and environment provisions in these earlier EU agreements, see Marín Durán and Morgera, *Environmental Integration in the EU's External Relations*, pp. 72–3, 80–1 and 114–15.

[23] Council of the European Union, 'Review of the EU Sustainable Development Strategy (EU SDS) – Renewed Strategy' (10917/06) 26 June 2006, p. 21; see, also, the preceding European Commission, *Communication on the 2005 Review of the EU Sustainable Development Strategy:*

by the Global Europe Strategy, endorsed in November 2006, which tackles the incorporation of 'cooperative provisions in areas related to labour standards and environmental protection'[24] in new FTAs, as part of the broader objective of using the EU's external trade policy more actively in order to enhance its competitiveness in a changing global economic order.[25] As the first example of this new trend, the T&SD chapter of the EU–Korea FTA complements the general exceptions clause,[26] with prescriptive provisions which reflect the policy goals of enhancing environmental and labour protection standards as a means to promote global sustainable development, while ensuring a level playing field in regulatory standards, so as to serve (EU) competitiveness interests.

Does this mean that T&SD chapters are, after all, just an attempt by the EU to export its own environmental and labour norms upon its regional partners and undermine their comparative advantage in international trade? And is the EU just imitating the US approach or, in fact, seeking to develop an alternative model to the regulation of trade and environmental/labour issues at the regional level? To shed some light on these questions, the next two sections proceed to examine the provisions of the T&SD chapter of the EU–Korea FTA through a comparative perspective.

2.2 Substantive provisions

The T&SD chapter of the EU–Korea FTA is placed, from the outset, within the global agenda on sustainable development, with explicit references being made to international instruments, such as Agenda 21 on Environment and Development of 1992,[27] the Johannesburg Plan of Implementation on Sustainable Development of 2002[28] and the 2006 Ministerial Declaration of the UN Economic and Social Council on Full Employment and Decent Work.[29] In line with this broader regulatory context, the Parties reiterate, in best-endeavour language, their undertakings at the international level, so as to ensure mutual supportiveness between trade and sustainable develop-

---

Initial Stocktaking and Future Orientations, Document COM (2005) 37 final, Brussels, 9 February 2005.

[24] European Commission, *Global Europe Strategy*, p. 9.

[25] On this point, see, further, Marín Durán, 'The Role of the EU in Shaping the Trade and Environment Nexus: Multilateral and Regional Approaches'.

[26] EU–Korea FTA, Article 2.15(1), whereby the Parties reaffirm their rights and obligations under Article XX GATT (see Footnote 14)

[27] Agenda 21, Document UN Doc A/CONF.151/26/Rev.1 vol.1, Annex II, 12 August 1992.

[28] See Footnote 11.

[29] ECOSOC (High-level Segment), 'Ministerial Declaration on Creating an Environment at the National and International Levels Conducive to Generating Full and Productive Employment and Decent Work for All, and its Impact on Sustainable Development', Document UN Doc A/61/3/Rev.1 chap III, paragraph 50; see, also, subsequent ECOSOC Resolution 2008/18, 'Promoting Full Employment and Decent Work for All', 14 July 2008.

ment: 'the Parties reaffirm their commitments to promoting the development of international trade in such a way as to contribute to the objective of sustainable development' and to 'strive to ensure that this objective is integrated and reflected at every level of their trade relationship'.[30] The Parties also 'recognize that economic development, social development and environmental protection are interdependent and mutually reinforcing components of sustainable development', and 'underline the benefit of cooperation on trade-related social and environmental issues as part of the global approach to trade and sustainable development'.[31]

However, it is also made clear from the outset that the purpose of bilateral cooperation under the T&SD chapter is not to harmonise standards of labour and environmental protection between the EU and Korea.[32] In a similar vein, it is stressed that the Parties' respective 'comparative advantage should in no way be called into question' and that environmental and labour standards 'should not be used' for protectionist trade purposes.[33] Notwithstanding the soft-law language that has been employed, these provisions are important in recognising the concerns that, as noted earlier, typically arise when environmental/labour issues are included in trade agreements, and particularly if these involve partners at different levels of development.

While regulatory integration or harmonisation is not, in principle, envisaged, the T&SD chapter seeks, nonetheless, to regulate the Parties' conduct in relation to environmental and labour protection standards, through two sets of substantive requirements. First, an obligation is laid down – albeit couched in best-endeavour language and subject to the Parties' right to regulate[34] – to 'seek to ensure' that domestic laws and policies 'provide for and encourage high levels of environmental and labour protection', which is defined as 'consistent with the internationally recognized standards or agreements'.[35] This best-endeavour obligation to ensure 'high levels' of environmental and labour protection should be read in conjunction with another set of provisions, which provide some guidance as to the international standards and agreements at issue.

With regards to labour standards, the Parties undertake, 'in accordance with their obligations deriving from membership'[36] of the International

---

[30] EU–Korea FTA, Article 13.1(1); see, also, Article 1(g), where sustainable development is recognised as an 'overarching objective' of the Agreement.

[31] Ibid. Article 13.1(2).

[32] Ibid. Article 13.1(3).

[33] Ibid. Article 13.2(3).

[34] Ibid. Article 13.3 reads: 'Recognising the right of each Party to establish its own levels of environmental and labour protection, and to adopt or modify accordingly its relevant laws and policies . . .'.

[35] EU–Korea FTA, Article 13.3.

[36] Ibid. Article 13.4(3). Note, however, that only EU Member States (not, in fact, the EU itself) are members of the ILO; see, further, Section on 'bilateral implications of the T&SD chapter'.

Labour Organisation, to respect and apply in their domestic laws and practices those core standards that are enshrined in the ILO Declaration on Fundamental Principles and Rights at Work (and its follow-up),[37] namely: freedom of association and the right to collective bargaining, the elimination of all forms of forced or compulsory labour, the effective abolition of child labour, and the elimination of discrimination in respect to employment and education.[38] Besides committing to adhere to these core labour standards, the Parties further 'reaffirm their commitment to effectively implementing the ILO Conventions' that they have each ratified and to make 'continued and sustained efforts' towards ratifying other key ILO Conventions.[39] Interestingly, for comparative purposes, these core ILO standards also serve as points of reference for the labour chapter in the Korea–US FTA, albeit, there, the Parties are under a clear obligation to adopt and maintain such standards within their domestic laws and practices.[40] Nonetheless, this obligation is only enforceable to the extent that violations occur in a 'manner affecting trade or investment between the Parties'.[41]

As to environmental standards, the Parties simply 'reaffirm their commitments to the effective implementation in their laws and practices of the multilateral environmental agreements to which they are party', without, however, specifying the agreements in question. This contrasts with the approach that is taken in the COPE FTA, which links, more specifically, domestic environmental performance with a closed list of core MEAs,[42]

---

[37] See Footnote 12. These core labour standards are to be observed by all ILO members, regardless of whether or not they have ratified the relevant ILO Conventions. For a critical assessment, see P. Alston, 'Core Labour Standards and the Transformation of the International Labour Rights Regime', *European Journal of International Law*, vol. 15 (2004), pp. 457–521.

[38] EU–Korea FTA, Article 13.4(3). The relevant eight ILO Conventions are: Convention C87 on Freedom of Association and Protection of the Right to Organise, 9 July 1948; Convention C98 on the Right to Organise and Collective Bargaining, 1 July 1949; Convention C29 on Forced Labour, 28 June 1930; Convention C105 on the Abolition of Forced Labour, 25 June 1957; Convention C138 on Minimum Age for Admission to Employment, 26 June 1973; Convention C182 on the Prohibition and Immediate Action for the Elimination of the Worst Forms of Child Labour, 17 June 1999; Convention C100 on Equal Remuneration, 29 June 1951; Convention C111 on Discrimination (Employment and Occupation), 25 June 1958.

[39] EU–Korea FTA, Article 13.4(3). Similar provisions are found in the COPE FTA, Articles 269(3) and (4), with the slightly stricter requirement of 'effective implementation' of the core ILO conventions.

[40] Korea–US FTA, Article 19.2 provides: 'Each Party *shall adopt* and maintain in its statutes and regulations, and practices thereunder, the following rights, as stated in the ILO Declaration on Fundamental Principles and Rights at Work and its Follow-Up (1998) . . .' (emphasis added).

[41] Korea–US FTA, Article 19.2, note 2.

[42] COPE FTA, Articles 268 and 270. For an overview of 'specific trade obligations' under these MEAs, see WTO Secretariat, 'Matrix on Trade Measures Pursuant to Selected Multilateral Environmental Agreements', Document WT/CTE/W/160/Rev.5., 15 June 2011.

namely: the Montreal Protocol on Substances that Deplete the Ozone Layer,[43] the Basel Convention on the Transboundary Movements of Hazardous Wastes and their Disposal,[44] the Stockholm Convention on Persistent Organic Pollutants,[45] the Convention on International Trade in Endangered Species of Wild Fauna and Flora,[46] the Convention on Biological Diversity[47] and its Cartagena Protocol,[48] the Kyoto Protocol[49] and the Rotterdam Convention on the Prior Informed Consent Procedure for Certain Hazardous Chemicals and Pesticides in International Trade.[50] The environment chapter of the Korea–US FTA also provides for a closed, but very different, list of MEAs (only including CITES and the Montreal Protocol from the above) and regional environmental agreements,[51] and, as for labour standards, there is a clear obligation upon regional partners to fulfil their obligations under the listed agreements.[52]

To a large extent, this first set of substantive rules in the T&SD chapter of the EU–Korea FTA can be seen as reiterating, in a regional context, commitments that both the EU and Korea have undertaken at the multilateral level, as part of the global agenda on sustainable development, to ratify and implement core labour and environmental conventions.[53] Yet, the furtherance of

---

[43] Montreal Protocol on Substances that Deplete the Ozone Layer (Montreal Protocol), 16 September 1987, 1522 UNTS 3.

[44] Basel Convention on the Transboundary Movements of Hazardous Wastes and their Disposal (Basel Convention), 22 March 1989, 1673 UNTS 57.

[45] Stockholm Convention on Persistent Organic Pollutants (POPs Convention), 22 May 2001, 2256 UNTS 119.

[46] Convention on International Trade in Endangered Species of Wild Fauna and Flora (CITES), 3 March 1973, 993 UNTS 243.

[47] Convention on Biological Diversity (CBD), 5 June 1992, 1760 UNTS 79.

[48] Cartagena Protocol on Biosafety (Cartagena Protocol), 29 January 2000, 2226 UNTS 208.

[49] Kyoto Protocol to the United Nations Framework Convention on Climate Change, 11 December 1997, 2303 UNTS 148.

[50] Rotterdam Convention on the Prior Informed Consent Procedure for Certain Hazardous Chemicals and Pesticides in International Trade (Rotterdam Convention), 10 September 1998, 2244 UNTS 337. Note that the JPOI highlights additional MEAs, including the Ramsar Convention on Wetlands of International Importance (2 February 1971, 996 UNTS 245), the Vienna Convention for the Protection of the Ozone Layer (22 March 1985, 1513 UNTS 293) in addition to the Montreal Protocol, the UN Framework Convention on Climate Change (4 June 1992, 1771 UNTS 107) in addition to the Kyoto Protocol, and the Convention to Combat Desertification (14 October 1994, 1954 UNTS 3).

[51] US–Korea FTA, Annex 20-A. While it does not encompass as many MEAs as those listed in the COPE FTA, it does include the 1971 Ramsar Convention.

[52] US–Korea FTA, Article 20.2 provides: 'A Party shall adopt, maintain, and implement laws, regulations, and all other measures to fulfil its obligations under the multilateral environmental agreements listed in Annex 20-A'. For a violation to be established, Parties must demonstrate that it occurs 'in a manner affecting trade or investment' between them (note 1).

[53] The JPOI explicitly refers to the 1998 ILO Declaration and 11 key MEAs; for an overview, see Cordonier-Segger and Khalfan, *Sustainable Development Law Principles, Practices and Prospects*, Tables 2.2 and 2.3, pp. 32–6.

this global agenda is not the only motive behind the T&SD chapter, which also sets out a second substantive obligation to 'uphold levels of protection', directly tackling the impact of differences in domestic environmental and labour standards upon bilateral trade and investment relations and, this time, using bold, mandatory language:

> A Party shall not fail to effectively enforce its environmental and labour laws, through a sustained or recurring course of action or inaction, in a manner affecting trade or investment between the Parties. A Party shall not weaken or reduce the environmental or labour protections afforded in its laws *to encourage trade or investment*, by waiving or otherwise derogating from, or offering to waive or otherwise derogate from, its laws, regulations or standards, in a manner affecting trade or investment between the Parties.[54]

Economic competitiveness considerations are, thus, the main rationale behind one of the few legally-binding obligations found in the T&SD chapter; that is, regional partners are specifically prohibited to lower (or fail to enforce) environmental and labour protection standards *as a means to* encourage trade and investment. In other words, the primary purpose of this bold prohibition is to prevent deregulatory pressures that would lead to a downward spiral of environmental and labour standards, and it seems to be based on the premise that a weakening of environmental and social protection regimes would create an unfair comparative advantage in the trade and investment relations between the EU and Korea – something which sits uneasily with the (hortatory) provisions to the contrary that were mentioned earlier.[55] Once again, the influence of the US–Korea FTA may be noticed, where a similar prohibition is found in the labour[56] and environmental[57] chapters of the agreement.

In addition to establishing these twofold obligations in relation to substantive standards, the T&SD chapter of the EU–Korea FTA also deals with the design and implementation of measures aimed at protecting the environment and social conditions that affect bilateral trade relations, albeit in soft-law terms. First, the Parties 'recognise the importance' of taking into account scientific and technical information and relevant international standards, guidelines or recommendations when preparing and implementing such

---

[54] EU–Korea FTA, Article 13.7 (emphasis added); see similar provisions in COPE FTA, Article 277.

[55] See Footnote 33.

[56] US–Korea FTA, Article 19.3.1(a), specifying that these include labour laws adopted to implement the core ILO Conventions. Article 19.3.1(b) imposes additional limitations on the enforcement discretion of the Parties, whereby a Party cannot defend a failure to enforce core labour standards on the basis of resource limitations or decisions to prioritise other enforcement issues.

[57] US–Korea FTA, Article 20.3.1(a), specifying that these include the laws to implement the environmental agreements listed in Annex 20A (see Footnote 5).

measures.[58] Further, the Parties agree to develop, introduce and implement any such measure in a transparent manner, with due notice and public consultation and with appropriate and timely communication to, and consultation of, non-state actors, including the private sector.[59]

Finally, the T&SD chapter provides for an indicative list of cooperative activities that the Parties commit to undertake, such as exchange views on the positive and negative impacts of their FTA on sustainable development and on measures to enhance or mitigate them (including sustainability impact assessments carried out by the Parties);[60] cooperation to promote the ratification of core and other ILO Conventions and multilateral environmental agreements with an impact on trade; cooperation in international fora responsible for social or environmental aspects of trade and sustainable development, including, in particular, the WTO, the ILO, the United Nations Environment Programme and MEA bodies; cooperation on the trade-related aspects of MEAs and of the ILO's Decent Work Agenda; and cooperation on the relationship between MEAs and international trade rules.[61]

In light of the above examination, the T&SD chapter of the EU–Korea FTA marks a new trend in the EU's regulatory approach to the integration of trade and environmental/labour issues at the bilateral level, which is likely to serve as a model in future FTA negotiations, including with other Asian countries.[62] Trade–labour and trade–environment linkages are no longer seen exclusively through the lens of exception clauses that are permissive and conditional in nature, but are further elaborated through positive commitments, as well as cooperative measures. While the Parties are still recognised as possessing a sovereign right to regulate, and national regulatory differences may emerge as a result, this right is restrained by a best-endeavour obligation to ensure high levels of environmental and labour protection, coupled with a bold prohibition against lowering (or failing to enforce) environmental and labour standards as a means to promote trade and/or investment. Yet,

---

[58] EU–Korea FTA, Article 13.8.

[59] Ibid. Article 13.9.

[60] On the EU's approach to sustainability impact assessments, see Marín Durán and Morgera, *Environmental Integration in the EU's External Relations*, Chapter 6.

[61] EU–Korea FTA, Article 13.11 and Annex 13. More specifically, cooperation is envisaged on the trade-related aspects of a number of global environmental issues, namely, the current and future international climate change regime (including issues relating to global carbon markets, ways to address adverse effects of trade on climate, as well as the means to promote low-carbon technologies and energy efficiency); biodiversity (in relation to biofuels); sustainable fishing practices; and deforestation (including addressing problems regarding illegal logging). In addition, the Parties commit to information exchanges and cooperation, in relation to corporate social responsibility and accountability, including on the effective implementation and follow-up of internationally agreed guidelines and on public and private certification and labelling schemes.

[62] See Footnote 4.

importantly, these novel prescriptive provisions of the T&SD chapter are anchored upon internationally recognised standards of environmental and social protection, which are set as the benchmark for assessing the regulatory performance of the Parties.

Accordingly, while the EU's competitiveness considerations flowing from the Global Europe Strategy have certainly played a role in the introduction of the T&SD chapter into the EU–Korea FTA, this has not translated into a concerted attempt by the EU to export its *own* environmental and social norms upon Korea, as a passive recipient. Furthermore, as will be shown in the following section, an essentially cooperative and non-confrontational approach has been favoured in the institutional mechanisms that have been put in place to oversee the implementation of the T&SD chapter.

2.3 Institutional provisions

When compared to EU practice under regional trade agreements concluded before the endorsement of the Global Europe Strategy,[63] another significant novelty of the EU–Korea FTA has been the creation of an institutional structure to deal specifically with matters falling under the T&SD chapter. The agreement establishes special bodies and procedures to monitor the application of the chapter and allows for independent expert advice and public participation in the decision-making processes.

A specialised Committee on Trade and Sustainable Development (exact composition of which is yet to be determined, but which is likely to involve not only trade officials, but also environmental and labour experts from both sides)[64] has been established to oversee the implementation of the T&SD chapter and to guide further bilateral cooperation, including in terms of realising the cooperative activities envisaged in the agreement.[65] To this end, this specialised committee should meet at least once a year and report to the general Trade Committee, which has the power to adopt decisions that are binding upon the Parties.[66]

---

[63] Under these older agreements, no particular institution was entrusted with the implementation of environmental and social cooperation provisions, and no specific procedures were provided for to settle disputes on these matters between the Parties. For an examination in relation to environment-related cooperation, see Marín Durán and Morgera, *Environmental Integration in the EU's External Relations*, pp. 73–4, 81 and 115–16. A similar approach has been followed under the EU–Korea Framework Agreement; see the contribution by Morgera to this volume.

[64] As the EU does not have exclusive competence for all matters covered by the T&SD chapter, the composition of this specialised committee may also include representatives from the EU Member States responsible for environmental and social policies.

[65] Ibid. Article 13.12(2). This is comparable to the Sub-committee on Trade and Sustainable Development established under the FTA with COPE, although the latter provides more details as to the Sub-committee's functions; see COPE FTA, Article 280, particularly 280(6).

[66] EU–Korea FTA, Articles 15.2(4) and 15.4.

In addition to this joint body, each Party is also required to set up a Domestic Advisory Group on sustainable development (comprising members from independent civil society organisations in a balanced representation of environment, labour and business organisations, as well as other stakeholders), with the task of advising on the chapter's implementation.[67] A mechanism (an annual Civil Society Forum) is also foreseen for conducting dialogue with these stakeholders, which may submit opinions to the Parties, regarding the sustainable development aspects of their trade relations.[68] Furthermore, the Parties commit to reviewing, monitoring and assessing the impacts of the implementation of the FTA on sustainable development through their respective participatory processes, as well as through instruments set up under the agreement, with specific reference to sustainability impact assessments.[69]

Any dispute between the EU and Korea concerning the T&SD chapter should be resolved solely through the specific dispute settlement procedure provided therein, as recourse to the general dispute settlement procedures available under the FTA is explicitly excluded for matters falling under the chapter.[70] Pursuant to this specific procedure, the Parties are first required to seek a mutually satisfactory resolution of the matter through consultations, including within the Committee on Trade and Sustainable Development. As a general rule, these consultations should not take longer than three months, and the Parties 'may' seek advice from Domestic Advisory Groups, as well as from competent international bodies.[71] Significantly, the Parties 'shall ensure' that the resolution arrived at 'reflects the activities of the ILO or relevant multilateral environmental organisations or bodies so as to promote greater cooperation and coherence between the work of the Parties and these organisations'[72] – regrettably, the FTA with COPE lacks such a nexus between regional and multilateral processes.[73]

Where these initial governmental consultations do not lead to a satisfactory resolution of the dispute, any Party may request that a Panel of Experts be convened, in order to examine the matter and subsequently present a report to the Parties within three months (as a general rule). Interestingly, all fifteen members of the Panel are required to have expertise in sustainable

---

[67] Ibid. Article 13.12(3)–(5).
[68] Ibid. Article 13.13
[69] Ibid. Article 13.10; see Footnote 60.
[70] EU–Korea FTA, Article 13.16; see, also, Chapter 14 of the FTA for the general dispute settlement procedures, which provide for arbitration proceedings and temporary remedies in cases of non-compliance, including compensation and suspension of trade obligations (Article 14.11). For a description and analysis of the dispute settlement provisions, see Chapter 4 of this volume.
[71] EU–Korea FTA, Article 13.14.
[72] Ibid. Article 13.14 (2).
[73] COPE FTA, Article 283.

development issues, be fully independent and not take instructions from either the Parties or the organisations represented in the Domestic Advisory Groups. At least five of the Panel's members must be non-nationals of either Party.[74] In its deliberations the Panel 'should seek advice' from Domestic Advisory Groups, as well as from competent international organisations.[75] There is, however, no strict obligation of compliance with the Panel's report: 'Parties shall make their best efforts to accommodate the advice or recommendations of the Panel of Experts'.[76] Nonetheless, the implementation of such recommendations is to be monitored by the Committee on Trade and Sustainable Development.[77]

It follows, therefore, that the institutional arrangements established under the T&SD chapter do not purport to serve as vehicle for the EU to use its relative economic size and leverage to enforce international standards of environmental and labour protection against its regional partner, but support, instead, a collaborative and non-confrontational approach to the integration of trade and environment/labour issues under the EU–Korea FTA. In this particular respect, the EU has (so far)[78] distanced itself from US practice, under the NAFTA Side Agreements and other FTAs concluded thereafter, where the enforcement of trade and environment/labour clauses is subject to dispute settlement procedures that include the possibility of monetary or trade sanctions, if a Party fails to comply with the decision of the arbitral panel.[79] For instance, under the Korea–US FTA, recourse to the general dispute settlement procedures (under Chapter 22) is available for matters falling under the environment and labour chapters, albeit only after exhaustion of consultation and panel procedures specifically provided for under each chapter.[80] The general dispute settlement procedures provide for arbitration before a panel with expertise in the social or environmental

---

[74] EU–Korea FTA, Article 13.15(3).

[75] Ibid. Article 13.15(1).

[76] Ibid. Article 13.15(2).

[77] Ibid. The COPE FTA (Articles 283–5) contains a similar dispute settlement procedure, dealing specifically with matters falling under its T&SD chapter, including inter-Party consultations and the establishment of a Group of Experts, whose recommendations are not strictly binding upon the Parties.

[78] However, one exception is the Economic Partnership Agreement with CARIFORUM States, where international environmental and labour standards could be theoretically enforced through sanctions, as part of the investment chapter (Part II, Title II, Chapter 2, Articles 72 and 73); see Marín Durán and Morgera, *Environmental Integration in the EU's External Relations*, pp. 107–8.

[79] For a comparative study of EU and US approaches, see C. Scherrer, T. Greven, A. Leopold and E. Molinari, 'An Analysis of the Relative Effectiveness of Social and Environmental Norms in Free Trade Agreements' (Brussels: European Parliament, 2009), www.europarl.europa.eu/activities/committees/studies.do?language=EN (accessed 27 April 2012). This study finds, however, that the stronger enforcement mechanisms in the US FTAs are not generally implemented in practice, but, rather, are used as a deterrent.

[80] Korea–US FTA, Articles 19.7(4), (5); 20.9(4), (5).

matters under dispute,[81] as well as for the payment of a 'monetary assessment' to, and the 'suspension of benefits' under the agreement by, the complaining Party, as remedies in cases of non-compliance with the panel's report.[82]

3 BILATERAL IMPLICATIONS OF THE T&SD CHAPTER

Being the first of its kind in EU practice, following the adoption of the Global Europe Strategy, and provisionally applied for less than a year at the time of writing, a number of legal and policy questions are likely to arise in the years to come, as bilateral cooperation develops under the T&SD chapter of the EU–Korea FTA. This section focuses on those that appear most pressing, namely, what are the tools available for carrying out such cooperation? And who is responsible for implementation on the EU side?

In terms of implementation tools, the regular dialogue within the joint Committee on Trade and Sustainable Development is, as we have seen, the key mechanism to follow-up and facilitate the implementation of the T&SD chapter, notably, in terms of assessing the fulfillment of the substantive obligations and realising the cooperative activities set out therein. This also provides a venue for the Parties to integrate, more systematically, environmental and labour issues into their trade and investment relations under the FTA, through the regular reporting to the general Trade Committee. The EU and Korea may equally use this institutional mechanism to further elaborate on certain aspects of the chapter, for instance, to clarify the MEAs that are the object of the best-endeavour obligation to maintain 'high levels' of environmental protection[83] or to identify new areas for cooperation.[84]

There is, however, a risk of overlap between the implementation of the T&SD chapter, for which the aforementioned committees are responsible, and that of the social and environmental cooperation provisions[85] of the Framework Agreement, which fall within the mandate of the Joint Committee established therein. While these bodies are meant to form part of a 'common institutional framework',[86] they, clearly, differ in terms of composition and expertise, and coordination challenges may arise as a result. In addition, a particular issue that could be potentially controversial is (serious) violations of core labour rights, which do not only fall under the T&SD chapter, but also under the 'essential elements' clause of the EU–Korea

---

[81] Ibid. Article 22.9(4).

[82] Ibid. Article 22.13.

[83] EU–Korea FTA, Articles 13.3 and 13.5.

[84] To those already identified in Annex 13, see Footnote 61.

[85] EU–Korea Framework Agreement, Articles 22 and 23, respectively. On environmental cooperation, see the contribution by Morgera to this volume.

[86] EU–Korea Framework Agreement, Article 43(3). On this point, see the contribution by Young Lo Ko to this volume.

Framework Agreement[87] – the latter being subject to enforcement through unilateral 'appropriate measures', which could include trade sanctions.[88]

Aside from these legal and institutional questions, there is an inherent tension between the bilateral character of the dialogue under the T&SD chapter and the fact that the EU may use this opportunity to advance its own interests and priorities in relation to trade and sustainable development issues. The EU has, indeed, an extensive practice of institutionalising dialogues with a growing number of third countries (including the high-level summits between the EU and Korea) and regions (including the Asia–Europe Meetings, in which Korea participates), covering different policy issues, with a view to both developing bilateral/regional cooperation, as well as forging common negotiating positions in international fora.[89] Yet, while allegedly based on 'shared values and common interests', such dialogues have been criticised for being tools for persuasion by the EU, rather than for truly bilateral/inter-regional negotiation.[90] Moreover, EU positions presented to third parties, in the context of these dialogues, result from a complex and lengthy process of internal negotiations among its (current) twenty-seven Member States, and there is often little flexibility to have such positions significantly altered through subsequent engagements with third parties.[91]

In our particular case, Korea can expect, for instance, that the EU would attempt to import into their T&SD chapter the list of core MEAs found in the COPE FTA,[92] as this appears to have become a sort of *acquis* in the integration of environmental concerns into EU external trade policy.[93] Nonetheless, concerns that the EU may successfully impose its own priorities and interests through institutionalised dialogue may be alleviated, at

---

[87] EU–Korea Framework Agreement, Article 1(1) provides: '. . . Respect for democratic principles and human rights and fundamental freedoms as laid down in the Universal Declaration of Human Rights and other relevant international human rights instruments, which reflect the principle of the rule of law, underpins the internal and international policies of both Parties and constitutes an essential element of this Agreement'. For further discussion of the 'essential elements' clause, see the contribution by Young Lo Ko to this volume.

[88] Ibid. Joint Interpretative Declaration, concerning Articles 45 and 46.

[89] For an examination of institutionalized dialogues in relation to environmental cooperation, see Marín Durán and Morgera, *Environmental Integration in the EU's External Relations*, Chapter 5; see, more generally, N. Alecu and E. Regelsberger, 'The EU and Inter-regional Cooperation', in C. J. Hill and M. H. Smith (eds), *International Relations and the European Union* (Oxford: Oxford University Press, 2005).

[90] See, for example, P. Leino, 'The Journey Towards all is Good and Beautiful: Human Rights and "Common Values" as Guiding Principles of EU Foreign Relations Law', in M. Cremona and B. De Witte (eds), *EU Foreign Relations Law* (Oxford: Hart Publishing, 2008), pp. 268; 273–8.

[91] Ibid. p. 297.

[92] See Section 2.2.

[93] See Marín Durán and Morgera, *Environmental Integration in the EU's External Relations*, pp. 123; 160, indicating that similar lists of MEAs are found in other EU agreements, as well as in the Generalised System of Preferences.

least to some extent, in the relations with Korea, which has greater bargaining power, vis-à-vis the EU, than most other countries and regions that are engaged in these dialogues, thanks to both its economic size[94] and relative importance to the EU as a trading partner,[95] as well as its limited dependence on EU external assistance.

This takes us to another tool that is generally important in supporting cooperation between the EU and third countries or regions – financial and technical assistance – but on which the T&SD chapter is silent. In fact, the significance of EU funding to the implementation of the chapter, and of other areas of EU–Korea cooperation, ought not to be overestimated, given that Korea is *a priori* excluded from eligibility of the main instruments (in quantitative terms) of EU external assistance, either on the basis of developmental[96] or geographical considerations.[97] EU–Korea institutionalised dialogue and cooperation activities under the T&SD chapter may, nonetheless, be supported through the EU financing instrument for cooperation with industrialised and high-income countries,[98] which disposes of an indicative financial envelope of €172 million for the period 2007–2013, to be split among 17 potential beneficiaries.[99] Not only are the resources that are

---

[94] Just as one indicator, Korea is ranked (number 15) within the 'very high human development' group, in terms of the 2011 Human Development Index.

[95] See Footnote 3.

[96] Regulation (EC) 1905/2006 of the European Parliament and of the Council establishing a financing instrument for development cooperation [2006] OJ L348/41 (DCI Regulation), with a total indicative financial envelope of €16, 897 million over the 2007–2013 period for thematic (including on the environment) and geographic (including for Asia) programmes covering all countries listed as 'ODA recipients' by the OECD Development Assistance Committee, which does not include South Korea (see Article 1 and Annexes 1 and 2 of the DCI Regulation).

[97] These are, notably, the Instrument for Pre-Accession Assistance (Regulation (EC) 1085/2006, [2006] OJ L210/82), with an indicative financial envelope of €11.5 billion for the period 2007–2013 and limited to candidates and potential candidates for EU membership; the European Neighbourhood and Partnership Instrument (Regulation (EC) 1638/2006, [2006] OJ L310/1), with an indicative envelope of €11.2 billion for the period 2007–2013 and limited to 17 countries falling within the European Neighbourhood Policy; and the European Development Fund (EU–ACP Council Decision 1/2006, [2006] OJ L247/22), with an indicative financial envelope of €22.7 billion for the period 2008–2013 and limited to the 78 African, Caribbean and Pacific (ACP) States and 21 'overseas countries and territories' that constitutionally depend on some EU Member States. For a detailed examination of these instruments, see G. Marín Durán, 'Environmental Integration in the EU Development Cooperation: Responding to International Commitments or Its Own Policy Priorities?', in E. Morgera (ed.), *The External Environmental Policy of the European Union: EU and International Law Perspectives* (Cambridge: Cambridge University Press, forthcoming 2012); Marín Durán and Morgera, *Environmental Integration in the EU's External Relations*, pp. 191–2.

[98] Council Regulation (EC) 1934/2006 establishing a financial instrument for cooperation with industrialised and other high-income countries and territories [2006] OJ L405/41 (ICI Regulation).

[99] Ibid. Article 16 and Annex.

available relatively limited, but financed cooperation activities are also likely to respond to the Union's 'strategic priorities and interests', given that there is no formal basis for input by the third countries concerned, when deciding on the allocation of these resources,[100] unlike under other EU financing instruments.[101]

It should also be noted that while Korea is not, in principle, eligible for funding under the EU Development Cooperation Instrument (even in the case of regional programmes for Asia),[102] resources from this instrument have been allocated to support the Asia–Europe Dialogue Facility, in which Korea participates and, thus, *de facto* benefits from this financial support.[103] Significant for our purposes, priority areas for such funding in 2011–2013 include 'employment and social policy' and 'environment, energy and climate change' as cross-cutting issues, as well as other specific issues that are also covered by the T&SD chapter of the EU–Korea FTA, notably 'corporate and social responsibility, decent work conditions and social protection in line with ILO conventions'.[104] Thus, it would be interesting to see how, as cooperation under the T&SD chapter develops, these bilateral and inter-regional dialogues interact and influence each other in forging positions on these issues.

As with any other mixed agreement jointly concluded by the EU and its Member States,[105] a key legal question that may arise is who, exactly, on the EU side, is responsible for implementing the T&SD chapter of the EU–Korea FTA? It appears that not all matters covered by the chapter fall within the exclusive competence of the EU as part of the common commercial policy[106] and that the inclusion of reciprocal commitments, in relation to the

---

[100] Ibid. Articles 5–6, particularly 5(2), whereby the ICI Regulation is implemented through (multiannual and annual actions) plans developed by the European Commission.

[101] Notably, for geographic programmes under the DCI Regulation (which are implemented through regional or country strategy papers that are drawn up by the European Commission in principle on the basis of dialogue with the partner country or region concerned) and for cooperation programmes under the European Development Fund (which are subject to a financing agreement between the Commission and the ACP countries concerned). See, further, Marín Durán, 'Environmental Integration in the EU Development Cooperation: Responding to International Commitments or Its Own Policy Priorities?'.

[102] See Footnote 96 and DCI Regulation, Article 34 (Korea not being eligible for assistance under any of the instruments mentioned therein).

[103] European Commission, 'Regional Strategy Paper for Asia 2007–2013 and Multi-annual Indicative Programme for Asia 2011–2013', 17 November 2010, www.eeas.europa.eu/deleg ations/south_korea/asia_eu/index_en.htm (accessed 27 April 2012).

[104] Ibid. p. 14.

[105] On mixed agreements, see, generally, C. Hillion and P. Koutrakos (eds), *Mixed Agreements Revisited – The EU and its Member States in the World* (Oxford: Hart Publishing, 2010) and, particularly, and in particular Chapter 10 on the issue of international responsibility.

[106] TFEU, Article 207(1); Joined Cases C-402/05 P and C-415/05 P *Yassin Abdullah Kadi and Al Barakaat International Foundation* v. *Council and Commission* [2008] ECR I-06351, paragraph 183, where the Court held that a measure falls within the common commercial policy 'only

implementation of core ILO conventions and MEAs, may not be considered as 'merely incidental' to the trade objectives of the EU–Korea FTA.[107] Pursuant to the TFEU, competence for environmental and social policies is shared between the EU and the Member States, albeit to different degrees.[108]

With regards to environmental matters under the T&SD chapter, responsibility for implementation will ultimately depend on the MEAs in question, which are not specified in the chapter, but is likely to be shared between the EU and the Member States, as both are parties to most key MEAs (with the notable exception of CITES).[109] Conversely, the EU is not formally a member of the ILO (only an observer), and its competence in relation to the core labour standards referred to in the T&SD chapter[110] is more limited and, notably, absent, in respect of 'freedom of association' and 'effective recognition of the right to collective bargaining'[111] – the Member States are, thus, individually responsible for implementing the relevant ILO Conventions (No. 87 and No. 98). Korea should, therefore, bear in mind this 'mixed' nature of the EU as an international actor and seek further clarification as to 'who is responsible for what' on the EU side, in terms of implementing the different provisions of the T&SD chapter.

4 CONCLUSIONS: AN ALTERNATIVE MODEL WITH BROADER RAMIFICATIONS?

The T&SD chapter of the EU–Korea FTA is the first concrete instance of the emerging shift in EU practice towards a more comprehensive regulation of trade–environment and trade–labour issues within regional trade agreements. As such, it is deemed to set the standard for other FTAs subsequently negotiated by the EU and, as we have seen, has already been influential in

---

if it relates specifically to international trade in that it is essentially intended to promote, facilitate or govern trade and has indirect and immediate effects on the trade in the products concerned'.

[107] Opinion 2/00 (re Cartagena Protocol) [2001] ECR I-9713, paragraph 23. Note, however, that the Council Decision, concluding the agreement on behalf of the EU ([2011] OJ L127/1), does not refer to the legal bases for environmental (Article 191 TFEU) and social (Article 153 TFEU) policies.

[108] TFEU, Articles 2(2) and 4(2)(b) and (e), respectively; see, also, Articles 191(1)–(2) TFEU and 153(1) TFEU, defining the scope of EU powers in these policy fields.

[109] Marín Durán and Morgera, *Environmental Integration in the EU's External Relations*, pp. 22–3 (for an overview of the MEAs to which the EU is a party), 9–20 (for an examination of the nature and scope of EU competence for environmental matters).

[110] EU–Korea FTA, Article 13.4.3(a).

[111] TFEU, Article 153(6). See, further, T. Novitz, 'Promoting Core Labour Standards and Improving Global Social Governance: An Assessment of EU Competence to Implement Commission Proposals', EUI Working Papers RSC No 2002/59, pp. 16–17, 25–6, noting, also, the absence of EU legislation, in relation to forced labour, www.eui.eu/RSCAS/WP-Texts/02_59.pdf (accessed 27 April 2012).

shaping the T&SD chapter of the 2011 FTA with Colombia and Peru. There is little doubt that the EU intends to have similar T&SD chapters included in its future FTAs,[112] including those that it is currently negotiating with several Asian countries, such as Malaysia and Singapore.[113]

As a direct competitor to the EU, the US FTA practice has certainly influenced the policy re-orientations and priorities enunciated in the Global Europe Strategy, including the identification of Korea as a priority partner.[114] Indeed, we have observed some ramifications of the labour and environment chapters of the 2007 US–Korea FTA on the T&SD chapter of the EU–Korea FTA. And, yet, in its own quest to ensure a certain level playing field as regards environmental and labour regulations, the EU has maintained a cooperative and non-confrontational approach, shying away from that of the US, which contemplates (at least, theoretically) the enforcement of environmental and labour standards through fines or trade sanctions.

Against this background, T&SD chapters have the potential to act as a laboratory for an alternative, less controversial model to regulate trade–environment and trade–labour linkages at the regional level. This potential may, however, be undermined by the new role of the European Parliament (since the entry into force of the Treaty of Lisbon on 1 December 2009)[115] as a co-legislator in the conclusion of FTAs, given that it has been advocating an EU move towards a binding and sanction-based mechanism to enforce environmental and labour standards, along the lines of US practice.[116] Such an enforcement mechanism risks increasing reluctance among partner countries towards including T&SD chapters in their FTAs with the EU, especially where there is no previous acceptance of a similar regime under FTAs with the US (for example, MERCOSUR countries).[117]

Looking beyond FTAs, there a number of ways in which EU–Korea cooperation under the T&SD chapter can be expected to build upon and

---

[112] See the recent European Commission, *Communication on Trade, Growth and World Affairs – Trade Policy as a Coherent Component of the EU's 2020 Strategy*, Document COM (2010) 612 final, Brussels, 9 November 2010, p. 8 (emphasising the implementation of T&SD chapters within current agreements), 9 (reiterating the ambition to include these chapters in future FTAs).

[113] After FTA negotiations between the EU and ASEAN group proved difficult, the European Commission received a mandate to start negotiations with individual countries, starting with Singapore (3 March 2010), followed by Malaysia (10 September 2010).

[114] European Commission, *Global Europe Strategy*, p. 9.

[115] TFEU, Article 218(6)(v). These new powers also extend to the adoption of EU autonomous measures in the field of commercial policy (Article 207(2)).

[116] European Parliament, *Resolution on Human Rights and Social and Environmental Standards in International Trade Agreements*, Document P7_TA (2010) 0434, 25 November 2010, paragraph 22(c).

[117] MERCOSUR countries (Argentina, Brazil, Paraguay and Uruguay) were also singled out in the Global Europe Strategy as priority partners (p. 9), and inter-regional FTA negotiations are ongoing.

interact with existing cooperation on trade–environment and trade–labour issues at the multilateral level. For instance, institutionalised dialogue under the T&SD chapter may be used by the EU and Korea, as a platform to forge common positions in international fora responsible for social, environmental and trade matters, notably the ILO, MEA bodies and the WTO. In addition, a procedural nexus has been established between the institutional mechanisms under the T&SD chapter and relevant multilateral processes (particularly, the ILO and MEA bodies), so as to promote coordination and positive synergies among the various levels of decision-making.

However, as we have also seen, the core purpose of the T&SD chapter is to add to the multilateral regulatory framework and, most notably, in terms of disciplining the use of environmental and labour standards as a means to encourage trade and investment. This prescriptive dimension of the T&SD chapter is unlikely to become multilaterally accepted in the WTO[118] or other international fora,[119] at least in the foreseeable future. There are, therefore, limits to the extent to which the T&SD chapter can serve as a stepping-stone for the development of new rules at the multilateral level, but this may not necessarily be a bad thing.

[118] See the discussion in Section on 'an insight into the broader context'.

[119] Similar concerns are expressed at the ILO; see, for example, 1998 ILO Declaration, paragraph 5: 'Stresses that labour standards should not be used for protectionist trade purposes, and that nothing in this Declaration and its follow-up shall be invoked or otherwise used for such purposes; in addition, the comparative advantage of any country should in no way be called into question by this Declaration and its follow-up'. In the MEA context, see, for example, UN Framework Convention on Climate Change, Article 3(5).

PART III

Beyond Trade and Economic Cooperation: Wider Issues in EU–Korea Relations

9

Overview of the EU–Korea Framework Agreement

James Harrison

1 INTRODUCTION

Negotiations for the Framework Agreement between the European Union and its Members States on the One Part and the Republic of Korea on the Other Part[1] were started at around the same time as the negotiations for the EU–Korea Free Trade Agreement (FTA). This reflects the policy of the EU that economic liberalisation should only be addressed as part of a broader agenda of cooperation with partner countries.[2]

The Framework Agreement was finally concluded in May 2010.[3] It provides a legal basis for cooperation between the EU and Korea in a range of subject areas, and it is central to the strategic partnership. Therefore, it is important to appreciate the nature and contents of the Framework Agreement, both to understand how it will influence the development of EU–Korea relations, as well as to comprehend how the model may be deployed in relation to other countries with which the EU wishes to form future partnerships.

The purpose of this chapter is to give an overview of the Framework Agreement and to highlight some of its main features. It will identify the types of action that may be taken by the EU and Korea, in implementing their commitments to pursue closer cooperation. The additional chapters in this Part will then explore in more detail what potential exists for collaboration between the EU and Korea under the Framework Agreement

---

[1] Framework Agreement between the European Union and its Member States on the one part, and the Republic of Korea, on the other part (EU–Korea Framework Agreement), www.eea s.europa.eu/korea_south/index_en.htm (accessed 20 April 2012).

[2] European Commission, *Communication on Global Europe: A Contribution to the EU's Growth and Jobs Strategy (Global Europe Strategy)*, Document COM (2006)567 final, Brussels, 4 October 2006, p. 12: 'FTA provisions should be an integral part of the overall relations with the country or region concerned'. The Communication was endorsed by the Council, *Conclusions on Global Europe – Competing in the World*, Document 14799/06, 13 November 2006.

[3] It will enter into force on the first day of the month, following the date on which the Parties have notified each other of the completion of the legal procedures necessary for that purpose. However, the Framework Agreement may be provisionally applied, pending formal entry into force with the agreement of the parties; EU–Korea Framework Agreement, Article 49.

in several specific policy areas and what particular challenges the partners may face.

2 SCOPE AND CONTENT OF THE FRAMEWORK AGREEMENT

2.1 Structure of the Framework Agreement

The Framework Agreement is intended to create a permanent institutional and legal framework for relations between the EU and Korea.[4] It 'updates and replaces'[5] the 1996 Framework Agreement for Trade and Cooperation, which will be repealed, once the 2010 Framework Agreement enters into force.[6] Unlike its predecessor,[7] the emphasis of the 2010 Framework Agreement is no longer on trade cooperation – an issue which is now dealt with in more detail by the FTA. Rather, the 2010 Framework Agreement addresses a much broader range of political, economic, social and cultural issues.

The Framework Agreement is a mixed agreement, which means that both the EU and its Member States are party to the agreement. This state of affairs inevitably complicates the implementation of the Framework Agreement, as it will become necessary to determine whether it is the EU or it's Member States which have competence for a particular policy matter. In practice, it is likely that such issues will have to be worked out on a case-by-case basis.[8]

The Framework Agreement is divided into 10 titles, as follows:

1. Basis and scope;
2. Political dialogue and cooperation;
3. Cooperation in regional and international organisations;
4. Cooperation in the area of economic development;
5. Cooperation in the area of sustainable development;
6. Cooperation in the area of education and culture;
7. Cooperation in the area of justice, freedom and security;
8. Cooperation in other areas;
9. Institutional framework;
10. Final provisions.

Even a brief glance at the structure of the Framework Agreement indicates that it covers almost all conceivable areas of government policy. However, whilst the Framework Agreement is broad in scope, it does not contain

---

[4] The Framework Agreement has effect, until either party expressly denounces it; EU–Korea Framework Agreement, Article 49(3).
[5] Ibid. Article 43(1).
[6] Ibid. Article 43(2).
[7] For an overview of the 1996 Framework Agreement, see Chapter 1 of this volume.
[8] See, further, Chapter 1 of this volume; see, also, C. Hillion and P. Koutrakos (eds), *Mixed Agreements Revisited – The EU and its Member States in the World* (Oxford: Hart Publishing, 2010).

particularly detailed obligations. Generally speaking, there are two types of provisions in the Framework Agreement.

2.2 The Framework Agreement as a locus of shared values

The first category of provisions found in the Framework Agreement establish obligations for the individual parties. These provisions identify the shared values of the two parties, and they outline the requirements of the parties, namely, to respect these values in their own actions. The most pertinent provision, in this respect, is Article 1 of the Agreement, which provides:

1. The Parties confirm their attachment to democratic principles, human rights and fundamental freedoms, and the rule of law. Respect for democratic principles and human rights and fundamental freedoms as laid down in the Universal Declaration of Human Rights and other relevant international human rights instruments, which reflect the principle of the rule of law, underpins the internal and international policies of both Parties and constitutes an essential element of this Agreement.
2. The Parties confirm their attachment to the Charter of the United Nations and their support for the shared values expressed therein.
3. The Parties reaffirm their commitment to promoting sustainable development in all its dimensions, economic growth, contributing to the attainment of international agreed development goals, and cooperating to address global environmental challenges, in particular climate change.
4. The Parties reaffirm their attachment to the principles of good governance and the right against corruption, notably taking into account their international obligations.
5. The Parties underline their shared attachment to the comprehensive nature of bilateral relations and to maintaining overall coherence in this regard.
6. The Parties agree to elevate their relations into a strengthened partnership and to develop cooperation areas at the bilateral, regional and global levels.
7. The implementation of this Agreement between Parties sharing the same values and respect shall therefore be based on the principles of dialogue, mutual respect, equal partnership, multilateralism, consensus and respect for international law.

The importance of the values and principles identified in Article 1(1) is emphasised by categorising then as 'essential elements' of the Agreement, which means that they are the very basis for the continuing application of the Agreement.[9] In other words, failure to respect these values and principles

---

[9] Article 4 of the Framework Agreement also classifies the obligation to counter the proliferation of weapons of mass destruction as an essential element of the Agreement. See, also, Chapter 11 of this volume.

could lead to the suspension of the Agreement.[10] Despite the fact that these provisions are somewhat vague in terms of what precisely the parties must do in order to respect these values, they cannot be dismissed as mere political rhetoric. In the first place, disputes arising over the implementation of the Agreement are to be considered by the Joint Committee, established under Article 44. Where a solution cannot be agreed by both the parties, Article 45 of the Framework Agreement establishes a specific mechanism for settling disputes arising over the implementation of the Agreement, including the essential elements clauses. Under this mechanism, the complaining party may take 'appropriate measures in accordance with international law' to seek to induce compliance with the Agreement,[11] but these actions may be challenged in arbitration. The arbitral tribunal has jurisdiction to consider both 'the basis for . . . the measure' and 'any other aspect . . . of the measure', including whether the measure is appropriate and proportionate.[12] This is an important development, because it means that the development of EU–Korea relations will not only be dictated by politics and diplomacy, but it may also be subject to legal scrutiny by an independent adjudicator.[13] This is an interesting illustration of the legalisation of the relationship between the EU and Korea, beyond the field of trade and investment.[14]

2.3 The duty to cooperate in specific policy areas

The second category of provisions in the Agreement create obligations for the parties to act together. The majority of the provisions of the Agreement fall into this category. Thus, the Framework Agreement has clauses calling for cooperation in a wide range of areas, including, *inter alia*, counterterrorism; small arms and light weapons; trade and investment; taxation; science and technology; energy; transport; consumer policy; health; employment and social affairs; environment and natural resources; climate change; agriculture, rural development and forestry; marine and fisheries; development assistance; culture and media; education; personal data protection;

---

[10] For a discussion of the essential elements clause, see Chapter 10 of this volume.
[11] EU–Korea Framework Agreement, Article 45(3).
[12] Ibid. Article 45(4).
[13] Arbitral tribunals are to be composed of three arbitrators – one appointed by each party and the third appointed by the Joint Committee. Unfortunately, the Agreement does not deal with the situation in which one of the parties fails to appoint an arbitrator or if the Joint Committee cannot reach agreement on the third arbitrator. Such a mechanism is important, so as to avoid the arbitral process being frustrated by one of the parties; see, for a similar situation, *Advisory Opinion on the Interpretation of Peace Treaties with Bulgaria, Hungary and Romania* (1950) ICJ Reports, p. 65. This situation could be remedied through the agreement of a 'detailed procedure for the speedy conduct of arbitration'; EU–Korea Framework Agreement, Article 46(1).
[14] For a discussion of the legalisation of EU–Korea relations, see Chapter 1 of this volume.

migration; combatting illicit drugs, money laundering, terrorism financing and cybercrime; tourism; and statistics.

In international law, it is well-established that a duty to co-operate 'does not imply an obligation to reach an agreement'.[15] Thus, these provisions of the Framework Agreement are programmatic, setting an agenda on which the parties must consult and exchange opinions, with a view to reaching agreement. Yet, international law does impose a duty to act in good faith, which means that negotiations must be 'meaningful'.[16]

The Framework Agreement is also important, in that it creates the institutional framework within which cooperation should take place. A Joint Committee is set up to 'facilitate the implementation and to further the general aims of [the Framework Agreement]'.[17] Whilst the Joint Committee is at the apex of the institutional structure, it is only one of the bodies which will be involved in the implementation of the Agreement. The Framework Agreement recognises that the parties may create other committees and bodies, in order to adequately deal with particular subject matters.[18] The following section will consider the types of actions that may be taken by the parties involved in implementing the Framework Agreement.

3 IMPLEMENTATION OF THE FRAMEWORK AGREEMENT

3.1 Introduction

As seen above, the Framework Agreement sets a basic framework for future cooperation between the EU and Korea. However, the development of closer EU–Korea ties will depend on concrete actions being taken on the basis of the Framework Agreement. There are several types of action that are foreseen by the Framework Agreement.

3.2 Cooperation, consultations and dialogues

The Agreement expressly calls for 'cooperation' and 'information exchange' on almost all of the issues that are included within the scope of the instrument. Generally speaking, the Agreement does not specify the form of cooperation, and it leaves it to the discretion of the parties to design an appropriate framework in which to cooperate, which meets their needs at any point in time. Clearly, the Joint Committee provides an institution

---

[15] *Advisory Opinion on Railway Traffic between Lithuania and Poland* (1931) PCIJ Reports 108, Series A/B, No. 42, p. 116.

[16] *North Sea Continental Shelf Case* (1969) ICJ Reports 3, paragraph 85.

[17] EU–Korea Framework Agreement, Article 44(2).

[18] Ibid. Article 44(3)(b). For an in-depth discussion of the institutional framework, see Chapter 10 of this volume.

through which cooperation and consultations can take place, although it does not have an exclusive role, and the parties may choose to cooperate through other avenues.

Generally speaking, the Framework Agreement leaves it to the discretion of the parties to decide upon the scale and frequency of cooperation. However, there are some areas which the Framework Agreement indicates should be subject to a regular process of consultation and cooperation from the outset. The use of the phrase 'dialogue' in these contexts suggests that there should be frequent meetings and exchange of information on these issues.

Most prominently, the Agreement expressly requires the parties to establish 'a regular political dialogue, based on shared values and aspirations . . . in accordance with procedures to be agreed between [Korea] and the [EU]'.[19] This political dialogue should explicitly address democracy and respect for human rights, international peace and security, arms control and other 'major international issues of common interest'.[20] It is foreseen that the dialogue will take place through a variety of channels, including summit meetings at leaders' level, consultations at ministerial level and briefings at senior officials' level.[21] Such dialogues may be either general or sectoral.[22] In this regard, it was announced at the sixth summit between the EU and Korea, which took place on 28 March 2012, that a high-level political dialogue would be held on an annual basis,[23] thus regularising what had previously been an *ad hoc* process in the past.[24]

If past practice is any guide, the high-level dialogue is likely to be general in nature, allowing political leaders to address a range of topical issues that are of interest to both sides. In particular, the political dialogue to date has addressed a range of important global issues, partly of an economic nature, but also touching on issues of international peace and security, both in the Korean peninsula, as well as in the wider world.[25]

There are other less high profile issues which are also highlighted by the Framework Agreement as essential topics for an ongoing dialogue. For example, the Agreement calls for the creation of an economic policy

---

[19]   Ibid. Article 3(1).
[20]   Ibid. Article 3(2).
[21]   Ibid. Article 3(3).
[22]   Ibid. Article 3(3)(e).
[23]   Republic of Korea–EU Summit Joint Press Statement, Document MEMO/12/224, 28 March 2012.
[24]   The history of EU–Korea relations is discussed in Chapter 1.
[25]   At the sixth summit, in March 2012, attended by President Lee Myung Bak, on behalf of Korea, and Herman Van Rompuy and Jose Manuel Barroso, on behalf of the EU, the leaders discussed, *inter alia*, peace and development in Afghanistan, the Iranian nuclear programme and the Syrian situation, as well as North Korea; see Republic of Korea–EU Summit Joint Press Statement, Document MEMO/12/224, 28 March 2012. See, also, Chapter 11 of this volume, in which Hae-Won Jun discusses the extent to which the two countries can develop a close relationship on issues of peace and security.

dialogue.[26] 'Regular dialogue' is also anticipated on the issue of development assistance,[27] and there shall also be 'dialogue' on climate change,[28] air transport[29] and maritime transport policy.[30] Dialogues are also suggested as possible strategies for engagement, in relation to issues surrounding employment and social affairs,[31] education[32] and international crimes.[33]

3.3 Joint projects

A second form of action foreseen under the Framework Agreement is the development of 'joint projects'.[34] Again, there is no particular form which such projects may take, and they could potentially occur across a number of different issues governed by the Framework Agreement.

One area in which projects may be undertaken is development assistance. At the sixth EU–Korea summit, the parties agreed to coordinate their engagement in in-country assistance,[35] and it is possible that the parties may design joint development assistance projects in a particular country, in order to make the most effective and efficient use of their development aid.

Another area where joint projects may be undertaken is in relation to energy, where the Framework Agreements talks about the 'conduct of joint studies and research'.[36] Joint scientific and technical projects are also encouraged under the Agreement on the Scientific and Technological Cooperation between the European Community and the Government of the Republic of Korea.[37] Indeed, science and technology may be a particularly profitable area for the development of joint projects, given the range of expertise of both parties in this regard. As noted in a UK parliamentary debate on the EU–Korea Framework Agreement:[38]

---

[26] EU–Korea Framework Agreement, Article 10.

[27] Ibid. Article 27(1).

[28] Ibid. Article 24(2).

[29] Ibid. Article 18(2)(b).

[30] Ibid. Article 19(6). This is an important issue for both parties, which has led to disputes in the past; see, for example, *Korea – Measures Affecting Trade in Commercial Vessels*, WTO Panel Report, 7 March 2005, Document WT/D273/R; *EC – Commercial Vessels*, WTO Panel Report, 22 April 2005, Document WT/DS301/R. In this context, a dialogue can be used in order to avoid future disputes before they arise.

[31] EU–Korea Framework Agreement, Article 22(4).

[32] Ibid. Article 29(2)(b).

[33] Ibid. Article 6(2).

[34] Framework Agreement, Article 2(1)(a).

[35] Republic of Korea–EU Summit Joint Press Statement, Document MEMO/12/224, 28 March 2012.

[36] Framework Agreement, Article 17(c).

[37] Agreement on the Scientific and Technological Cooperation between the European Community and the Government of the Republic of Korea, Article 3(4). This Agreement is cross-referenced in Article 16 of the Framework Agreement.

[38] Debate on the Draft European Union (Definition of Treaties) (Republic of Korea Framework

South Korea is world-leading in many technologies and has been at the forefront of scientific and technological innovation in recent years. Sections of the agreement call for greater cooperation on science and technology, energy and environmental matters; that will be of great benefit to the United Kingdom and the rest of the European Union, not only in the development of new technology, but because of job creation that it will bring.

As is implied by this quote, science and technology cooperation is not an end in itself, but it is likely to have a positive impact upon the economies of both parties, thus complementing the objectives of the FTA. Moreover, such cooperation may also have implications for other policy areas, where scientific or technological developments may aid specific policy objectives. For example, this could be the case for environmental protection[39] or peace and security.[40]

The organisation of joint projects in the field of science and technology has been facilitated by the negotiation of a Cooperation Roadmap in Science, Technology and Innovation. A second Roadmap was adopted at the third meeting of the Joint Science and Technology Cooperation Committee in July 2011, in which the parties agreed to reinforce their cooperation in a number of key sectors, notably, green energy, nanotechnologies, information and computer technologies and the mobility of researchers.[41] Under the Roadmap, the parties agreed to organise a series of workshops, in which they would seek to identify the areas where potential collaborations and joint projects could take place.

The Framework Agreement also highlights the potential for joint projects in the areas of statistics,[42] employment and social affairs[43] and education.[44]

3.4 Cooperation through international and regional organisations

A third type of action under the Framework Agreement is the promotion of collective efforts in relevant regional and international fora and organisations.[45] In other words, the Framework Agreement and its institutions may be used as a coordinating process, prior to negotiations on issues of common concern. Article 8 requires that the Parties:

Agreement) Order 2012, Sixth Delegated Legislation Committee, Session 2010–2012, Thursday 26 January 2012, col. 4.

[39] See Chapter 12 of this volume.

[40] See Chapter 11 of this volume.

[41] Available at www.ec.europa.eu/research/iscp/pdf/korea_roadmap_2011-2013.pdf (accessed 30 May 2012).

[42] EU–Korea Framework Agreement, Article 42(2).

[43] EU–Korea Framework Agreement, Article 22(4).

[44] Ibid. Article 29(2)(a).

[45] Ibid. Article 2(1)(b).

cooperate and exchange views in regional and international fora and organisations, such as the United Nations, the International Labour Organisation (ILO), the Organisation for Economic Cooperation and Development (OECD), the WTO, the Asia–Europe Meeting (ASEM) and ASEAN Regional Forum (ARF).[46]

This type of action is also relevant in the environmental context, where both the EU and Korea are parties to the same multilateral environmental agreements.[47]

3.5 The negotiation of additional agreements

The Framework Agreement also explicitly provides for the possibility for the parties to adopt additional 'specific agreements in any area of cooperation falling within its scope'.[48] Such agreements are one way in which the parties can develop a more detailed legal framework for their mutual relations, and this mechanism highlights the dynamic nature of the relationship. There are already a number of specific agreements which the parties have concluded, including the 2010 Free Trade Agreement, the 2009 Competition Agreement, the 2007 Science and Technology Agreement and the 1997 Customs Agreement. All of these agreements form part of the common institutional framework established by the Framework Agreement,[49] and they should be implemented in a coherent and coordinated manner.[50]

Some other areas in which specific agreements may be useful are highlighted in the Framework Agreement itself, for example, in relation to the regulation of shipping agency activities[51] or illegal migration.[52] Moreover, specific agreements may be negotiated in other areas, where a need is subsequently identified by the parties. Indeed, the ability to conclude additional agreements means that the legal framework for EU–Korea relations will remain dynamic, and the partners will be able to respond to new and emerging challenges, as time goes on.

---

[46] Ibid. Article 8.
[47] Ibid. Article 23. See the discussion in Chapter 12 of this volume, in which Morgera explains how dialogues can be a useful mechanism to build alliances, in order to influence the development of international environmental law.
[48] Ibid. Article 43(3).
[49] Ibid. Article 43(4): 'Existing agreements relating to specific areas of cooperation falling within the scope of this Agreement shall similarly be considered part of the overall bilateral relations as governed by this Agreement and as forming part of a common institutional framework'.
[50] Ibid. Article 43(3). See, also, Chapter 10 of this volume, in which Young Lo Ko argues that the Framework Agreement can be understood as a constitutional instrument, which sets the parameters of any further agreements. He also considers the challenges for maintaining coherence in EU–Korea relations.
[51] EU–Korea Framework Agreement, Article 19(5).
[52] Ibid. Article 33(3).

3.6 *Business cooperation and people-to-people contacts*

The Framework Agreement is not only expected to lead to closer ties between the governments and officials of the two parties, but it is also aimed at 'encouraging cooperation between businesses'[53] and 'promoting people-to-people contacts and understanding'.[54] One way in which such cooperation can take place is through exchanges of delegations between the European Parliament and the Korean National Assembly.[55] Given that the Framework Agreement is a mixed agreement, it is also important that national parliamentarians from the EU Member States should also be engaged in this sort of exchange activity, in order to increase cross-cultural understanding in areas that are not covered by EU competence.

The Framework Agreement also recognises 'the role and potential contribution of organised civil society in the dialogue and cooperation process under [the Agreement]', and the parties 'agree to promote effective dialogue with organised civil society and its effective participation'.[56] It is possible that this provision will lead to the active involvement of civil society in the dialogues mentioned above, as well as providing a legal basis for facilitating the involvement of civil society in the work of the Joint Committee.[57] This will not only provide for a more enriched discussion and debate of the issues, but it will also provide a means of legitimising any actions taken by the EU and Korea, as part of their strategic partnership.[58]

4 CONCLUSION

The Framework Agreement is an attempt to set out, in a rudimentary way, some of the shared values that will underpin the relationship between the EU and Korea in the long-term. Yet, the conclusion of the Framework Agreement is only the first step in a long journey of strengthening EU–Korea relations over the years to come. The building of trust and mutual understanding will be vital, if there is going to be real and meaningful cooperation

---

[53] Ibid. Article 2(1)(e); see, also, Article 11.

[54] Ibid. Article 2(1)(h).

[55] Ibid. Article 3(3)(e).

[56] Ibid. Article 40.

[57] Unlike the Trade Committee under the FTA, the Joint Committee is not under an explicit obligation to communicate with all interested parties; see J. Harrison, 'Transparency and Public Participation in International Economic Law: A Case Study of the Korea–EU Free Trade Agreement', *Sungkyunkwan Journal of Science and Technology Law*, vol. 5 (2011), pp. 6–9.

[58] On the role of non-state actors in promoting the legitimacy of international decision-making, see A. E. Boyle and C. Chinkin, *The Making of International Law* (Oxford: Oxford University Press, 2007), pp. 26–7. On the importance of public participation in treaty-making and implementation, see, also, the comments of Younsik Kim in Chapter 3 of this volume.

on the important domestic and foreign policy issues that are addressed by the Framework Agreement.

Arguably, the development of increased contact and communication between Koreans and Europeans, whether between governments or between parliamentarians and civil society, will be one of the key factors in determining the success of the strategic partnership established by the EU and Korea. It is this human element which underpins diplomacy and which will be vitally important, in order to 'consolidate, deepen and diversify relations in areas of mutual interest'.[59] It can be expected that cooperation will, therefore, develop step-by-step, on the basis of the legal and institutional framework established by the Framework Agreement and related instruments. The following chapters will highlight some of the opportunities and challenges for strengthening relations in particular policy areas.

---

[59] EU–Korea Framework Agreement, Preamble.

10

A Common Institutional Framework for EU–Korea Relations

Young Lo Ko

1 INTRODUCTION

As part of the agreement to upgrade their bilateral relations to a strategic partnership, the EU and Korea signed the Free Trade Agreement[1] and a new Framework Agreement[2] in 2010. These agreements, together with other sectoral agreements, form part of the so-called 'common institutional framework' (CIF). The unique form of the EU–Korea CIF is the outcome of a compromise, accommodating the diverging demands of Korea and the EU. On the one hand, the EU wished to construct a unified framework, which placed the FTA in a wider context of overall bilateral relations, following the EU's Global Europe Strategy.[3] On the other hand, the Korean government wished the FTA to be independent of political legal frameworks. The EU–Korea CIF reflects the demands of both sides, by establishing the specific agreements, including the FTA, as separate regimes. At the same time, the Framework Agreement organises those regimes into a unified and consistent governing system. There are two principal ways in which this is achieved.

First, the parties established an institutional interaction mechanism. Under this arrangement, the institutions established under the specific agreements of the CIF, including the FTA, are to report on their activities to the Joint Committee, which is the management institution of the Framework Agreement, and the CIF as a whole.

Second, the parties agreed on common principles, which underpin the CIF. These common principles are enshrined in the so-called essential

---

[1] Free Trade Agreement between the European Union and its Member States of the one part, and the Republic of Korea of the other part (EU–Korea FTA) [2011] OJ L127/6, 14 May 2011.

[2] Framework Agreement between the European Union and its Member States on the one part, and the Republic of Korea, on the other part (EU–Korea Framework Agreement), www.eeas.europa.eu/korea_south/index_en.htm (accessed 20 April 2012).

[3] European Commission, *Communication on Global Europe: Competing in the World. A Contribution to the EU's Growth and Job Strategy (Global Europe Strategy)*, Document COM(2006)567 final, Brussels, 4 October 2006, endorsed by the Council, 'Conclusions on Global Europe – Competing in the World' (14799/06) 13 November 2006.

element clauses in the Framework Agreement, which apply not only to the Framework Agreement, but also to the CIF in its entirety, through the necessary link that was established between the Framework Agreement and the specific agreements.

This chapter explains the emergence, and the structure, of the EU–Korea CIF and explores whether those two methods are adequately designed to serve the aims of the CIF, as a unified governing system of independent regimes, established and governed by the specific agreements.

2 THE EMERGENCE OF THE EU–KOREA COMMON INSTITUTIONAL FRAMEWORK

Following the Global Europe Strategy, the EU sought the conclusion of a FTA with Korea, which had been identified in the Strategy as one of the priority countries with which the EU wanted to pursue closer relations.[4] Having had two preliminary meetings in 2006, Korea and the EU announced the official launch of negotiations for the FTA in May 2007. On that occasion, the Union also proposed an upgrade of political ties between them to a strategic partnership and the revision of the existing Framework Agreement. Both sides basically agreed that the new Framework Agreement for facilitating the strategic partnership was necessary, in order to correspond to upgraded economic and trade relations, which will be facilitated by the FTA. However, there were differences of positions, regarding the content and form of a new Framework Agreement.

The EU's bilateral legal framework varies from country to country, but a distinguishable pattern can be discerned, according to the status of economic development, geographical proximity and accession candidacy of the other party to the bilateral relations.[5] With non-neighbouring countries, the EU has concluded bilateral legal frameworks which consist in (a) a non-binding instrument, such as joint declarations and an action plan (for example, with Australia, Japan and the United States); (b) a combination of a binding agreement for socio-economic relations and a non-binding instrument for political relations (for example, with Canada and India); or (c) a single agreement, with human rights conditionality, which conditions overall bilateral relations in respect for human rights, democratic principles and the rule of law (for example, with Mexico and Chile). Though not relevant to all cases, it is generally considered that EU's bilateral legal frameworks with developed

---

[4] European Commission, *Communication on Global Europe: Competing in the World. A Contribution to the EU's Growth and Job Strategy (Global Europe Strategy)*, p. 9.

[5] For a detailed analysis on the typology of frameworks for the bilateral cooperation of the EU with third states, see A. Ward, 'Frameworks for Cooperation between the European Union and Third States: A Viable Matrix for Uniform Human Rights Standards?', *European Foreign Affairs Review*, vol. 3 (1998), p. 3.

countries fall under category (a) or (b), while those with developing countries tend to have a form that could be characterised as category (c).

The EU had taken the negotiations for an upgrade of the Framework Agreement with Korea as an opportunity to construct a bilateral legal framework that was fully reflective of the Global Europe Strategy and set a precedent to show consistency of its practice in terms of the use of human rights conditionality.[6] Accordingly, it proposed a draft text of the Framework Agreement, which could be generally characterised as a type (c) agreement. The proposed draft text of the new EU–Korea Framework Agreement provided conditionality, stipulating not only respect for human rights, but also cooperation in non-proliferation of Weapons of Mass Destruction (WMD) as essential elements of the Agreement, on the one hand,[7] and established legal and institutional links between the Framework Agreement and the FTA, on the other hand.[8]

It seems quite reasonable to imagine that Korea might have preferred to have an (a) or (b) type agreement, given its strong political and economic achievements, which parallel those of the countries which have concluded those types of agreements with the EU. As an alternative, a Framework Agreement including both the human rights and WMD clauses, without giving them essential elements status, could have been an acceptable option. Resistance might not have been as strong as in the negotiations of the FTA with India, which has human rights and WMD concerns.[9] Nevertheless,

---

[6] The EU has inserted a human rights conditionality clause in its agreements with third countries since the early 1990s. Thereunder, the parties may suspend the agreement, on the basis of those clauses where it considers that the other party has failed to fulfil obligations in respect for the conditions provided in the clauses. For a detailed discussion of the human rights conditionality clause, see Section 5 of this chapter.

[7] The EU has adopted the policy of including the non-proliferation clause in every mixed agreement of the EU, which provides cooperation in, and contribution towards, countering the proliferation of weapons of mass destruction (WMD) as an essential element of the Agreement, since the adoption of the 2003 Council policy note on the fight against the proliferation of weapons of mass destruction. See Council of the European Union, *Fight against the Proliferation of Weapons of Mass Destruction: Mainstreaming Non-Proliferation Policies into the EU's Wider Relations with Third Countries*, Council Note, 14997/03, 19 November 2003. See, also, Section 3.2 of this chapter. For a further discussion of the WMD clause, see, also, Chapter 11 of this volume.

[8] L. Grip, 'The EU Non-Proliferation Clause: A Preliminary Assessment', *SIPRI Background Paper*, 11 November 2009, www.books.sipri.org/files/misc/SIPRIBP0911.pdf (accessed 9 April 2012).

[9] India has nuclear weapons, but is not a party to the Non-Proliferation Treaty (NPT). In the 2007 negotiating mandate of the FTA with India, the European Council authorised the European Commission to negotiate an upgrade of the existing framework agreement into the new agreement, with the human rights and WMD clauses, and set up the link between the new framework agreement and the FTA. India refused such a proposal, and the EU–India FTA has thus been being negotiated as a pure trade agreement, without attendant political elements. See Ibid.

the EU's attempt to insert those clauses and establish a strong link between the Framework Agreement and the FTA could have faced challenges from Korea. The fact that no EU agreement having both the human rights and WMD clauses has ever been concluded with a country with no imminent human rights and WMD concerns posed a critical question concerning why Korea should conclude an agreement containing those clauses as essential elements of the Framework Agreement. Furthermore, the possibility of the suspension of the entire bilateral legal framework, including the FTA, on the basis of a failure to fulfil human rights and non-proliferation obligations was enough to give rise to a concern that the human rights and WMD clauses would serve as an instrument to extend EU's political influence over Korea.

On the other hand, the EU had, in the past, always insisted on the inclusion of essential elements clauses in its agreements on external relations. The example of the collapse of FTA negotiations with Australia and New Zealand, due to the refusal of those countries to insert a human rights conditionality clause into the FTAs, clearly illustrates that consistency in the use of human rights conditionality clauses is one of the prime concerns of the EU in the negotiations of its international agreements.[10] The Global Europe Strategy, which refers to the need for a wider institutional architecture that accommodates FTAs and other political provisions, also reflects such concerns.[11] Furthermore, the former EU–Korea Framework Agreement for Trade and Cooperation already contained a human rights conditionality clause, so it would have been a downgrade, rather than an upgrade, for the EU to conclude a Framework Agreement, without human rights conditionality.[12]

The circumstances of the negotiations also provided the EU with grounds to press for the proposed text. The relatively low profile of the negotiations of the Framework Agreement may have rendered it possible to avoid public attention to, and opposition against, the insertion of the human rights and WMD clauses in the Framework Agreement. The strategy of the EU was to downplay the historical meaning of human rights conditionality clauses and, instead, emphasise a modern meaning of the human rights conditionality, as an expression of the like-mindedness of Korea and the EU, in respect to human rights. The preoccupation of the Korean government with concluding the FTA could also render the issues of human rights conditionality less problematic. It seems that the EU had actually drawn on the preoccupation of the Korean government for the conclusion of the FTA, by conditioning progress of the FTA negotiations, on the progress of negotiations of the

[10] K. Smith, *European Union Foreign Policy in a Changing World* (2nd edn) (Cambridge: Polity Press, 2008), p. 130.

[11] *Global Europe Strategy*, p. 10.

[12] See Framework Agreement for Trade and Cooperation between the European Community and its Member States on the one hand and the Republic of Korea on the other hand (1996 Framework Agreement) [2001] OJ L 90/46, 30 March 2001, Article 1.

Framework Agreement.[13] On the other hand, Korea, which did not have imminent human rights or WMD concerns, did not seem to have such strong incentives to reject the proposed text, which could put the negotiations of the FTA into deadlock.

The final text of the Framework Agreement includes both human rights and WMD within its essential elements clauses,[14] which is one important element of the common institutional framework which currently governs EU–Korea relations.

3 STRUCTURE OF THE COMMON INSTITUTIONAL FRAMEWORK

The EU–Korea CIF has a constitutional structure in which the Framework Agreement, as a 'constitutional' agreement, provides for general cooperation and common principles of the CIF. In turn, the specific agreements give effect to the Framework Agreement. Such a structure has been adopted, in order to serve the aim of the CIF as a unified governing system of separate regimes.

The constitutional structure of the CIF is set out in the provisions of the Framework Agreement on the relations between the agreements of the CIF. Of primary importance, in this regard, is Article 43(3) of the Framework Agreement, which reads:

> The Parties may complement this Agreement by concluding specific agreements in any area of cooperation falling within its scope. Such specific agreements shall be an integral part of the overall bilateral relations as governed by this Agreement and shall form part of a common institutional framework.

This provision of the Framework Agreement foresees the establishment of a network of agreements and instruments falling under the umbrella of the CIF. An example of an agreement integrating itself into the CIF is the FTA, which provides, in Article 15.14(2):[15]

> The present Agreement shall be an integral part of the overall bilateral relations as governed by the Framework Agreement. It constitutes a specific Agreement giving effect to the trade provisions within the meaning of the Framework Agreement.

The shape of the Korea–EU CIF sketched out by these provisions is reminiscent of the facade of Greek temples, with pillars surmounted by

---

[13] This has been hinted in the interview of Lina Grip with an unidentified EU official, who holds that the progress in the FTA negotiations was predicated on progress in the negotiations of the Framework Agreement; see Grip, 'The EU Non-Proliferation Clause', p. 11.

[14] EU–Korea Framework Agreement, Articles 1 and 4.

[15] See, also, EU–Korea Framework Agreement, Article 9(2), which provides '. . . the Parties shall give effect to their cooperation in the trade and investment area through the agreement establishing a free trade area. The aforementioned agreement shall constitute a specific agreement giving effect to the trade provisions of this Agreement, within the terms of Article 43'.

a pediment. The Framework Agreement, as a constitutional agreement, constitutes a pediment, which is supported by the pillars of the specific agreements. At the time of writing, specific agreements constituting the CIF include (1) the FTA; (2) the Agreement concerning Cooperation on Anti-competitive Activities;[16] (3) the Agreement on the Scientific and Technological Cooperation;[17] and (4) the Agreement on Cooperation and Mutual Administrative Assistance in Customs Matters.[18]

Yet, it is necessary to ask what it means to say that an agreement is 'an integral part of the overall bilateral relations as governed by [the Framework Agreement]'. The following sections will explore this question, in relation to two issues. First, it will consider the institutional links between the institutions established by the Framework Agreement and those of the specific agreements. Second, it will examine the common principles that are set out in the Framework Agreement and to what extent they are also applicable to the other 'pillars' of the CIF.

4 THE EU–KOREA COMMON INSTITUTIONAL FRAMEWORK: A UNIFIED GOVERNING SYSTEM?

4.1 *Institutional oversight of the common institutional framework*

One mechanism for ensuring a unified governing system is the establishment of institutional links between the various agreements making up the CIF. This section will consider those institutions and how they interrelate.

The principal managing institution of the Framework Agreement is the Joint Committee. The role of the Joint Committee is to maintain overall coherence in bilateral relations and ensure the smooth and proper functioning of bilateral agreements between Korea and the EU.[19] For that purpose, the Joint Committee is mandated to seek methods of forestalling problems and receives reports from the management institutions relating to the other specific agreements, including the Trade Committee established under the FTA, on their activities.[20] The Joint Committee meets once a year at deputy

---

[16] Agreement between the European Community and the Government of the Republic of Korea concerning cooperation on anti-competitive activities (Competition Agreement) [2009] OJ L202/36, 4 August 2009.

[17] Agreement on the Scientific and Technological Cooperation between the European Community and the Government of the Republic of Korea (STC Agreement) [2007] OJ L106/44, 24 April 2007.

[18] Agreement between the European Community and the Republic of Korea on cooperation and mutual administrative assistance in customs matters (Customs Agreement) [1997] OJ L121/14, 13 May 1997.

[19] EU–Korea Framework Agreement, Article 44.

[20] EU–Korea FTA, Article 15.1(5).

minister level.[21] It also serves as a forum of consultations for settling disputes over the essential element clauses.[22]

Political dialogues supplement the Joint Committee as consultation forums, where issues on *inter alia* democracy and human rights, international and regional conflicts, international security and other international issues of common interest are discussed. Political dialogues take place at ministerial and senior official levels. Summit meetings are held whenever the parties deem it necessary, and ministerial meetings take place on an annual basis. In addition, sectoral dialogues and exchanges of delegations between the European Parliament and the National Assembly of Korea have been institutionalised.[23]

Some of the other agreements also have their own institutional frameworks. However, they are designed to feed into the main institutional framework that is set up under the Framework Agreement.

The FTA has the Trade Committee as its managing institution.[24] The Trade Committee meets once a year at ministerial level, which is co-chaired by the Minister for Trade of Korea and the Commissioner for Trade of the European Union.[25] The Trade Committee supervises and facilitates the implementation and application of the FTA and supervises the work of all specialised committees, working groups and other bodies established under the FTA.[26] It receives information and reports from the specialised committees and working groups, concerning their schedule and agenda in advance of the meetings of those bodies and also concerning their activities at regular meetings of the Trade Committee.[27] It assumes responsibility to report its own activities, as well as the activities of its specialised committees, working groups and other bodies, to the Joint Committee at each regular meeting of the Joint Committee.[28]

Specialised committees established at the signing of the FTA include:

---

[21] The EU and Korea have held nine Joint Committee meetings, as of 2011, and the latest meeting was held in Seoul, Korea, in June 2011. The agenda of the meeting covered cooperation *inter alia* in customs administration, research and development, education, environment, sanitary and phytosanitary matters and trade. See Press Release of the Korean Ministry of Foreign Affairs and Trade on the Result of 9th Korea–EU Joint Committee, www2.korea.kr/newsWeb/pages/brief/partNews2/view.do?call_from=extlink&call_from=extlink&dataId=155760533 (accessed 17 February 2012). The text is provided only in Korean.

[22] EU–Korea Framework Agreement, Article 44(3)(g). See, also, Section 5.1 of this chapter and Chapter 9 of this volume.

[23] Ibid. Article 3(3)(e).

[24] EU–Korea FTA, Article 15.1.

[25] The first EU–Korea Trade Committee was held in 12 October 2011, where implementation of the agreement and management of the Trade Committee and institutional framework established by the FTA have been discussed. See European Commission – Press Release, 'EU Trade Chief Welcomes Progress from First Europe-South Korea Trade Committee', www.trade.ec.europa.eu/doclib/docs/2011/october/tradoc_148268.pdf (accessed 17 February 2012).

[26] EU–Korea FTA, Article 15.1(3).

[27] Ibid. Article 15.2(4).

[28] Ibid. Article 15.1(5).

(1) the Committee on Trade in Goods; (2) the Committee on Sanitary and Phytosanitary Measures; (3) the Customs Committee (and Joint Customs Cooperation Committee, when the matters at issue are exclusively covered by the EU–Korea Customs Agreement, which has been in force since 1997); (4) the Committee on Trade in Services, Establishment and Electronic Commerce; (5) the Committee on Trade and Sustainable Development; and (6) the Committee on Outward Processing Zones on the Korean Peninsula. The list of the specialised committees is not exhaustive, and the Trade Committee may decide to establish other specialised committees.[29] Specialised committees are to meet once a year at senior official level. These specialised committees are to inform and report on their activities to the Trade Committee, which, in turn, informs and reports such activities to the Joint Committee.

Institutions for other specific agreements, as an integral part of overall bilateral relations and part of the common institutional framework, are also linked to the Framework Agreement.

The Competition Agreement gives effect to Article 14 of the Framework Agreement on competition policy and complements Article 11.6.2 of the FTA in relation to the enforcement of competition laws.[30] The Agreement does not have a management institution, and the implementation of the Agreement is managed by ongoing meetings and contacts between the competition authorities of the respective parties.[31] Issues relating to the competition chapter of the FTA are also handled by competition authorities.

Article 16 of the Framework Agreement refers to the STC Agreement as the basic legal framework of cooperation in science and technology cooperation. The STC Agreement has established the Joint Committee on Scientific and Technological Cooperation (JCSTC), which oversees and facilitates implementation of the STC Agreement.[32] It meets on a biennial basis at deputy minister level. The JCSTC forms part of the CIF, by assuming responsibility to report to the Joint Committee of the Framework Agreement on the status, achievements and effectiveness of the cooperative activities made within the framework of the Agreement.[33]

The Customs Agreement gives effect to Article 13 of the Framework Agreement on customs cooperation. A Joint Customs Cooperation Committee (JCCC) has been established by the Agreement, which would

---

[29] Ibid. Article 15.2.2.

[30] For a more in-depth discussion of competition cooperation between the EU and Korea, see Chapter 6 of this volume.

[31] See, however, the Memorandum of Understanding between the Fair Trade Commission of the Republic of Korea and the Competition Directorate-General of the European Commission, www.ec.europa.eu/competition/international/legislation/korea.pdf (accessed 7 June 2012).

[32] STC Agreement, Article 6.

[33] STC Agreement, Article 6(3)(4).

replace the specialised Customs Committee established under the FTA, where the subjects under discussions are exclusively covered by the Customs Agreement.[34] It meets on a biennial basis at senior official (Director General) level. The JCCC also assumes the obligation to inform and report to the Joint Committee of the Framework Agreement, at the request of the Joint Committee.[35] Where it replaces the specialised Customs Committee of the FTA, it also assumes the same obligation to inform and report to the Trade Committee, as with other specialised committees of the FTA.[36]

4.2 Institutional interactions in the common institutional framework

As has been seen above, institutional interactions in the CIF are to be facilitated by the information and reporting arrangements established between the Joint Committee and the management institutions of the specific agreements. This establishes a clear institutional link between the bodies, with the Joint Committee occupying a position at the apex of the institutional architecture. Yet, it begs the question concerning what powers may be exercised by the Joint Committee, vis-à-vis the other organs within the CIF? Can it adopt decisions which bind the other institutions within the CIF? Or is its role simply one of receiving information and making recommendations to the other institutions?

In the first place, it would seem appropriate to assume that the Joint Committee has the power to adopt decisions containing procedural rules to implement the information exchange and reporting arrangements. Given that the specific agreements lay down an obligation on the respective institutions to report to the Joint Committee, it is reasonable to conclude that the Joint Committee, to which those obligations are owed, is in a position to decide upon how such obligations are to be discharged and what consequences will follow from a failure to fulfil the obligations. In this respect, the decisions of the Joint Committee could be held to be legally binding on the institutions of the CIF.

Whether the Joint Committee has the power to make binding decisions on substantive issues is, however, unclear at present. Institutions created under other EU agreements have been expressly granted formal powers to make binding decisions. For example, the Joint and Association Councils in the EU–Mexico Agreement[37] and EU–Chile

---

[34] EU–Korea FTA, Article 15.2(1)(c).
[35] EU–Korea Framework Agreement, Article 44(3)(c).
[36] EU–Korea FTA, Article 15.2(4).
[37] Economic Partnership, Political Coordination and Cooperation Agreement between the European Community and its Member States, of the one part, and the United Mexican States, of the other part – Final Act – Declarations (EU–Mexico Agreement) [2000] OJ L276/45 28 October 2000.

Agreement[38] have been explicitly provided with powers to make legally binding decisions.[39] The decisions, as such, are considered to be binding under international law and form an integral part of the EU legal order.[40] They are also to be fully binding on the institutions of the Agreements. The EU–Korea FTA also provides that the Trade Committee has such decision-making powers.[41] The Framework Agreement, in contrast, is silent on this issue.

It is hard to say, decisively, that decisions of the Joint Committee have binding legal effects, given that no provision in the Framework Agreement provides for such powers of the Joint Committee. Nevertheless, the constitutional function of the Joint Committee suggests that we should not rush to the conclusion that the decisions of the Joint Committee on issues other than implementation of the information and reporting arrangements would be purely hortatory. It must be remembered that, as a matter of international law, international institutions and their organs have those powers which are necessary for them to effectively carry out their functions.[42] It can, therefore, be argued that, without substantive means to coordinate policies produced in the independent regimes established by the specific agreements, the Joint Committee would not be able to effectively perform its function of maintaining the coherence of overall bilateral relations. Indeed, there are a number of functions of the Joint Committee, which would seem to presuppose the power to make decisions, which would have resulting consequences across the CIF. For example, the Joint Committee is charged with setting priorities, in relation to the aims of the Framework Agreement,[43] seeking appropriate methods of forestalling problems in areas covered by the Agreement[44] and resolving disputes regarding the application or interpretation of the Framework Agreement.[45] These functions presuppose certain types of decision-making powers. With no substantive power to facilitate coherence of overall bilateral relations, the Joint Committee would amount to no more than a consultation forum for the ready exchange of information.

---

[38] Agreement establishing an association between the European Community and its Member States, of the one part, and the Republic of Chile, of the other part – Final Act (EU–Chile Agreement) [2002] OJ L352/3 30 December 2002.

[39] EU–Mexico Agreement, Article 47; EU–Chile Agreement, Article 5(2).

[40] *S.Z. Sevince v. Staatssecretaris van Justice*, ECJ Case C-192/89 [1990] ECR I-3461, paragraph 9.

[41] EU–Korea FTA, Article 15.4(2).

[42] The so-called doctrine of implied powers has been endorsed by the International Court of Justice, which held, in relation to the United Nations, that 'the Organisation must be deemed to have those powers which, though not expressly provided in the Charter, are conferred upon it by necessary implication as being essential to the performance of its duties'; *Advisory Opinion on Reparation for Injuries Suffered in the Service of the United Nations Case* (1949) ICJ Reports, p. 174.

[43] EU–Korea Framework Agreement, Article 44(3)(e).

[44] Ibid. Article 44(3)(f).

[45] Ibid. Article 44(3)(g)–(h).

The issue is complicated by the fact that other institutions within the CIF do have formal decision-making powers. The most prominent example is the Trade Committee, which manages what is, arguably, the most important aspect of EU–Korea bilateral relations. The Trade Committee is an institution that holds the requisite power to adopt interpretations of, and amendments to, the provisions of the FTA and to adopt its own rules of procedure.[46] Most notably, the Trade Committee has the power to make legally binding decisions.[47] It is an independent body, which holds and assumes exclusive powers and responsibilities over matters of the FTA. Thus, the Joint Committee cannot exercise any decision-making powers, which would deprive the Trade Committee of its own functions. Nevertheless, it can still be assumed that the Joint Committee may have a role to play in guiding the decisions of the Trade Committee on matters which have a broader consequence for bilateral relations. The need for a power to make binding decisions is even more important, given that the Joint Committee is composed of senior officials, whereas the Trade Committee is constituted by ministers. The Joint Committee, in this circumstance, would hardly exert any substantive influence over the Trade Committee, if its decisions were purely hortatory.

Though not explicitly provided in the agreements constituting the CIF, it is tenable to suggest that the constitutional function assigned to the Joint Committee to maintain coherence of overall bilateral relations would allow it to address decisions to the Trade Committee in exercising its decision-making power. Decisions of the Joint Committee, in that sense, would have certain constitutional effects, which would bind the Trade Committee to make decisions in line with those of the Joint Committee.

5 COMMON PRINCIPLES OF THE EU–KOREA COMMON INSTITUTIONAL FRAMEWORK

5.1 The essential elements clause

Another mechanism for ensuring a unified governing system is the establishment of common principles, which underpin bilateral relations between Korea and the EU. Common principles of the CIF are enshrined in the essential element clauses of the Framework Agreement. Article 1 of the Framework Agreement provides that respect for human rights constitutes an essential element of the Framework Agreement, which reads:[48]

---

46 EU–Korea FTA, Article 15.1(4).
47 Ibid. Article 15.4.
48 The need for standard human rights conditionality clauses having human rights and non-execution clauses and joint interpretative declaration was first raised when dealing with Yugoslav wars in the mid-1990s. Facing grave human rights violations in Yugoslavia, the

The Parties confirm their attachment to democratic principles, human rights and fundamental freedoms, and the rule of law. Respect for democratic principles and human rights and fundamental freedoms as laid down in the Universal Declaration of Human Rights and other relevant international human rights instruments, which reflect the principle of the rule of law, underpins the internal and international policies of both Parties and constitutes an essential element of this Agreement.

Moreover, Article 4 provides that cooperation in the non-proliferation of WMD also constitutes an essential element of the Framework Agreement.[49] The non-execution clause and the Joint Interpretative Declaration give effect to these essential element clauses, by specifying the legal effects of a breach of the essential element clause. The non-execution clause (Article 45(3) of the Framework Agreement) states:

> If either Party considers that the other Party has failed to fulfil its obligations under this Agreement, it may take appropriate measures in accordance with international law. Before doing so, except in cases of special urgency, the Party shall present all the information required to the Joint Committee for a thorough examination of the situation. The Parties shall hold consultations within the Joint Committee and, if both Parties agree, these consultations may be facilitated by a mediator appointed by the Joint Committee.

The Joint Interpretative Declaration on Articles 45 and 46 spells out that 'cases of special urgency', in Article 45 of the Framework Agreement, refers to a material breach of the Framework Agreement, which consists of a repudiation of the Framework Agreement not sanctioned by the general rules

---

EU suspended the cooperation agreement with Yugoslavia, by having recourse to the principle of *rebus sic stantibus* provided in Article 62 of the 1969 Vienna Convention on the Law of Treaties (VCLT). The EU did so after only one-and-half months after its notification of intention to suspend the Yugoslav government. However, Article 65(3) of the VCLT requires the aggrieved party to allow the contested party at least three months for raising objections about notified measures before taking measures, and there was criticism that the EU failed to comply with this provision in this instance. In order to address such a flaw in suspending the agreement, the European Council and the Member States adopted a resolution on human rights, which mandated insertion of human rights clauses in every EU mixed agreement, in order to provide the legal basis for suspension of the agreement, in cases of grave violations of human rights. For an analysis of the Yugoslavia crisis and the human rights conditionality clauses, see L. Bartels, *Human Rights Conditionality in the EU's International Agreements* (Oxford: Oxford University Press, 2005), p. 20. For detailed analyses on the historical background and evolution of the essential element clauses, see, also, Der-Chin Horng, 'The Human Rights Clause in the European Union's External Trade and Development Agreements', *European Law Journal*, vol. 9 (2003), p. 677; V. Miller, 'The Human Rights Clause in the EU's External Agreements', *House of Commons Research Paper* 04/33 (2004).

[49] See, also, Chapter 11 of this volume.

of international law or a particularly serious and substantial violation of an essential element of the Agreement.

According to these provisions, a breach of the essential element clauses may constitute a material breach of the Framework Agreement, within the meaning of Article 60 of the Vienna Convention on the Law of Treaties (VCLT), which means that the unilateral measures taken against the breach of the essential element clauses include the suspension of the Framework Agreement.[50]

Not only may a party suspend the Framework Agreement as a response to a breach of the essential elements clause, but it is also possible that it may suspend one of the other agreements of the CIF, because those other agreements are considered an 'integral part of the bilateral relations'. The Joint Interpretative Declaration concerning Articles 45 and 46 confirms that the specific agreements of the CIF are linked to the Framework Agreement, in relation to the failure to fulfil obligations of the Framework Agreement and the essential element clauses. The second paragraph of the Joint Interpretative Declaration provides that the measures taken in response to a failure to fulfil obligations of the Framework Agreement may relate to the Framework Agreement or to a specific agreement falling under the CIF. In addition, the fourth paragraph provides for dispute settlement on the measures taken in relation to a specific agreement for a material breach of the Framework Agreement.[51]

Implementation of the essential element clauses is underpinned by an enforcement mechanism in the EU–Korea CIF, comprising consultation and arbitration procedures. Before taking action to suspend an agreement, except in cases of special urgency, the complaining party shall have recourse to the consultation in the Joint Committee, and, for that purpose, shall present all the information that is required to the Joint Committee for a thorough examination of the relevant situation. The parties may appoint a mediator for facilitating consultations.[52] In cases of special urgency, which refers to, *inter alia*, serious and substantial violations of the essential elements of the Framework Agreement, the other party shall be notified immediately, as to

---

[50] Article 60 of the VCLT reads: '1. A material breach of a bilateral treaty by one of the parties entitles the other to invoke the breach as a ground for terminating the treaty or suspending its operation in whole or in part . . . 3. A material breach of a treaty, for the purposes of this article, consists in: (a) a repudiation of the treaty not sanctioned by the present Convention; or (b) the violation of a provision essential to the accomplishment of the object or purpose of the treaty'.

[51] The fourth paragraph of the Joint Interpretative Declaration does not explicitly state 'the measures' in the paragraph referring to the measures taken for a material breach of the Framework Agreement. However, it is implied, by Article 46.4 of the Framework Agreement, which provides that arbitration tribunal is a forum of dispute settlements on the measures taken in special urgency cases, which means a material breach of the Framework Agreement.

[52] EU–Korea Framework Agreement, Article 45(3).

the measure taken. Consultations in cases of special urgency shall be held at the request of the other party, for up to twenty days. The measure shall apply after this period, and the party which is subject of the measure may request arbitration to examine any aspect of, or the basis for, the measure.[53]

The arbitration tribunal consists of three arbitrators: one is appointed by each party and the third is appointed by the Joint Committee. The Joint Committee shall appoint a third arbitrator within fourteen days from the day of a request of arbitration. The decision of the arbitration tribunal shall be taken by a majority vote within three months from the date of the appointment of the arbitrators. The parties must take the steps required to implement the decision of the arbitrators, and, by request of the parties, the arbitrators shall issue recommendations on how to implement the decision.[54]

5.2 The content of the essential element clauses

At the heart of the question as to how effectively the common principles enshrined in the essential element clauses could govern the CIF, is whether those clauses carry a normative effect, which could effectively bind the parties to the commitments laid down by the clauses.

The standard human rights clause refers to various international instruments as reference instruments of human rights norms, within the meaning of the clause. Such instruments include, *inter alia*, the Universal Declaration on Human Rights (UDHR), the Helsinki Final Act and the Charter of Paris for a New Europe.[55] References to international human rights instruments in the human rights clause have the effect of incorporating norms established in those instruments into the essential elements of the human rights clause.[56] Accordingly, the parties are required to respect the norms pronounced and established by those instruments. The non-execution clause proclaims that the human rights clause lays down legal obligations on the parties to respect such norms. A party that considers that the other has failed to fulfil such obligations may take unilateral measures, which includes suspension of the Agreement. By making reference to the international instruments, the standard human rights clause defines the norms, for which the parties are required to respect, whose effect is to be ensured by the non-execution clause and Joint Interpretative Declaration.

The normative effect of the human rights clause of the EU–Korea CIF is to be ensured by the same mechanism of the standard human rights clause.

---

[53] Ibid. Article 45(4).
[54] Ibid. Article 46.
[55] European Commission, *The Inclusion of Respect for Democratic Principles and Human Rights In Agreements Between the Community and Third States*, Document COM(95) 216 final, p. 8.
[56] Bartels, *Human Rights Conditionality in the EU's International Agreements*, p. 90.

However, the human rights clause of the EU–Korea CIF obscures the norms that the parties are required to respect under the human rights clause, by referring to 'other relevant human rights instruments' as reference instruments.[57] The most plausible reading seems that the instruments, as such, refer to the human rights instruments of which all the parties to the Framework Agreement are parties. Such instruments would include the main human rights instruments, which cover most of the fundamental human rights norms.[58] However, there is some ambiguity in the human rights essential elements clause, which has the potential to undermine its application, by rendering uncertain precisely what obligations the parties are required to respect.

The WMD clause – another essential element clause of the EU–Korea CIF – does not incorporate the norms by referring to specific WMD instruments, however, it sets out the steps to be taken to incorporate the norms in a relatively concrete manner.[59] The WMD clause provides that the parties assume the obligation of cooperating in, and contributing towards, countering the proliferation of WMD. For fulfilling such obligations, the parties are to (1) fully implement their respective, existing legal obligations, regarding disarmament and non-proliferation and other relevant instruments agreed by parties; (b) take steps to sign, ratify or accede to and fully implement all other international instruments; and (c) establish an effective system of national export controls to prevent proliferation of WMD and related goods and technologies.[60] The WMD clause incorporates, as its norms, existing non-proliferation obligations of the parties, those of other relevant instruments agreed by the parties and the international WMD instruments to be proposed for accession. In addition, the WMD clause provides for the means to clarify the norms of the WMD clauses and the obligations laid down by those norms, by indicating the official position of the relevant international agencies as a reference point for assessing material breaches of the WMD clause.[61]

---

[57] EU–Korea Framework Agreement, Article 1(1).

[58] Those instruments would include, *inter alia*, the International Covenant on Civil and Political Rights; the International Covenant on Economic, Social and Cultural Rights; the International Convention on the Elimination of All Forms of Racial Discrimination; the Convention on the Elimination of All Forms of Discrimination against Women; the Convention against Torture and Other Cruel, Inhumane or Degrading Treatment or Punishment; and the Convention on the Rights of the Child.

[59] The EU has succeeded in inserting WMD clauses into its mixed agreements with almost 100 countries. Recently, the EU has agreed to insert the clause in its Partnership and Cooperation Agreement with Vietnam, and negotiations with Armenia, Azerbaijan, Georgia, Malaysia, Russia, Singapore and Thailand are ongoing at the time of writing. See Council of the European Union, *Six-monthly Progress Report on the implementation of EU Strategy against Proliferation of Weapons of Mass Destruction* (2010-II). For further discussion, see Chapter 11 of this volume.

[60] See EU–Korea Framework Agreement, Article 4.

[61] Framework Agreement, Joint Interpretative Declaration Concerning Articles 45 and 46.

Nevertheless, certain points still need to be clarified even further. Many of the international conventions concerning WMD are only open to participation by states, thus the obligations of the WMD clause are to be implemented mostly by the Member States of the EU. All of the Member States are parties to most, but not all, international conventions on these issues. For instance, France, Estonia and Lithuania are not parties to the Seabed Arms Control Treaty, whilst all the other Member States have joined the Treaty.[62] This implies that the obligations laid down by the WMD clause may sometimes be different from Member State to Member State. It should also be addressed, in this respect, whether the parties in the WMD clause refer to the EU and its Member States or just the Member States on the European side. If the parties in the WMD clause refer to only the Member States, there would be little room for the EU to manoeuvre to coordinate Member States' WMD policies, and the essential element mechanism would be working only in relation to individual Member States.

6 CONCLUSION

The EU–Korea CIF is the first international instrument that Korea has ever had which governs trade and political foreign policies within a unified framework. For the EU, the EU–Korea CIF is its first bilateral legal framework (as opposed to non-binding instrument) that it has concluded with a developed state, which conditions overall bilateral relations in respect for both human rights and cooperation in the non-proliferation of WMD. In this sense, the EU–Korea CIF is expected to constitute a good reference point for negotiations of EU's future bilateral legal framework, with third countries which are in a similar position to Korea, in economic and political terms.

The EU–Korea CIF has some shortcomings, which fail to make it a fully unified governing system. First, it fails to provide measures to give effect to the information and reporting arrangements and to explicitly confer on the Joint Committee the necessary powers to facilitate information and reporting arrangements and to effectively perform its constitutional function of maintaining the coherence of overall bilateral relations. Nevertheless, as has been shown above, the constitutional function of the Joint Committee of maintaining the coherence of overall bilateral relations implies that the Joint Committee has those powers that are necessary to facilitate information and reporting arrangements. Second, there is also some ambiguity in the essential elements clauses, which underpin the CIF. The lack of clarity over which human rights norms fall within the scope of the human rights essential elements clause can also be addressed by an interpretation of the parties. Such

---

[62] A full list of the parties to the Seabed Arms Control Treaty is available at www.state.gov/w ww/global/arms/treaties/seabed3.txt (accessed 17 February 2012).

an initiative would also support the idea that the human rights clause was intended to reflect the common values of the partners.

Despite the diverging stances of Korea and the EU on the nature of the CIF during the negotiations of the Framework Agreement, the mechanisms for the institutional interaction and application of the common principles seem to be capable of supporting the constitutional structure of the CIF as a unified governing system. In that light, what is necessary for the CIF to effectively operate as a unified governing system seems to be the determination of the parties to exploit the potential of such mechanisms to the maximum extent.

11

Cooperation in the Field of International Peace and Security: A Newcomer to the Legal Framework for EU–Korea Relations

Hae-Won Jun*

1 INTRODUCTION

The inclusion of international peace and security is one of the most notable developments in the new EU–Korea Framework Agreement, in comparison with the 1996 Framework Agreement for Trade and Cooperation. The 1996 Agreement largely focused on the economic aspects of cooperation, leaving security issues largely untouched. By contrast, security cooperation is mentioned frequently in the preamble to the new EU–Korea Framework Agreement, and this issue is incorporated into several substantive articles. Moreover, to mark the importance of security cooperation, the articles on security cooperation appear earlier than that on economic cooperation, that is, from Articles 4 to 7.

Such a marked difference between the two agreements begs two crucial questions: (1) what are the reasons for the extension of the Korea–EU cooperation towards security issues? and (2) what is the potential for further cooperation in this area?

Focusing on the first question, one should note that the security issues inserted in the new Framework Agreement are rather selective and do not cover a comprehensive range of security problems. In particular, traditional defence issues are not covered by the new Framework Agreement. Why did the two parties choose these issues to be covered by the Framework Agreement, but not others? To answer this question, it is necessary to investigate the changes in the security perspectives of both Korea and the EU, during the period since the conclusion of the 1996 Framework Agreement.

The second question relates to the effectiveness of the new Framework Agreement. Will the new Framework Agreement lead to substantial security cooperation between the two parties? Or is it a mere declaration of their shared interests, without clear means for implementation? As the new Framework Agreement has a relatively weak mechanism for dispute

* The views expressed in this chapter are the author's sole responsibility and are not to be construed as representing those of the Korea National Diplomatic Academy.

settlement and enforcement, the clauses on cooperation in relation to security issues amount to little more than an announcement of the willingness for the two parties to make an effort to work together for international peace and security in the global context. Its effective implementation depends on the voluntary cooperation by both parties. In short, the depth of cooperation based on the Framework Agreement is open to future progress, potentially ranging from a possible regular, but, ultimately, empty, discussion to a common action, with clear, concrete objectives.

The aim of this chapter is to answer these two questions. The next section explains the implications of the new Framework Agreement for the EU–Korea cooperation on international peace and security. Sections 3 and 4 then attempt to explain why the new Framework Agreement offers the potential for further cooperation.

2 CHOICE OF AREAS FOR SECURITY COOPERATION

2.1 *Scope of cooperation: traditional and non-traditional security issues*

The EU–Korea Framework Agreement is based on a set of shared values, which include 'democratic principles, human rights and fundamental freedoms and the rule of law'.[1] These values imply a normative universality, as there is a basic assumption that everyone in the world is eligible to possess these values. Moreover, to make a secure environment for these values to flourish within a specific country, they must be spread to other countries. Otherwise, constant threats to the stability of these values persist.

Therefore, with these shared interests at the core of their strategic partnership, it is natural that Korea and the EU committed themselves to promoting international peace and security. Recognising this, the Framework Agreement comprises a broad scope of security threats, including terrorism, serious crimes of international concern, the proliferation of weapons of mass destruction and their means of delivery, climate change, energy and resources insecurity, poverty and financial crisis. To respond to such threats, the Framework Agreement calls for cooperation:

> in sectors of mutual interest, notably promoting democratic principles and respect for human rights, countering the proliferation of weapons of mass destruction; combating illicit trade in small arms and light weapons; taking measures against the most serious crimes of concern to the international community; combating terrorism; cooperation in regional and international organisations.[2]

---

[1] Framework Agreement between the European Union and its Member States on the one part, and the Republic of Korea, on the other part (EU–Korea Framework Agreement), Article 1(1), www.eeas.europa.eu/korea_south/index_en.htm (accessed 20 April 2012).

[2] Ibid. Preamble.

In addition to this, it also calls for cooperation in the areas of 'personal data protection; migration; combating illicit drugs; combating organised crime and corruption; combating money laundering and terrorism financing; combating cyber-crime; law enforcement'.[3] These issues imply that the border between internal security and external security is blurred, at best. It also illustrates that the achievement of the shared values, in the area of security cooperation, is only possible by taking a global approach.

2.2 Substantive provisions on security cooperation

2.2.1 The EU's standard clauses and their application to the EU–Korea relationship

Countering the proliferation of weapons of mass destruction, small arms and light weapons, the most serious crimes of concern to the international community and cooperation in combating terrorism are all included, as a standard practice, in relation to the EU's promised cooperation with third countries. The EU has set rules and norms for its agreements with third countries, in relation to its security objectives. Consequently, the EU–Korea Framework Agreement incorporates such rules and norms. Nonetheless, it is still worth closely examining the four major areas of cooperation mentioned in the Agreement, since it indicates the potential for cooperation between the two parties, in comparison to those between the EU and other countries. Moreover, clauses dealing with these issues do not always appear in an identical form in the EU's agreements with third countries. Some modifications are required, in order to adjust the clauses to a given third countries' policy preferences. The more the policy difference between the EU and the given third country, the more the standard EU clause is modified, as a result. In extreme cases, the two parties agree to omit some clauses altogether. Therefore, the form of the EU's clauses shows the degree of compatibility between the two parties in the given policy area.

2.2.2 Countering the proliferation of weapons of mass destruction

With the backdrop of the 9/11 crisis in 2001 and the subsequent war in Iraq in 2003, the Council decided to incorporate non-proliferation policies into the EU's wider relations with third countries.[4] For this purpose, a WMD clause was required to be either inserted in new (or revised) mixed agreements or to become part of parallel political agreements, depending on the legal basis. A standard EU clause on Weapons of Mass Destruction (WMD) was endorsed by the Council of the European Union in November 2003,

---

[3] Ibid.

[4] See, generally, M. Cremona, 'External Relations and External Competence of the European Union', in P. Craig and G. de Burca (eds), *The Evolution of EU Law* (2nd edn) (Oxford: Oxford University Press, 2011), pp. 239–40.

strictly for this purpose.[5] Since that time, WMD non-proliferation clauses have been inserted in all new or renewed mixed agreements and agreements negotiated with third countries.[6]

A clause on countering the proliferation of weapons of mass destruction is found in Article 4 of the EU–Korea Framework Agreement, which provides:

> 1. The Parties consider that the proliferation of weapons of mass destruction and their means of delivery, both to state and non-state actors, represents one of the most serious threats to international stability and security.
>
> 2. The Parties therefore agree to cooperate in and contribute towards countering the proliferation of weapons of mass destruction and their means of delivery through full implementation of their respective existing legal obligations relating to disarmament and non-proliferation and other relevant instruments agreed by both Parties. The Parties agree that this provision constitutes an essential element of this Agreement.
>
> 3. The Parties furthermore agree to cooperate and to contribute to countering the proliferation of weapons of mass destruction and their means of delivery by:
> a) taking steps to sign, ratify, or accede to, as appropriate, and fully implement all other relevant international instruments;
> b) the establishment of an effective system of national export controls to prevent the proliferation of weapons of mass destruction and related goods and technologies, including end-user controls and appropriate civil and criminal penalties for breaches of export controls.
>
> 4. The Parties agree that their political dialogue will accompany and consolidate these elements.

This text is marginally different from the standard clause adopted in 2003. There are two major differences of note.

The first difference is found in paragraph 2, which refers to the 'full implementation of their respective existing legal obligations relating to disarmament and non-proliferation and other relevant instruments agreed by both Parties', rather than 'compliance with and national implementation of their existing obligations under international disarmament and non-proliferation treaties and agreements and other relevant international obligations'. This difference merely reflects the depth of both parties' existing commitments to the international efforts to countering WMD. The EU established the WMD clause, in order to put pressure on those countries which do not

---

[5] Council of the European Union, *Fight against the Proliferation of Weapons of Mass Destruction – Mainstreaming Non-Proliferation Policies into the EU Wider Relations with Third Countries*, Document 149973/03, 19 November 2003. This document sets the standard EU policy on the non-proliferation issue in the EU.

[6] L. Grip, 'The EU Non-Proliferation Clause: A Preliminary Assessment', *SIPRI Background Paper*, November 2009, www.books.sipri.org/files/misc/SIPRIBP0911.pdf (accessed 12 June 2012).

comply and to implement such international obligations. While the EU's agreements with third countries contains a number of policy areas for cooperation, by inserting the WMD clause in those agreements, the EU tries to use other areas of cooperation as a carrot to induce these countries to make significant efforts to counter the proliferation of the WMD. In the case of Korea, the EU finds little need for such pressure, as both Korea and all Member States of the EU have already signed and implemented the Non-Proliferation Treaty[7] and other international commitments, regarding countering the WMD.

Instead, the reference to 'instruments agreed by both Parties' indicates two things. On the one hand, this wording acknowledges that both Korea and the EU are on an equal footing, regarding their respective implementation of, and compliance with, international legal obligations. On the other hand, it implies the possibility for both parties to deepen their cooperation in countering the WMD. Such cooperation can take place both bilaterally and through joint efforts for further international cooperation.

The second difference is found in paragraph 3(b), which simply reflects the parties' existing system of export controls. In this regard, the Framework Agreement is more sophisticated than the standard EU clause.

2.2.3 Small arms and light weapons

The EU's standard Small Arms and Light Weapons (SALW) clause originates from the meeting of the European Council, which took place on 15–16 December 2005, where the European Council adopted the EU Strategy to combat illicit accumulation and trafficking of SALW and their ammunition.[8] The 2005 Strategy made a reference to the need for a SALW clause in agreements with third states. This strategy aimed to develop an integrated approach and a comprehensive plan, so as to combat the illicit trade in SALW and their ammunition. At its meeting on 8–9 December 2008, the Council concluded the text of a standard SALW clause.[9] The conclusion, as in the case of non-proliferation clauses, obliged the EU to include the SALW clause in the provisions relating to CFSP in all relevant international agreements with third countries.

Article 5 of the EU–Korea Framework Agreement contains a modified form of EU's standard SALW clause, as shown below:

> 1. The Parties recognise that the illicit manufacture, transfer and circulation of small arms and light weapons, including their ammunition, and their excessive accumulation, poor management, inadequately secured stockpiles and

---

[7] Treaty on the Non-Proliferation of Nuclear Weapons (NPT) (1 July 1968) 729 UNTS 169.

[8] Council of the European Union, *EU Strategy to Combat Illicit Accumulation and Trafficking of SALW and their Ammunition*, Document 5319/06, 13 January 2006.

[9] Council of the European Union, *Conclusions on the Inclusion of a SALW Article in Agreements between the EU and Third Countries*, Document 17186/08, 17 December 2008.

uncontrolled spread continue to pose a serious threat to peace and international security.

2. The Parties agree to implement their respective commitments to deal with the illicit trade in small arms and light weapons, including their ammunition, within the framework of international instruments including the UN Programme of Action to Prevent, Combat and Eradicate the Illicit Trade in Small Arms and Light Weapons in All Its Aspects (UN PoA) and the International Instrument to Enable States to Identify and Trace, in a Timely and Reliable Manner, Illicit Small Arms and Light Weapons (ITI), as well as obligations deriving from UN Security Council resolutions.

3. The Parties undertake to cooperate and to ensure coordination, complementarity and synergy in their efforts to deal with the illicit trade in small arms and light weapons and ammunition, at global, regional, sub-regional and national levels.

Like the non-proliferation clause, the inclusion of the SALW clause is in line with the interests of Korea. Korea and the EU Member States commonly participate in, and implement, the existing international instruments and programmes.[10] There are, however, some exceptions in this area, because of Korea's security difficulties. The Convention on the Prohibition of the Use, Stockpiling, Production and Transfer of Anti-Personnel Mines and their Destruction[11] and the Convention on Cluster Munitions (CCM)[12] entered into force in March 1999 and August 2010, respectively, and the EU Member States are parties to these treaties. However, Korea does not participate in these two conventions, because of the peculiar security situation in the Korean Peninsula. On the other hand, Korea does participate in the process of the Convention on Prohibition or Restriction on the Use of Certain Conventional Weapons which May Be Deemed to Be Excessively Injurious or to Have Indiscriminate Effects.[13]

2.2.4 International crimes and counter-terrorism

International crimes and counter-terrorism are two other areas which the EU has sought to include in its agreements with third states. These are also issues which Korea has prioritised in recent years. In March 2009, the Korean Presidential Office ('Cheong Wa Dae') published a foreign and security policy paper, 'Global Korea: The National Security Strategy of the

---

[10] See the website of the UN Office for Disarmament, www.un.org/disarmament/convarms/SALW/ (accessed 5 June 2012).

[11] Convention on the Prohibition of the Use, Stockpiling, Production and Transfer of Anti-Personnel Mines and their Destruction (18 September 1997) 2056 UNTS 211.

[12] Convention on Cluster Munitions (20 May 2008).

[13] Convention on Prohibition or Restriction on the Use of Certain Conventional Weapons which May Be Deemed to Be Excessively Injurious or to Have Indiscriminate Effects (10 October 1980) 1342 UNTS 137.

Republic of Korea'.[14] The paper acknowledged new security challenges, such as international/transnational crimes, proliferation of weapons of mass destruction, terrorism, drugs and arms trade, piracy, cyber-crime, trafficking and money laundering, with the concept of human security and the 'comprehensive security threat'. It is notable that the paper emphasises the importance of the responsibility of a state in international affairs. It argues that national interests are inseparable from peace and prosperity in the wider global world. As one of four strategic aims, an advanced security system is established, comprising not only territorial defence against North Korea, but also international partnerships for the protection of significant sea lanes, the provision of humanitarian aid and reconstruction and counter-terrorism and the non-proliferation of WMDs. Thus, the inclusion of the clauses on the most serious crimes of concern to the international community[15] and cooperation in combating terrorism[16] in the Framework Agreement was also based on mutual shared interests between Korea and the EU.

In relation to international crimes, the EU systematically seeks the inclusion of a clause supporting the International Criminal Court (ICC) in negotiating mandates and agreements with third countries.[17] The revised Cotonou Agreement of 2005,[18] which applies to 79 African, Caribbean and Pacific countries and the EU, was the first binding legal instrument including an ICC-related clause, and it has provided a model for subsequent agreements, although some adjustments to the clause are required, as a specific position of the given third country on the ICC is to be considered for its agreement with the EU. This issue is dealt with in Article 6 of the EU–Korea Framework Agreement, which provides:

> 1. The Parties reaffirm that the most serious crimes of concern to the international community as a whole must not go unpunished and that their effective prosecution must be ensured by taking measures at the national level and by enhancing international cooperation, as appropriate, including the International Criminal Court. The Parties agree to fully support the universality and integrity of the Rome Statute of the International Criminal Court and related instruments.
> 2. The Parties agree that a dialogue between them on these matters would be beneficial.

---

[14] Office of the President, *Global Korea: The National Security Strategy of the Republic of Korea* (Seoul: Office of the President 2009) (Korean).

[15] EU–Korea Framework Agreement, Article 6.

[16] Ibid. Article 7.

[17] See Council Decision 2011/168/CFSP of 21 March 2011 on the International Criminal Court and repealing Common Position 2003/444/CFSP [2011] OJ L76/56 22 March 2011.

[18] Second Revision of the Cotonou Agreement, Agreed Consolidated Text of 11 March 2010, Article 11(7), www.ec.europa.eu/development/icenter/repository/second_revision_cotonou _agreement_20100311.pdf (accessed 29 May 2012).

Article 6 of the Framework Agreement presented above illustrates deeper cooperation between Korea and the EU than shown in the Cotonou Agreement. The ICC clause in the Cotonou Agreement emphasised the necessity to ratify the Rome Statute,[19] because not all parties to the agreement had done so. On the contrary, Korea and the EU Member States were both active in the establishment of the ICC and had already ratified the Statute. Therefore, the article in the framework agreement merely confirms their mutual commitment to address international crime.

As for Article 7 on counter-terrorism, the Framework Agreement shows the two parties' commitment to address terrorism in a more global context than the EU standard clause on counter-terrorism. On 21 September 2001, shortly after 9/11, the European Council approved the Plan of Action on Combating Terrorism.[20] The Action Plan raised the need to systematically evaluate EU relations with third countries, in the light of counter-terrorism. In the European Council meeting in Seville in June 2002, a global approach to fighting terrorism was emphasised. As a part of such approach, the Seville Council acknowledged that all EU agreements with third countries were to incorporate counter-terrorism clauses.[21] The EU's standard clause on counter-terrorism provides:

> The Parties reaffirm the importance of the fight against terrorism, and in accordance with international conventions and with their respective legislation and regulations agree to co-operate in the prevention and suppression of terrorist acts. They shall do so in particular:
> • In the framework of the full implementation of Resolution 1373 of the UN Security Council and other relevant UN resolutions, international conventions and instruments;
> • by exchange of information on terrorist groups and their support networks in accordance with international and national law; and,
> • by exchange of views on means and methods used to counter terrorism, including in technical fields and training, and by exchange of experiences in respect of terrorism prevention.

Compared to this standard clause, the article in the Framework Agreement is far more advanced, as shown below:

> 1. The Parties, reaffirming the importance of the fight against terrorism, and in accordance with applicable international conventions, including international humanitarian, human rights and refugee law, as well as with their respective legislation and regulations, and, taking into account the UN Global Counter-

---

[19] Rome Statute establishing the International Criminal Court (17 July 1998) 2187 UNTS 3.

[20] See, generally, D. Casale, 'EU Institutional and Legal Counter-terrorism Framework', *Defence Against Terrorism Review*, vol. 1 (2008), pp. 49–78.

[21] Presidency Conclusions, Seville European Council 21–22 June 2002, Document 13463/02, 24 October 2002, Annex V, paragraph 4.

Terrorism Strategy, contained in the UN General Assembly Resolution no.60/288 of 8 September 2006, agree to cooperate in the prevention and suppression of terrorist acts.

2. The Parties shall do so in particular:

a) in the framework of implementation of Resolutions of the UN Security Council and their respective obligations under other relevant international conventions and instruments;

b) by exchange of information on terrorist groups and their support networks, in accordance with international and national law;

c) by exchanges of views on means and methods used to counter terrorism, including in technical fields and training, and by exchange of experiences in respect of terrorism prevention;

d) by cooperating to deepen the international consensus on the fight against terrorism including the legal definition of terrorist acts, as appropriate, and in particular by working towards an agreement on the Comprehensive Convention on International Terrorism;

e) by sharing relevant best practices in the area of protection of human rights in the fight against terrorism.

There are several elements to note, as regards this provision. First, the article in the Framework Agreement has incorporated an express reference to the protection of human rights in the context of combating terrorism. Concern for undermining human rights became acute in the process of strengthening measures to track and investigate terrorists. Violation of privacy is another issue of human rights, as enhancing internal security involved establishing mechanisms for collecting and exchanging information. For instance, the EU–US Passenger Name Records (PNR) Agreement[22] resulted from the difference between the EU and US on data protection. Article 7 of the Framework Agreement shows that achieving a balance between security and human rights became a key legal element in the EU's agreement on counterterrorism with third countries.

Second, the article also extends to cooperation in a more global context, by adding a commitment to establish a Comprehensive Convention on International Terrorism. The negotiation of a convention on this subject is currently deadlocked, because the participating countries could not agree on the definition of terrorism.[23] Combating terrorism necessitates global efforts,

---

[22] Agreement between the United States of America and the European Union on the use and transfer of Passenger Name Records to the United States Department of Homeland Security, Document 17434/11, 8 December 2001, replacing an earlier agreement, which had been provisionally applied since 2007.

[23] See, for example, J. M. Sorel, 'Some Questions about the Definition of Terrorism and the Fight against its Financing', *European Journal of International Law*, vol. 14 (2003), pp. 365–78; M. Di Filippo, 'Terrorist Crimes and International Co-operation: Critical Remarks on the Definition and Inclusion of Terrorism in the Category of International Crimes', *European*

since terrorism often takes place across borders. As justice, intelligence and police matters are deeply rooted in sovereignty, countries are often reluctant to cooperate in a regular and voluntary fashion. Even the EU, which has pooled and shared sovereignty for the last 60 years, has only recently made progress in the fields of justice and home affairs.[24] Different legal systems are severe obstacles for cooperation in this area. A minimum level of mutual recognition and harmonisation of national laws is necessary for effective international cooperation to counter terrorism. For many countries, a clear definition of terrorism does not exist in their legal system. Under such circumstances, the commitment by Korea and the EU to the Comprehensive Convention on International Terrorism means their willingness to share common elements, not only in the international cooperation for combating terrorism, but also in the progress of their national law on terrorism.

The fight against terrorism and other areas of security policy also require cooperation in related areas. In this regard, the Framework Agreement covers cooperation in combating illicit drugs,[25] organised crime and corruption,[26] money laundering and terrorism financing,[27] cyber-crime[28] and law enforcement.[29] Although the means for cooperation in these areas remain vague, the Framework Agreement provides the potential for the coordination of both parties' actions in these fields. Since even national policies in these fields are underdeveloped, mere dialogues between Korea and the EU and its Member States may contribute to the adoption of similar policies and, eventually, lead to more concrete cooperation.

2.2.5 Evaluation

The EU and Korea have included some areas for security cooperation in the Framework Agreement, partly because the EU is self-obliged to include them with a number of standard clauses. In order to adopt a coherent approach in the Common Foreign and Security Policy, the EU has established principles for its agreements with third countries. From the point of view of the EU's counterparts, these standard clauses may limit its room for manoeuvre when negotiating an agreement with the EU, since the adoption of these clauses can be a precondition for a successful agreement.

Journal of International Law, vol. 19 (2008), pp. 533–70; R. Young, 'Defining Terrorism: The Evolution of Terrorism as a Legal Concept in International Law and its Influence on Definitions in Domestic Law', *Boston College International and Comparative Law Review*, vol. 29 (2006), pp. 23–106.

[24] See, generally, S. Peers, *EU Justice and Home Affairs Law* (Oxford: Oxford University Press, 2011).

[25] EU–Korea Framework Agreement, Article 34.

[26] Ibid. Article 35.

[27] Ibid. Article 36.

[28] Ibid. Article 37.

[29] Ibid. Article 38.

However, the reality is far from the EU's unilateral demand for automatic inclusion of the clauses in agreements. In most of the EU's agreements with third countries, the clauses were modified, so as to take into account the particular foreign policies of the EU's counterparts. In some cases, the EU and its counterparts simply exclude some standard clauses entirely, due to the sensitiveness of the given issue for the latter.

Therefore, the security areas included in the Framework Agreement are those on which both the EU and Korea have common interests for cooperation, even though the level of interests may not be equal for the two parties. Also, the degree of policy specification in the given areas may not be the same for them, either. The mutual interests of the two, however, can be found in the fact that the standard clauses are modified for deeper and stronger cooperation in the Framework Agreement. Also, the inclusion of non-traditional security issues – for example, cyber-crime, money launder-ing and organised crime – indicates that the two parties have willingness for comprehensive security cooperation.

3 GAPS IN SECURITY COOPERATION

Despite a long list of areas of security cooperation in the Framework Agreement, certain areas of security cooperation are missing. Anti-piracy actions, UN peace-keeping operations, peace building and development in conflict areas and R&D cooperation in defense procurements are not mentioned in the Framework Agreement, even though both parties actively contribute to international peace and security in those particular areas. Especially, in the above-mentioned Global Korea paper, the Korean gov-ernment made it clear that cooperation on research and development for defence procurements and cooperation on peace building and development for conflict areas are its two major interests in its relationship with Europe, apart from its commitment to the Asia–Europe Meeting (ASEM). Of course, one may argue that these are implicitly included in the Framework Agreement by some expressions, such as cooperation in 'regional and inter-national organisations',[30] 'maritime transport policy'[31] and 'development assistance'.[32] However, these words are short of concrete commitments to cooperation in those fields.

There may be two reasons for the exclusion of these areas from the Framework Agreement. On the one hand, the anti-piracy actions, UN peace-keeping operations, peace building and development in conflict areas and research and development cooperation in defence procurements are not exclusive competences of the EU. Of course, most security cooperation

[30] EU–Korea Framework Agreement, Article 8.
[31] Ibid. Article 19.
[32] Ibid. Article 27.

featured in the Framework Agreement is not solely in the hands of the EU. However, in practice, the EU may find it easier to include clauses relating to those areas in which the EU has already established standard clauses. In addition, the EU also might have had less difficulty with generating consensus among the Member States on those areas which are subject to the so-called 'community method'.[33] Indeed, the EU has already produced common rules in the security areas covered by the Framework Agreement – such as illicit drugs, organised crime and corruption, money laundering and terrorism financing, cyber-crime and law enforcement cooperation. In contrast, the EU's common foreign and security policy is less developed, and the Member States continue to have a lot of individual influence in its ongoing development.[34]

On the other hand, due to their respective military allies, the EU and the Korea may have attempted to avoid committing themselves to cooperation which would have military implications. Especially since most of the EU member states are the members of the North Atlantic Treaty Organization (NATO). The military role of the EU, in the presence of the NATO, has been a controversial and unsettled issue thus far. Although the EU has strengthened its roles on defence issues, the division of labour between the EU and the NATO is still unclear.[35] The external dimension of the EU's military cooperation is even more underdeveloped than the cooperation among the Member States. Therefore, the sensitivity of military cooperation may have induced the EU and Korea to focus on the non-military dimension of security cooperation.

The absence of cooperation with military instruments in the Framework Agreement does not permanently prevent the two parties from acting together in this area. Their cooperation in anti-piracy and crisis management is possible on *an ad* hoc basis, when their willingness is strong enough to overcome the complexity of their security ties. Indeed, leaders at the sixth EU–Korea Summit in March 2012 pledged to explore possibilities for closer cooperation in efforts to counter Somalia-based piracy in the Gulf of Aden.[36]

Looking to the future, the EU's empowered foreign and security policy

[33] In other words, the areas which used to fall within the first pillar of the EU.
[34] Consolidated Version of the Treaty on the European Union (TEU) [2010] OJ C83/13, 30 March 2010, Article 42(1) calls for the 'progressive framing of a common Union defence policy', through unanimous decisions of the European Council. Article 42(2) further provides that '[the common security and defence policy] of the Union . . . shall not prejudice the specific character of the security and defence policy of certain Member States and shall respect the obligations of certain Member States'. . . in the NATO.
[35] TEU, Article 42(2) provides that the EU 'shall respect the obligations of certain Member States, which see their common defence realised in the North Atlantic Treaty Organisation (NATO), under the North Atlantic Treaty and be compatible with the common security and defence policy established within that framework'.
[36] Republic of Korea–EU Summit Joint Press Statement, Document MEMO/12/224, 28 March 2012.

is likely to create many more opportunities for partnership with Korea. With shared interests in crisis management and peace-keeping missions, there is much room for Korea and the EU to cooperate for a securer world. Mixing civilian and military operations and avoiding combat missions is the general direction of the EU. Korea takes a similar approach to overseas peace-keeping operations. In the operations supported by the UN Security Council, Korea and the EU will increasingly work together.[37] Korea could also potentially take part in an EU operation as a foreign partner, as Russia did in Chad in 2008.[38] The EU Member States are highly experienced in peace-keeping missions in Eastern Europe, Africa and the Middle East. As the EU is open to non-member countries joining its overseas operations, participating in those missions would help Korea access the EU's expertise in the multilateral operations and knowledge concerning those regions and strengthen its ties with European countries, which have dominated by economic cooperation so far.

In the meantime, the exchange of information and experience will be the main component of their cooperation, in relation to military operations. The most likely cooperation in defence is on R&D for defence procurement. With highly developed science and technology fields, both in Korea and the EU, the gains for cooperation in these fields will be extensive, in aspects of both economy and security. Also, the relatively long history of cooperation in science and technology[39] can be easily extended to cooperation in research and development for defence procurement. Mutual economic interests in the reconstruction of post-conflict areas are also easily recognisable. Although the Framework Agreement does not put much weight on this issue, frequent exchanges may allow cooperation to materialise over time.

4 POTENTIAL FOR FUTURE DEVELOPMENT AND ITS LIMITS

The EU–Korea Framework Agreement creates a stepping stone for an upgraded relationship between the two partners. It introduces security as a new arena for their cooperation. The scope of such cooperation envisaged in the Framework Agreement currently remains merely consultative and subject to future agreement. The depth of cooperation depends on the mutual willingness of the two parties. As the Framework Agreement aims for the development of a long-term relationship, it is understandable that the contents of cooperation are vague, and it focuses on coordination, dialogue

---

[37] Korean and European troops are both already working in the International Security Assistance Force in Afghanistan; see www.isaf.nato.int/troop-numbers-and-contributions/index.php (accessed 4 June 2012).

[38] See the Agreement between the European Union and the Russian Federation on the participation of the Russian Federation in the European Union military operation in the Republic of Chad and in the Central African Republic (EUFOR Tchad/RCA) [2008] OJ L 307/16.

[39] On cooperation in the field of science and technology, see Chapter 9 of this volume.

and information exchange. Moreover, such methods of cooperation will produce meaningful outcomes and, possibly, common actions, only if they are based on shared principles and interests in specific issues, and if the parties are able to form common positions on the details of objectives and instruments.

In this light, how can one assess the potentials for further development on security cooperation between Korea and the EU? One way of examining the compatibility of the interests between the two is to evaluate the similarities and differences of public opinion on specific security issues in the two parties.

Public opinion may be changeable and is often rooted in emotional responses. Moreover, the influence of public opinion is generally weakest in foreign policies, compared to other policy areas. Nevertheless, it is not negligible in policy-making in a democratic country, because the policy-makers cannot ignore the general trend of public opinion. Despite the possible gap between the elite and the public, public opinion can still be used to compare the attitudes of a country with that of another one. The difference between the two countries may lead to different policies.

Among various security issues covered by the Framework Agreement, this section looks at public opinion on non-proliferation and counter-terrorism, as these are the most familiar issues for the general public. To begin with, Table 11.1 shows the public opinion on a country's right to develop nuclear fuel. The table shows the public opinions of Korea and certain EU Member States, as well as that of the US. With Iran and North Korea, the development of nuclear programmes has been an increasingly sensitive issue for both Korea and the EU. Such sensitivity is clearly reflected in the attitude of Koreans, where security concern for the North Korean nuclear programme has persisted for a long time. Under these circumstances, Korea became highly cautious in allowing new countries to develop nuclear fuel. Seventy-six per cent of the Korean respondents agreed that the UN should try to stop new countries from producing nuclear fuel and provide a substitute, because of the possibility of developing nuclear weapons. In contrast, objection to new countries' nuclear programmes are less strong in France, Germany, Italy, Poland, Spain, the UK and the US. In particular, public opinion in France is almost evenly divided.

Moving on to perceptions on terrorism, the levels of concern in major European countries are much higher than in Korea, as shown in Table 11.2. Whereas the majority of respondents see terrorism as a big problem in their own countries in the UK, France, Germany, Italy, Spain and Poland, the public opinion in Korea is almost evenly split. However, in Sweden, Bulgaria, the Czech Republic and Slovakia, the degree of concern for terrorism is lower than in Korea. Thus, although the 10 countries in the table do not represent all of the Member States of the EU, one may infer that the public attitude to the threat from terrorism in Korea does not significantly differ from Europe.

Table 11.1 *Attitudes towards the development of nuclear fuel (%).*

Country	All countries should be free to produce nuclear fuel under the UN oversight, because of their right to nuclear energy and energy independence	The UN should try to stop new countries from producing nuclear fuel, but provide a substitute, because of the possibility to develop nuclear weapons	Neither/ Depends	Don't know/ No answer
France	44	46	6	5
Germany	28	63	6	4
Italy	29	57	12	2
Poland	32	49	6	14
Spain	14	61	13	12
UK	36	55	6	3
South Korea	22	76	1	1
United States	29	56	7	7

Source: Council on Foreign Relations, *Public Opinion on Global Issues: A Web-Based Digest of Polling from around the World* (November 2009), Chapter 4b, www.cfr.org/public_opinion (accessed 4 June 2012).

Finally, Table 11.3 illustrates a critical difference between four European countries and Korea on the implementation of counter-terrorism actions. In France, Poland, Spain and the UK, generally, the people firmly object to undermining human rights, even for the purpose of security. In contrast, with a small margin, the majority of Korean respondents accept that some degree of torture can be allowed, in order to gain information for saving innocent lives. This is a striking difference over the balance between security and human rights.

In sum, looking at public opinion in Europe and Korea on various security issues, the potential compatibility of positions between the EU and Korea is far from perfect. This does not mean that cooperation in these areas would not be possible. Rather, it indicates that the Framework Agreement rightly commits to dialogue on them. The dialogues will provide opportunities for the EU and Korea to upgrade their similarities in principles to similarities in practice. Furthermore, to overcome the differences in public opinion, the two parties should invest in public diplomacy. The dialogues should not stop at the official level. After all, the Framework Agreement is an agreement comprising 28 democratic countries. The cooperation between the EU and Korea should, therefore, be based on the broad involvement of the peoples and civil society of both parties.

Table 11.2 *Attitudes towards terrorism as a problem in one's own country (%).*

Country	Very big problem	Moderately big problem	Small problem	Not a problem at all	Don't know/No answer
UK	30	41	23	4	2
France	54	29	15	1	0
Germany	31	43	18	7	1
Italy	73	20	6	1	0
Spain	66	26	5	1	1
Sweden	3	10	48	34	4
Bulgaria	24	18	31	21	7
Czech Republic	16	26	40	16	2
Poland	35	30	22	10	3
Slovakia	17	17	42	23	2
South Korea	12	34	36	13	5

Source: Council on Foreign Relation, *Public Opinion on Global Issues: A Web-Based Digest of Polling from around the World* (November 2009), Chapter 4a, www.cfr.org/public_opinion (accessed 4 June 2012).

Table 11.3 *Attitudes towards the torturing of prisoners (%).*

Country	Allowing some degree of torture to gain information that saves lives	Clear rules against torture should be maintained	Don't know/ No answer
France	16	82	2
UK	16	82	3
Poland	27	62	11
Spain	11	82	7
South Korea	51	48	1

Source: Council on Foreign Relation, *Public Opinion on Global Issues: A Web-Based Digest of Polling from Around the World* (November 2009), Chapter 4a, www.cfr.org/public_opinion (accessed 4 June 2012).

5 CONCLUSION

The Framework Agreement is an important instrument for the future cooperation on international peace and security between the EU and Korea, as it creates a basis for future cooperation on counter-terrorism, non-proliferation, cyber-terrorism and human security. It is up to the two parties involved, as to whether their cooperation will remain simply a rhetorical exchange or whether it will lead to substantial activities.

What could bring Korea and the Europe Union together in the efforts to enhance global security based on the new Framework Agreement? There are three main ways for them to work more closely on security issues. First, they should develop more concrete conceptions of their shared values, such as human rights, democracy, prosperity and the rule of law, all of which are the backbone of global security issues. Second, they should continue to search for those global security issues, in which, as relatively distant actors in geographical terms, Korea and the EU have mutual, shared interests. Third, facing the pressure of limited resources and increasing demands to contribute to global security, both parties have interests to enhance efficiency and effectiveness through wider cooperation. This requires cooperation on the aspect of infrastructure for security, for example, in respect to research and development on defence procurement, facilities for information sharing and so on.

In addition to contributing to global security, the two parties can also help enhance the stability of each other. Geographical distance, preoccupation with their own security issues and complex relationships with their immediate neighbours have often precluded Korea and the EU from cooperating on each other's security challenges. Indeed, the Framework Agreement seems to be rather ambiguous on the cooperation in relation to their regional security concerns. However, constant interaction on broad security issues may increase the opportunities for them to improve their mutual understanding and provide political support for each other's regional security. Especially with the rise of China and the US emphasis on the strategic importance of the Asia–Pacific region, the lack of geopolitical interests between the regions places them in a unique position to play a role as an honest normative actor. Against such a backdrop, the extent of cooperation based on the Framework Agreement will, undoubtedly, grow over time.

12

Environmental Cooperation between the EU and Korea

Elisa Morgera

1 INTRODUCTION

This chapter will discuss environmental cooperation between the EU and Korea against the background of the law and practice of the EU's external relations. It will identify environment-related provisions in the EU–Korea Framework Agreement[1] and contrast them with other bilateral agreements concluded by the EU with third countries. It will then discuss two means of implementation: political dialogue and EU external funding. By fostering better understanding of the peculiarities and ambitions of the EU's approach to environmental integration in its external relations, the chapter will conclude by emphasising the opportunities and limitations of dialogue to strengthen environmental cooperation between the EU and Korea.

2 THE BASES OF ENVIRONMENTAL COOPERATION IN THE FRAMEWORK AGREEMENT

2.1 Overview

The environmental dimension of the Framework Agreement with Korea can be assessed from the viewpoint of environmental integration – a treaty-based requirement for the EU to integrate environmental concerns into the definition and implementation of its policies, including its external relations.[2] To fulfill this obligation, the EU aims to include in its general bilateral agreements both environmental cooperation clauses (dealing solely with the environment) and environmental integration clauses (mandating or encouraging the incorporation of environmental concerns into other cooperation areas).

[1] Framework Agreement between the European Union and its Member States, on the one part, and the Republic of Korea, on the other part (EU–Korea Framework Agreement), www.eeas.europa.eu/korea_south/index_en.htm (accessed 20 April 2012).

[2] Consolidated Version of the Treaty on the Functioning of the European Union (TFEU) [2010] OJ C83/47, 30 March 2010, Article 11. For a discussion of the relevance of this provision in EU external relations, see G. Marín Durán and E. Morgera, *Environmental Integration in the EU's External Relations: Beyond Multilateral Dimensions* (Oxford: Hart Publishing, 2012), Chapter 1.

The former have the function of including the environment as a specific area of EU external relations as a whole, while the latter serve to 'green' individual EU policies covered by a given agreement, beyond the area of environmental cooperation.[3] In analysing these provisions, in light of the differentiation that characterises environmental clauses in EU bilateral agreements, attention should be paid to the specific legal wording and environmental standards utilised, the choice of priority issues for environmental cooperation, the selection of cooperation areas in which environmental integration is ensured and the trade and environment nexus.[4] In the specific case of EU–Korea relations, the environmental clauses of the Framework Agreement are significantly complemented by the environment-related provisions of the trade and sustainable chapter of the EU–Korea Free Trade Agreement,[5] which are discussed at length in Marín Durán's contribution to this volume.[6]

2.2 Environmental cooperation clauses

Environmental concerns are integrated from the outset in the Framework Agreement, with preambular language reaffirming parties' commitment to 'promote sustainable development in its economic, social and environmental dimensions'[7] and to 'ensure a high level of environmental protection'.[8] In addition, environmental protection forms part of the basis for bilateral cooperation, whereby the parties reiterate their commitment 'to cooperate to address global environmental challenges, and in particular climate change',[9] and is also listed as one of the central aims of the Agreement.[10]

Two key provisions on environmental cooperation can then be found in the title dealing with 'cooperation in the area of sustainable development':[11] one of general scope, entitled 'environment and natural resources',[12] and one specifically addressing climate change, which is recognised as a 'common global threat'.[13] The latter reflects the increasing political priority that has become attached to climate change in the EU's bilateral external relations[14]

---

[3] Marín Durán and Morgera, 'Environmental Integration on the EU's External Relations', p. 56.
[4] Ibid. p. 57.
[5] Free Trade Agreement between the European Union and its Member States of the one part, and the Republic of Korea of the other part (EU–Korea FTA) [2011] OJ L127/6, 14 May 2011.
[6] See Chapter 8 of this volume.
[7] EU–Korea Framework Agreement, Preambular Recital 15.
[8] Ibid. Preambular Recital 16.
[9] Ibid. Article 1(3).
[10] Ibid. Article 2(2)(d).
[11] Ibid. Title V.
[12] Ibid. Article 23.
[13] Ibid. Article 24.
[14] K. Kulovesi, E. Morgera and M. Muñoz, 'Environmental Integration and Multi-Faceted International Dimensions of EU Law: Unpacking the EU's 2009 Climate and Energy

and is discussed more specifically in Rossati's contribution to this volume.[15] The Framework Agreement also indicates that the principal modalities for implementation of the environmental provisions are regular dialogue at policy and technical levels and the mutual exchange of information, expertise and best practices, including, where possible, participation in each other's relevant environmental programmes.[16]

Under the general provision on environment and natural resources, the parties 'agree on the need to conserve, and manage in a sustainable manner, natural resources and biological diversity as a basis for the development of current and future generations'.[17] This is complemented by another, qualified statement to the effect that the 'outcome of the World Summit on the Sustainable Development and the implementation of relevant multilateral environmental agreements shall be taken into account, as relevant'.[18] Furthermore, the parties identify a list of priority environmental issues, on which they 'shall endeavour to strengthen their cooperation', including in a regional context, such as climate change and energy efficiency; environmental awareness; participation in, and implementation of, multilateral environmental agreements, particularly emphasising those dealing with biodiversity and biosafety and also specifically mentioning the Convention on International Trade in Endangered Species[19]; promotion of environmental technologies, products and services, including environmental management systems and eco-labelling; prevention of illegal transboundary movement of hazardous substances, hazardous wastes and other forms of waste; protection of the coastal marine environment; soil and land management; and local participation in environmental protection.[20]

When compared to other EU bilateral agreements, the outlined clause on environmental cooperation is not particularly detailed or stringent. A useful comparison can be drawn, for instance, with the Association Agreement with Central American countries,[21] which was concluded shortly after the Framework Agreement with Korea and is also representative of the new generation of EU bilateral agreements (so-called post-Global

Package', *Common Market Law Review*, vol. 48 (2011), pp. 829–91; K. Kulovesi, 'Climate Change in EU External Relations: Please Follow My Example (or I Might Force You To)', in E. Morgera (ed.), *The External Environmental Policy of the European Union: EU and International Law Perspectives* (Cambridge: Cambridge University Press, 2012), pp. 115-48.

[15] See Chapter 13 of this volume.
[16] EU–Korea Framework Agreement, Articles 2, 23(i), 24(2) and 45(2).
[17] Ibid. Article 23(1).
[18] Ibid. Article 23(3).
[19] Convention on International Trade in Endangered Species of Wild Fauna and Flora (CITES) (3 March 1973) 993 UNTS 243.
[20] EU–Korea Framework Agreement, Article 23(2)(a)–(h).
[21] Agreement establishing an Association between the EU and its Member States, on the one hand, and Central America on the other, 22 March 2011 (hereinafter, EU–Central America Association Agreement).

Europe agreements)[22] and which has a comparably wide subject matter. In the Association Agreement, the priorities for environmental cooperation are identified through legally binding language, expressly including the protection of ecosystems, forests and fisheries;[23] pollution prevention in all environmental media (freshwaters, sea, soil and air); as well as sound management of chemicals, deforestation and the depletion of the ozone layer.[24] In addition, the measures to carry out environmental cooperation are spelt out, albeit in soft language, and include capacity building and institutional strengthening, technology transfer, integration of environmental considerations in land-use management, promotion of sustainable production and consumption patterns and strengthening environmental management, monitoring and control systems.[25] It should also be noted that the Association Agreement includes a provision on indigenous peoples and other ethnic groups, according to which, cooperation is required, so as to ensure the effective participation of these groups in the sustainable management and use of land and natural resources and in environmental protection.[26] Biodiversity cooperation between the EU and Korea, including cooperation on matters of interest to indigenous and local communities, could, however, become more prominent in the near future; as implementation of the 2010 Nagoya Protocol on Access and Benefit-Sharing[27] gets underway, new EU legislation is likely to be developed, with inherent transboundary dimensions.[28] In addition, the EU had already provided some indication of its

[22] The new generation of EU bilateral agreements were launched by the 2006 Global Europe Strategy; European Commission, *Communication on Global Europe: Competing in the World. A Contribution to the EU's Growth and Job Strategy* (*Global Europe*), Document COM (2006)567 final, Brussels, 4 October 2006, endorsed by the Council, 'Conclusions on Global Europe – Competing in the World' (14799/06) 13 November 2006. See, further, Marín Durán and Morgera, *Environmental Integration in the EU's External Relations*, pp. 50–1, 138–40; R. Zvelc, 'Environmental Integration in EU Trade Policy: The Generalised System of Preferences, Trade Sustainability Impact Assessments and Free Trade Agreements', in E. Morgera (ed.), *The External Environmental Policy of the European Union: EU and International Law Perspectives* (Cambridge: Cambridge University Press, 2012), pp. 174-203.

[23] Although, see the discussion below (Section 2.3) on environmental integration clauses, in relation to forests and fisheries.

[24] EU–Central America Association Agreement, Article 50(3).

[25] Ibid. Article 50(1).

[26] Ibid. Article 45(3).

[27] Nagoya Protocol on Access to Genetic Resources and the Fair and Equitable Sharing of Benefits Arising from their Utilization to the Convention on Biological Diversity, UN Doc. UNEP/CBD/COP/DEC/X/1, 29 October 2010.

[28] When the Nagoya Protocol enters into force, countries such as the EU Member States using genetic resources originating from third countries will be mandated to ensure that genetic resources and traditional knowledge utilised within their jurisdiction have been accessed, in accordance with the legislation and requirements of the third country that provided these resources. The European Commission has already indicated the need to propose new EU legislation to implement the Nagoya Protocol in the EU's 2020 Biodiversity Strategy (European Commission, *Communication on Our Life Insurance, Our Natural Capital: An EU Biodiversity*

interest in exploring, through its bilateral relations with third countries, the trade-related aspects of biodiversity, as part of an effort to ensure biodiversity mainstreaming through its full economic valuation.[29]

More generally, it can be noted that there is no reference in the EU–Korea Framework Agreement to approximation of environmental laws to those of the EU, which is the approach that is used in the Euro–Mediterranean context and in the case of the Partnership and Cooperation Agreements between the EU and CIS countries. In contrast, in the case of EU–Korea relations, there seems, instead, to be (explicit and implicit) reliance on *international* environmental standards. This is the trend of the new generation of EU bilateral agreements, where a more systematic approach can be detected in the utilisation of international environmental standards as the benchmark for assessing domestic environmental performance, with increased emphasis on questions related to implementation and enforcement. This appears as a more appropriate course of action to legitimise the EU's efforts to promote environmental protection outside its borders and avoid criticisms on the grounds of extra-territoriality or even neo-colonialism. There is, however, no consistency in referring explicitly to multilateral environmental treaties across EU bilateral agreements,[30] although an incipient trend has been detected in certain post-Global Europe Agreements to rely on the list of multilateral environmental agreements included in the special-incentive arrangement for sustainable development and good governance under the EU's Generalised System of Preferences.[31]

2.3 Environmental integration clauses

Apart from the specific environmental cooperation clauses discussed above, environmental concerns have also been integrated into four other specific

---

Strategy to 2020, Document COM (2011)244 final, Brussels, 3 May 2011, p. 16, 'Action 20'; endorsed by the Council, 'Conclusions – EU Biodiversity Strategy to 2020', 23 June 2011). For a discussion of the Nagoya Protocol from an EU perspective, see M. Buck and C. Hamilton, 'The Nagoya Protocol on Access to Genetic Resources and the Fair and Equitable Sharing of Benefits Arising from their Utilisation to the Convention on Biological Diversity', *Review of European Community and International Environmental Law*, vol. 20 (2011), p. 47.

[29] E. Morgera, 'The Trajectory of EU Biodiversity Cooperation: Supporting Environmental Multilateralism Through EU External Action', in E. Morgera (ed.), *The External Environmental Policy of the European Union: EU and International Law Perspectives* (Cambridge: Cambridge University Press, 2012), pp. 235–59.

[30] Marín Durán and Morgera, *Environmental Integration in the EU's External Relations*, pp. 135–6.

[31] Regulation (EC) 732/2008 of 22 July 2008, applying a scheme of generalised tariff preferences for the period from 1 January 2009 to 31 December 2011 and amending Regulations (EC) 552/97, (EC) 1933/2006 and Commission Regulations (EC) 1100/2006 and (EC) 964/2007 [2008] OJ L211/1; see Marín Durán and Morgera, *Environmental Integration in the EU's External Relations*, Chapter 3.

provisions under the Framework Agreement with Korea, namely agriculture, fisheries, energy and transport. Unlike in most of the other EU bilateral agreements, however, there is no cross-cutting clause on environmental integration, which is significant in the absence of specific reference to environmental concerns in other cooperation areas, such as tourism[32] and industrial development.[33]

In the fields of agriculture, rural development and forestry, the EU and Korea undertake to exchange information and develop cooperation on, *inter alia*, the integration of environmental requirements into agricultural policy; sustainable forest management to prevent deforestation and encourage the creation of new woodland, 'including due regard to the interests of developing countries where timber is sourced'; and, more generally, on the links between these three policy fields and the environment.[34] This is in line with EU practice in other bilateral contexts, where clauses providing for environmental integration in the agriculture sector are frequent, but tend to remain quite general.[35] Cooperation on forestry issues, in particular, is dealt through specialised bilateral negotiations in the context of the EU Forest Law Enforcement, Governance and Trade (FLEGT) initiative.[36] FLEGT-related negotiations are in place with certain Asian countries[37] and represent a particularly interesting co-regulatory experiment, whereby the EU engages third countries in assessing their own national legal framework on forests against international standards and stakeholder concerns on sustainable forest management.[38] While Korea, as a timber-importing, rather than exporting, country,[39] is not directly concerned with FLEGT and its implications for access to the EU market,[40] it may still find the model of regulatory

---

[32] Compare with EU–Central America Association Agreement, Article 65.

[33] Compare with EU–Central America Association Agreement, Article 64.

[34] EU–Korea Framework Agreement, Article 25(f), (g) and (i).

[35] Marín Durán and Morgera, *Environmental Integration in the EU's External Relations*, p. 137.

[36] Regulation (EC) 2173/2005 on the establishment of a FLEGT licensing scheme for imports of timber into the European Community [2005] OJ L347/1. See the discussion in Marín Durán and Morgera, *Environmental Integration in the EU's External Relations*, pp. 272–6.

[37] European Forestry Institute–EU FLEGT Facility, FLEGT in Asia, www.euflegt.efi.int/portal /home/vpa_countries/in_asia/ (accessed 1 May 2012).

[38] See Morgera, 'Ambition, Complexity and Legitimacy of Pursuing Mutual Supportiveness through the EU's External Environmental Action' in B. Van Vooren, S. Blockmans and J. Wouters (eds), *The EU's Role in Global Governance: The Legal Dimension* (Oxford: Oxford University Press, forthcoming 2013), Chapter 13. On the links between FLEGT and the role of forests in international climate change negotiations, see A. Savaresi, 'EU External Action on Forests: FLEGT and the Development of International Law', in E. Morgera (ed.), *The External Environmental Policy of the European Union: EU and International Law Perspectives* (Cambridge: Cambridge University Press, 2012), pp. 149–73.

[39] The International Tropical Timber Organisation classifies Korea as a 'timber-consuming' country; see www.itto.int/itto_members/ (accessed 1 May 2012).

[40] The EU placed an obligation of due diligence on operators placing timber and timber products on the EU market to ensure the legal origin of their timber products and established a

cooperation a useful inspiration for developing other areas of environmental cooperation with the EU or for developing a similar approach to environmental cooperation with other countries.

In the area of fisheries, parties are required to 'encourage marine and fisheries cooperation, at bilateral and multilateral levels, particularly with a view to promoting sustainable and responsible marine and fisheries development and management'.[41] In comparison with the Association Agreement with Central America, the provision on fisheries cooperation appears quite general. In EU–Central America relations, cooperation has the more specific aims of data collection, monitoring, control and surveillance, the fight against illegal, unregulated and unreported fishing and reinforced cooperation with international and regional organisations, so as to ensure 'better understanding of the added value of international legal instruments in achieving a proper management of marine resources'.[42] The difference can be explained by Korea's high level of development and its distant-fishing activities in areas where EU distant-fishing vessels also operate. It may, therefore, be expected that fisheries-related cooperation between Korea and the EU could, in practice, focus on the exchange of information and best practices. Moreover, the EU and Korea are both party to several regional fisheries management organisations, including, *inter alia*, the North Atlantic Fisheries Organisation (NAFO), the Commission on the Conservation of Antarctic Marine Living Resources (CCAMLR), the International Commission for the Conservation of Atlantic Tuna (ICCAT), the Western and Central Atlantic Fishery Commission (WCAFC) and the Inter-American Tropical Tuna Commission (IATTC). It follows that mutual cooperation may include formulating joint positions on issues raised within these bodies.

In terms of EU–Korea cooperation in the energy sector, best-endeavour language is utilised, in relation to information exchange and joint studies aimed at, *inter alia*, developing new sustainable, innovative and renewable forms of energy, including biofuels and biomass, wind and solar energy, as well as hydropower generation; promoting energy efficiency in the production, transportation, distribution and end-use of energy; and fostering the transfer of technology aimed at sustainable energy production and energy efficiency.[43] While a similar provision in the EU–Central America Association Agreement is couched in voluntary terms, it is directly related to activities for, rather than studies on, the 'promotion of energy

---

presumption of compliance for timber originating from a country licensed under the FLEGT scheme: Regulation (EU) 995/2010 of 20 October 2010, laying down the obligations of operators who place timber and timber products on the market [2010] OJ L295/23, Articles 3–4.

[41] EU–Korea Framework Agreement, Article 26.
[42] EU–Central America Association Agreement, Article 59.
[43] EU–Korea Framework Agreement, Article 17(1)(a), (c) and (d).

saving, energy efficiency, renewable energy and assessing the environmental impacts of energy production and consumption, in particular its effects on biodiversity, forestry and land use change'.[44] Generally, energy is the area in which the EU more systematically includes environmental integration requirements, with particular emphasis on renewable energy and energy efficiency.[45] This approach is now reflected in a treaty-based environmental integration requirement for the EU's internal and external energy policy.[46]

The specific reference to biofuels in the EU–Korea Framework Agreement is particularly significant, because the EU has adopted biofuels production sustainability criteria applicable to imported biofuels, on the basis of an internal piece of legislation that provides for cooperation with third countries.[47] The criteria have been unilaterally set by the EU, but were expressly based on international reference documents.[48] Lack of compliance with these criteria does not lead to a ban on imports or use within the EU, but rather to a series of disincentives.[49] Through a combination of international legislation and external action at different levels,[50] the EU hopes to influence ongoing multilateral negotiations by systematically referring to the biofuels sustainability criteria in its negotiating position at the multilateral level,[51] but also using its internal legislation, in combination with bilateral tools of external relations, as a basis for building alliances with individual third countries, with a view to arriving at common/closer negotiating positions at the multilateral level or inspiring domestic action beyond its borders.[52] Dialogues between the EU and third countries or regions have provided an avenue for the discussion of respective negotiating positions on biofuels and have sometimes led to commitments to hold bilateral high-level meetings

---

[44] Central America Association Agreement, Article 65(2)(c).

[45] Marín Durán and Morgera, *Environmental Integration in the EU's External Relations*, p. 137.

[46] TFEU, Article 194(1)(c).

[47] Directive (EC) 2009/28 of the European Parliament and of the Council on the promotion of the use of energy from renewable sources [2009] OJ L 140/16 (Renewables Directive), Article 18(4).

[48] Ibid. Preambular, recitals 69, 73 and 77.

[49] See the detailed discussion in Kulovesi, Morgera and Muñoz, 'Environmental Integration and Multi-Faceted International Dimensions of EU Law: Unpacking the EU's 2009 Climate and Energy Package', pp. 883–4.

[50] Marín Durán and Morgera, *Environmental Integration in the EU's External Relations*, pp. 269–71; Morgera, 'Ambition, Complexity and Legitimacy of Pursuing Mutual Supportiveness through the EU's External Environmental Action'.

[51] For example, 'Summary of the Fourteenth Meeting of the Subsidiary Body on Scientific, Technical and Technological Advice to the CBD: 10–21 May 2010', *Earth Negotiations Bulletin*, vol. 9, no. 514 (2010), p. 12.

[52] EUROLAT – Resolution of 15 May 2010, 'Tackling Climate Change Challenges Together: For an EU–LAC Coordinated Strategy in the Framework of the UNFCCC Negotiations' (2010), paragraphs 37–8.

in the run-up to key negotiating sessions.[53] In addition, the Sustainability Impact Assessments that precede the conclusion of EU bilateral agreements have addressed the issue of certification for biofuels among policy recommendations to ensure sustainability,[54] occasionally making express reference to the EU criteria as guidance for third countries.[55]

With regards to EU–Korea cooperation in the field of transport, a provision on environmental integration in that sector is framed in best-endeavour terms, but it is quite elaborate. Environmental protection appears as one of the specific objectives of bilateral cooperation in this field,[56] with a requirement to promote, *inter alia*, regulatory convergence on the environmental aspects of transport policy, the reduction of greenhouse emissions in the transport sector and the implementation of pollution prevention standards (notably, as regards maritime transport and aviation) 'in line with the relevant international conventions applicable to both Parties, including cooperation in the appropriate international fora aimed at ensuring better enforcement of international regulations'.[57] This is certainly a more sophisticated provision than its counterpart in the EU–Central America Association Agreement, although the latter also points to cooperation in appropriate international fora, so as to ensure better enforcement of international standards.[58] Both instances clearly relate to the EU's multilateral and unilateral stances on climate change mitigation in the aviation sector. Given delays at the multilateral level to agree on climate change-related action in this sector, as supported by the Union, the EU included aviation activities in its own scheme for greenhouse gas emission allowance trading, with significant extraterritorial implications for third-country airlines flying to and from EU airports.[59]

---

[53] Third European Union–Brazil Summit, Stockholm, 6 October 2009 – Joint Statement (14137/09 (Presse 285) 2009), paragraphs 2–12.

[54] IARC, Institute for Development Policy and Management, 'Trade Sustainability Impact Assessment of the Association Agreement under Negotiation between the European Community and MERCOSUR' (Final Report, 2009), p. 99; ECORYS Research and Consulting, 'Trade Sustainability Impact Assessment of the Association Agreement to be negotiated between the EU and Central America' (Draft Final Report, 2009), pp. 90–1.

[55] ECORYS Research and Consulting, 'Trade Sustainability Impact Assessment of the FTA between the EU and ASEAN' (Final Report, 2009) Volume I, Main Findings and Recommendations, pp. 60–1.

[56] EU–Korea Framework Agreement, Article 18(1).

[57] Ibid. Article 18(2)(b),(c) and (e).

[58] EU–Central America Association Agreement, Article 68(2)(d).

[59] On the EU action on aviation, see the Court of Justice of the European Union, C-366/10 *Air Transport Association of America and Others*, Judgement of 21 December 2011 (not yet reported); J. Scott and L. Rajamani, 'EU Climate Change Unilateralism: International Aviation in the European Emissions Trading Scheme', *European J. Int'l Law*, vol. 23 (2012), pp. 469–94; K. Kulovesi, '"Make Your Own Special Song, Even if Nobody Else Sings Along": International Aviation Emissions and the EU Emissions Trading Scheme', *Climate Law*, vol. 2 (2011), p. 535. See, also, the relevant discussion in Chapter 13 of this volume.

2.4 Assessment

Some commentators have criticised the environmental provisions of EU bilateral agreements for their open-ended nature, often avoiding details as regards the procedures and time frames for implementation.[60] In fact, most of the clauses of EU bilateral agreements simply provide an indication of the general aims and possible key areas for cooperation, but concrete cooperation activities are left to be developed through regular dialogue between the Parties, on the basis of mutual interests and needs and on the variable capabilities to meet those needs. Thus, the agreements fail to establish clear benchmarks and indicators of success in implementing environmental clauses, as well as precise monitoring and evaluation procedures, which, for instance, would specify the frequency of and the actors involved in reviews of progress in order to ensure that implementation is proceeding according to the intention of the parties.[61]

Thus, the impact of these bilateral commitments on actual environmental cooperation also needs to be verified in the context of other EU external relations tools. Formal differences in the wording of environmental clauses in EU bilateral agreements do not necessarily have an impact on implementation, which, instead, rests with the provision of funding and the continued momentum provided by policy dialogue between the parties.[62] The EU, however, has generally been reluctant to undertake contractual commitments on its financial and technical assistance to third countries. The following sections will, thus, turn to other tools of the EU's external relations, which are of relevance in the environmental cooperation with Korea, namely, institutionalised dialogue and EU financial and technical assistance.

3 TOOLS FOR IMPLEMENTATION

3.1 Dialogue

Dialogues[63] are presented by the EU as a tool for the periodic exchange of views with third countries, although they are essentially organised at the initiative of the EU. They are primarily used to follow up on environmental cooperation commitments included in bilateral agreements; they allow for

---

[60] B. Chaytor, 'Environmental Issues in Economic Partnership Agreements: Implications for Developing Countries', *ICTSD Issue Paper* (2009), pp. 34–5.

[61] Marín Durán and Morgera, *Environmental Integration in the EU's External Relations*, pp. 142–3.

[62] T. Greven, A. Leopold and E. Molinari, 'An Analysis of the Relative Effectiveness of Social and Environmental Norms in Free Trade Agreements', European Parliament Study (2009), pp. 25–6.

[63] This section draws upon Marín Durán and Morgera, *Environmental Integration in the EU's External Relations*, Chapter 5.

a further prioritisation of the specific areas for environmental cooperation identified in these agreements, but not in-depth or systematic monitoring of past and ongoing cooperation activities. When dialogues effectively contribute to further defining the priorities for environmental cooperation on the basis of a bilateral exchange of views, they lead to the elaboration of action plans. Only in a few instances, however, have these action plans provided for specific objectives and timelines for environmental cooperation or for more detailed monitoring and follow-up institutional arrangements.[64] Monitoring is also limited by the scant level of involvement of civil society in the dialogues.[65] EU funding, in addition, is not necessarily linked to the implementation of such action plans, rather, these are generally expected to be funded through a variety of sources, which may include EU aid, but also include other sources.

There are several avenues for dialogue between the EU and Korea. First of all, dialogue can occur within the institutional framework set up by their bilateral agreements. The EU–Korea Framework Agreement contains provisions on a joint institutional framework that is relevant for the implementation of its environment-related clauses.[66] It establishes a general Joint Committee that is entrusted with facilitating the implementation and furthering the general aims of the agreement, as well as ensuring coherence with other specific agreements concluded by the parties, such as the Free Trade Agreement.[67] The Joint Committee is mandated to ensure the proper operation of the Framework Agreement. Of particular relevance to the current discussion, the Joint Committee is mandated to set priorities, in relation to the implementation of the Agreement, and to make suggestions on future actions.[68] Therefore, the Joint Committee presents an opportunity for the partners to pursue a dialogue on environmental cooperation, in order to give more specific content to the environmental provisions in the Framework Agreement.[69]

In addition, dialogue can also occur in parallel, through *ad hoc*, self-standing institutional structures. This is the case for dialogues that may be institutionalised between the EU and groups of countries that do not have a

---

[64] This is, for instance, the case of EU–China cooperation, in relation to carbon capture and storage: 13th EU–China Summit Joint Press Communiqué, Brussels, 6 October 2010, paragraphs 1 and 7.

[65] P. Leino, 'The Journey Towards all that is Good and Beautiful: Human Rights and "Common Values" as Guiding Principles of EU Foreign Relations Law', in M. Cremona and B. De Witte (eds), *EU Foreign Relations Law* (Oxford: Hart Publishing, 2008), p. 283.

[66] EU–Korea Framework Agreement, Article 43(4).

[67] For a discussion of achieving coherence in EU–Korea relations, see Chapter 10 of this volume.

[68] EU–Korea Framework Agreement, Article 44.

[69] Marín Durán and Morgera, *Environmental Integration in the EU's External Relations*, pp. 127–9.

common agreement with the EU, like the Asia–Europe Meetings (ASEM), in which Korea also participates. ASEM have been held at the summit level every second year since 1996, as an informal and multi-dimensional dialogue and cooperation process. It encompasses political, economic and cultural cooperation with 18 Asian countries,[70] the ASEAN Secretariat[71] and, since 2010, the Russian Federation, New Zealand and Australia.[72] The ASEM outcomes tend to highlight environmental areas of common interest, for instance, calling for concrete and result-oriented dialogue on sustainable forest and water resource management.[73] ASEM produced a High-level Statement on Climate Change, encouraging the continuation of dialogue on the implementation of the international climate change regime[74] and the Beijing Declaration on Sustainable Development.[75] Priorities for dialogue and cooperation are updated by heads of state and government at their Summit meetings, forming the basis of two-year work programmes, which are drawn up by foreign ministers on the occasion of each Summit and are then reviewed and updated at the foreign ministers' meetings, which take place between Summits.[76] Also, the economic ministers' meetings include an environmental component, focusing on dialogue and cooperation in priority industrial sectors, including agro-technology, food processing, bio-technology, information and telecommunication (including e-commerce), transport, energy and environmental engineering.[77]

On the sidelines of ASEM meetings, the EU and Korea have also convened bilateral summits since 2002. These summits have mostly provided opportunities to set priorities for environmental cooperation, notably, on climate change, green growth,[78] energy technologies and energy efficiency, particularly within multilateral frameworks, such as the International

---

[70] Brunei, Burma/Myanmar, Cambodia, China, Indonesia, Japan, Laos, Korea, Malaysia, the Philippines, Singapore, Thailand, Bulgaria, Romania, India, Mongolia, Pakistan and Vietnam.

[71] See European External Action Service, 'ASEM', www.eeas.europa.eu/asem/index_en.htm (accessed 9 April 2012).

[72] Eighth Asia–Europe Meeting, 'Chair's Statement', Brussels, 4–5 October 2010, paragraph 3. See the comments by N. Alecu de Flers and E. Regelsberger, 'The EU and Inter-regional Cooperation', in C. Hill and M. Smith (eds), *International Relations and the European Union* (Oxford: Oxford University Press, 2005), p. 332.

[73] Eighth Asia–Europe Meeting, 'Chair's Statement', Brussels, 4–5 October 2010, paragraph 37.

[74] Sixth Asia–Europe Meeting, 'Declaration on Climate Change', Helsinki, 10–11 September 2006.

[75] Seventh Asia–Europe Meeting, 'Declaration on Sustainable Development', Beijing, 24–5 October 2008.

[76] Ibid. paragraph 20.

[77] Ibid. paragraph 16.

[78] EU–Korea Fifth Summit, Joint Press Statement, Brussels, 6 October 2010. Climate change was also included in the EU–Korea Second Summit, Joint Press Statement, Hanoi, 9 October 2004. No mention of environment, sustainable development or climate change was made in the First Summit Joint Press Statement, Copenhagen, 24 September 2002.

Energy Agency and the International Partnership for Energy Efficiency Cooperation.[79] This appears in line with the Europe 2020 strategy for smart, sustainable and inclusive growth, whereby the EU commits to increase its outreach on the bilateral level, with a view to building mutual understandings with third countries, in the search of a global solution to climate change, through regulatory dialogues with partner countries, in order to promote equivalence, mutual recognition and convergence in regulatory approaches and tools related to green growth and climate change and the use of high-level strategic dialogues on energy and climate, access to raw materials and global poverty.[80] Along similar lines, in the 2020 Trade Strategy, the European Commission proposed that the EU external trade policy continue to support and promote green growth around the globe, based on dialogue with other countries, in order to ensure coherence with the development objectives of poverty eradication and good governance.[81] The EU's notion of green growth, however, remains elusive: there are clear indications that it refers to low-carbon development,[82] but the weight of other dimensions varies.[83]

Finally, dialogue has been used by the EU for facilitating a process of coordination with third countries of negotiating positions related to ongoing multilateral environmental negotiations. While the EU has been able to obtain firm political commitment from some partner countries, such as Japan, South Africa and Mexico, to preparing joint negotiating positions

---

[79] EU–Korea Fourth Summit, Joint Statement, Seoul, 23 May 2009.

[80] European Commission, *Communication on Europe 2020 – A Strategy for Smart, Sustainable and Inclusive Growth (Europe 2020)*, Document COM(2010)2020 final, Brussels, 3 March 2010 pp. 21–2; endorsed by the Council, 'Conclusions', Brussels, 17 June 2010.

[81] European Commission, *Communication on Trade, Growth and World Affairs – Trade Policy as a Core Component of the EU's 2020 Strategy (Trade, Growth and World Affairs Communication)*, Document COM (2010) 612 final, Brussels, 9 November 2010, pp. 8, 11 and 14.

[82] This emerges quite clearly from *Europe 2020*. See the discussion in E. Morgera, 'Relevance beyond Borders: Recent Developments in the EU', *Environmental Policy and Law*, vol. 40, no. 5 (2010) pp. 234–46.

[83] For instance, the Commission suggests that the concept of the green economy 'applies in particular to developing countries' and should be implemented through the economic valuation of natural resources, sustainable consumption and production, market-based mechanisms and greater private sector involvement: European Commission, *Communication on Rio+20: Towards the Green Economy and Better Governance (Communication Rio+20)*, Document COM (2011)363 final, Brussels, 20 June 2011, p. 5. In other policy documents, however, the Commission gave different indications. In the 2020 Trade Strategy, the Commission linked green growth with energy, resource efficiency and biodiversity protection (*Trade, Growth and World Affairs Communication*, pp. 8, 11 and 14), whereas in its thematic strategies for external environmental funding, the Commission indicated that the 'green economy' is largely limited to sustainable chemicals management (European Commission, *Environment and Natural Resources Thematic Programme – 2011–2013 Strategy Paper and Multiannual Indicative Programme (ENRTP Strategy 2011–2013)*, 29 October 2010, p. 25.

through these dialogues,[84] this is, so far, not the case for Korea. It remains to be seen whether this will change, following the conclusion of the Framework Agreement.

3.2 Funding

The legal framework for EU external assistance[85] is composed of a series of internal EU legal instruments, whereby environment-related financial and technical support to third countries is provided on a thematic or geographic basis and is mostly sourced from the EU budget.

In principle, Korea is not eligible under the thematic environment instruments, which are open to developing countries, as defined by the EU.[86] Instead, Korea is covered by the EU's Instrument for Cooperation with Industrialised/High-Income Countries,[87] which supports cooperation between the EU and a group of countries that are characterised by an advanced level of development, rather than geographical proximity. A total of 17 industrialised and other high-income countries are covered by this instrument,[88] including countries that are considered 'strategic partners' by the EU (such as Canada and the United States), other long-standing, developed country partners of the EU (such as Japan, Australia and New Zealand), as well as high-income countries from Asia (Korea) and from the Gulf Cooperation Council. The Instrument seeks to strengthen links with countries that 'share similar political, economic and institutional structures and values' to the Union,[89] particularly by promoting dialogue with them on bilateral and regional bases, as well as within multilateral fora, while fostering the Union's specific interests.[90]

The Instrument for Cooperation with Industrialised/High-Income Countries disposes of an indicative financial envelope of €172 million for the period 2007–2013.[91] Spending is not formally programmed on the basis of dialogue with partner countries, but, rather, through (multi-annual and

---

[84]   Marín Durán and Morgera, *Environmental Integration in the EU's External Relations*, p. 266.

[85]   This section draws upon Marín Durán and Morgera, *Environmental Integration in the EU's External Relations*, Chapter 4. See, also, G. Marín Durán, 'Environmental Integration in EU Development Cooperation: Responding to International Commitments or its Own Policy Priorities?', in E. Morgera (ed.), *The External Environmental Policy of the European Union: EU and International Law Perspectives* (Cambridge: Cambridge University Press, 2012), pp. 204-34.

[86]   See Annex I of the Regulation (EC) 1905/2006 of the European Parliament and of the Council establishing a financing instrument for development cooperation [2006] OJ L348/41.

[87]   Council Regulation (EC) 1934/2006 establishing a financial instrument for cooperation with industrialized and other high-income countries and territories [2006] OJ L405/41.

[88]   Ibid. Annex.

[89]   Ibid. Article 2(1).

[90]   Ibid. Article 16.

[91]   Ibid. Article 16.

annual) action plans developed by the European Commission, thus primarily reflecting the Union's 'strategic priority and interests'.[92] As to the areas for cooperation, emphasis is placed on, *inter alia*, the promotion of cooperative projects in research, science and technology, energy, transport and environmental matters, with specific reference to climate change, as well as the promotion of dialogue between political, economic and social actors and non-governmental organisations.[93] Thus, these resources can serve to support institutionalised dialogue and environmental cooperation activities, including in a multi-stakeholder framework, in a broad array of areas under the Framework Agreement with Korea.

4 CONCLUSIONS

Environmental clauses are found in all the EU bilateral agreements, because of the treaty-based requirement of environmental integration that is binding upon the EU. In the specific case of the EU–Korea Framework Agreement, provisions on environmental cooperation are framed more generally, particularly when compared and contrasted with those in the Association Agreement between the EU and Central America. This divergence can be most likely explained by Korea's more significant bargaining power and limited dependency on EU assistance. These provisions, however, are also the product of the EU's own environmental priorities and broader interests towards a given country or region; the regional strategy paper for EU–Asia cooperation, in fact, emphasises sustainable production and consumption[94] and green growth.[95]

In making the most of environmental cooperation opportunities with the EU, Korea should keep in mind the peculiarities of the EU as a bilateral partner, notably, its tendency to establish and institutionalise stable external governance systems in a multiplicity of areas, through non-hierarchical, iterative, 'transnational, participatory regulatory frameworks', in order to pursue proactive or preventative longer-term strategies that entail the creation of further 'policy-making, norm-generating, coordinating and monitoring institutions', in the context of which, the pursuance of self-interest can be more easily exposed.[96] Against this background, given the open-ended nature of the environmental cooperation provisions in the EU–Korea Framework

---

[92] Ibid. Articles 5–6, particularly 5(2).

[93] Ibid. Article 4.

[94] Regional Strategy Paper for EU–Asia Cooperation 2007–2013, p. 13: 'assist[ing] Asian manufacturers in responding to higher environmental quality standards to produce environmental friendly products and services both in the production process and in the use of goods'.

[95] Regional Strategy Paper for EU–Asia Cooperation 2007–2013, p. 13.

[96] G. De Burca, 'EU External Relations: The Governance Mode of Foreign Policy', in B. Van Vooren, S. Blockmans and J. Wouters (eds), *The EU's Role in Global Governance: The Legal Dimension* (Oxford: Oxford University Press, forthcoming 2013), Chapter 3.

Agreement, dialogue between the parties will be the essential tool to enable and operationalise their environment-related commitments and prioritise action for mutually beneficial environmental action and, possibly, to elicit EU funding to that end.

Another salient feature of the EU as a bilateral partner is its constitutional requirement for coherence in its external policy, which translates into a legal obligation for the Union to 'actively pursue' a multiplicity of objectives, including environmental protection at different levels, human rights and trade liberalisation – all under the overall ambit of contributing to multilateralism.[97] Thus, in its environmental cooperation activities, the EU is mandated to help develop international measures to preserve and improve the quality of the environment and the sustainable management of global natural resources[98] and to promote an international system based on stronger multilateral environmental cooperation and stable global environmental governance.[99] In addition, the EU's external environmental action is expected to contribute to the other objectives of the Union's external relations, such as supporting human rights, preventing conflicts and encouraging the integration of all countries into the world economy.[100] To achieve these objectives, the Union has put in place three modalities to support the development and implementation of international environmental law.

First, the EU seeks to use external action in order to politically, technically and financially support the implementation of existing multilateral environmental agreements beyond its borders, particularly in developing countries. While this modality may not necessarily target Korea, as a highly developed country, it may provide the ground for joint activities between the EU and Korea, thus supporting implementation in developing countries (so-called 'triangular cooperation').[101]

[97] Consolidated Version of the Treaty on the European Union (TEU) [2010] OJ C83/13, 30 March 2010, Article 21; see, further, J. Larik, 'Entrenching Global Governance: The EU's Constitutional Objectives Caught Between a Sanguine Worldview and a Daunting Reality', in B. Van Vooren, S. Blockmans and J. Wouters (eds), *The EU's Role in Global Governance: The Legal Dimension* (Oxford: Oxford University Press, forthcoming 2013), Chapter 1.

[98] TEU, Article 21(2)(d) and (f).

[99] Ibid. Article 21(2)(h), read in conjunction with the above-mentioned provisions, and TFEU, Article 11 on environmental integration: 'Environmental protection requirements must be integrated into the definition and implementation of the Union policies and activities, in particular with a view to promoting sustainable development'.

[100] For discussion on this, see M. Cremona, 'Coherence and EU External Environmental Policy', in E. Morgera (ed.), *The External Environmental Policy of the European Union: EU and International Law Perspectives* (Cambridge: Cambridge University Press, 2012), pp. 33-54; and for a specific discussion on human rights obligations, concerning the EU's external environmental action, see D. Augenstein, 'The Human Rights Dimension of Environmental Protection in EU External Relations Post-Lisbon', in E. Morgera (ed.), *The External Environmental Policy of the European Union: EU and International Law Perspectives* (Cambridge: Cambridge University Press, 2012), pp. 263-86.

[101] The EU has, for instance, discussed with Mexico opportunities for triangular environmental

Second, the EU is using its external action tools to build alliances with third countries, regions or groups of countries, with a view to influencing ongoing international environmental negotiations.

Third, the EU is using these tools to make progress on environmental issues on which the international community has been unable to launch negotiations towards an international legally binding agreement; in the absence of multilateral environmental negotiations, the EU wishes to pursue certain environmental goals with other willing countries, with a view to building international consensus from the bottom up.[102] This strategy has the potential to promptly respond to the changing multilateral landscape, so that EU external environmental action switches from one of the above-outlined modalities of interaction with environmental multilateralism to the other, depending on the progress or lack thereof at the multilateral level. Against this background, dialogue can be used to jointly assess the outcomes of multilateral environmental negotiating sessions or major global environmental summits and to better understand reciprocal negotiating priorities and proposed action for implementation. However, the special nature of the EU as an international actor would render it difficult, if not impossible, for these dialogues to influence the negotiating position of the EU in the short term. The EU position that is presented to third countries through dialogue is 'already relatively final', due to the fact that it is the result of lengthy intra-EU negotiations between its twenty-seven Member States, so that it cannot really be affected by the outcome of dialogues.[103] Indeed, as Marise Cremona underlines, for the EU, it is:

> easier to exercise its external regulatory competence when it has already worked out a position at the internal level, and once that position has been worked out, the EU will have an incentive not to engage in international commitments which represent a significant departure from the policy balance achieved internally.[104]

Along these lines, the EU is also increasingly creating complex interactions between its internal environmental regulation and its unilateral and bilateral external action, in a combined attempt to influence ongoing multilateral environmental negotiations. In that regard, once again, dialogues, particularly, but not exclusively, regulatory ones, can be particularly useful, in order to better understand certain internal environmental regulatory acts

---

cooperation towards African countries: see EU–Mexico Fifth Summit, 'Mexico–EU Strategic Partnership Joint Executive Plan', Comillas, 16 May 2010, p. 2.

[102] Marín Durán and Morgera, *Environmental Integration in the EU's External Relations*, Chapter 7.

[103] Leino, 'The Journey towards all that is Good and Beautiful: Human Rights and "Common Values" as Guiding Principles of EU Foreign Relations Law', p. 279.

[104] M. Cremona, 'Expanding the Internal Market: An External Regulatory Policy for the EU?', in B. Van Vooren, S. Blockmans and J. Wouters (eds), *The EU's Role in Global Governance: The Legal Dimension* (Oxford: Oxford University Press, forthcoming 2013), Chapter 10.

of the EU and their extraterritorial implications.[105] Without necessarily leading to a process of mutual recognition or cooperation in the elaboration of national standards, these exchanges can be useful as mutual learning opportunities, in particular, with a view to identifying best practices in eco-innovation and green growth. In this connection, Korea can make the most of the EU's 'willingness to . . . share sovereignty with a view to achieving collective goals'.[106] Benefiting from these periodic opportunities for dialogue, particularly when they involve a variety of stakeholders, expert and independent international entities, such as multilateral environmental agreement bodies and UN specialised agencies, the EU and Korea can together explore innovative opportunities to act, as co-generators of environmental norms.[107]

---

[105] As opposed to measures with an extraterritorial 'effect'; see distinction that is drawn by A. G. Kokott, with regards to EU internal measure, that does not embody a concrete rule of conduct for subjects beyond the territory of the EU, but still creates an indirect incentive for them: Opinion, C-366/10 Air Transport Association of America and Others (6 October 2011), paragraphs 145–7.

[106] De Burca, 'EU External Relations: The Governance Mode of Foreign Policy'.

[107] See Morgera, 'Ambition, Complexity and Legitimacy of Pursuing Mutual Supportiveness through the EU's External Environmental Action'.

13

The Legal Framework for EU–Korea Climate Change Cooperation: Opportunities and Challenges under the Framework Agreement and Free Trade Agreement

David Rossati

1 INTRODUCTION

Climate change is a threat of global dimensions requiring concerted action at the international level. The first global initiative to address the matter by the international community dates from 1992, when delegates at the UN Conference on Environment and Development signed the United Nations Framework Convention on Climate Change (UNFCCC).[1] Following its entry into force in 1994, state parties initiated a negotiating path, in order to implement the principles and the ultimate goal of the Convention.[2] In 1997, this culminated in the adoption of the Kyoto Protocol, which imposes quantified greenhouse gasses (GHGs) limitations and reductions on developed countries for a five year commitment period.[3] The reach of the Protocol was limited by the refusal to ratify by the United States – one of the major global emitters. However, the Kyoto Protocol eventually entered into force in 2005, following the ratification of Russia, partly thanks to strong EU advocacy. After almost twenty years, the multilateral legal framework to fight global warming has developed into a highly complex regulatory regime, and states are also on a negotiating path to reach a new and even more ambitious global agreement on climate change. However, state parties have still not converged on an agreed pathway towards individual emission reductions. Nevertheless, the negotiations, which took place within the Conferences of the Parties (COP and CMP) of the UNFCCC and the Kyoto Protocol,[4] are proving successful in creating a solid basis for a pos-

---

[1] United Nations Framework Convention on Climate Change (UNFCCC) (9 May 1992) 1771 UNTS 107.

[2] See the *Bali Action Plan*, December 1/CP.13, paragraph 1, UN Doc. FCCC/CP/2007/6/Add.1. All COP decisions are available at www.unfccc.int (accessed 11 April 2012).

[3] Kyoto Protocol to the United Nations Framework Convention on Climate Change (Kyoto Protocol) (11 December 1997) 2303 UNTS 148, Article 3.

[4] The Conference of Parties and the Conference of the Parties serving as the Meeting of the Parties are the respective supreme bodies of the UNFCCC and the Kyoto Protocol. See UNFCCC, Article 7; and Kyoto Protocol, Article 13.

sible future agreement.[5] Among those steps, the agreement to continue the Kyoto Protocol, until at least 2017, gives a clear sign of the will of many developed countries to continue on an internationally binding mitigation path.[6]

As for many other countries, climate change is a crucial component of both the EU and Korea's sustainable development policies, since mitigating greenhouse gasses emissions and adapting to the adverse effects of global warming inevitably impact on other important national and bilateral interests: economic growth, employment and health, to name but a few. Against this background, the climate change related provisions, contained in the recent – but not yet in force – 2010 Framework Agreement[7] between the EU and Korea, represent a pathway of implementation, which can be deemed complementary to the multilateral regime established under the UNFCCC.

The aim of this chapter is to explore how international and national laws aimed at curbing greenhouse gasses (GHGs) emissions interact with the recent bilateral obligations stemming from the Framework Agreement and the EU–Korea Free Trade Agreement liberalising trade and investment.[8] The chapter will start by noting the dynamic nature of climate change law and policy, both at the international and domestic level, sketching out recent developments in the global climate change regime and in domestic climate change policies of the EU and Korea. The chapter will then consider the possible actions that can be taken at the bilateral level and tensions that may arise between the commitments of the parties to cooperate on climate change and other policy goals within their bilateral relations. Three specific issues will be canvassed:

1. The linking of the EU and the future Korean emissions trading schemes.
2. The creation of a crediting mechanism for so-called National Appropriate Mitigation Actions (NAMAs) in Korea.
3. The consequences for the use of 'carbon equalisation' measures enshrined in the EU Emissions Trading Scheme (ETS) Directive.[9]

The general finding is that the different impacts of EU and Korean mitigation policies on their respective energy intensive sectors could lead to the

---

[5] L. Rajamani, 'The Cancun Climate Agreements: Reading the Text, Subtext and Tea Leaves', *International and Comparative Law Quarterly*, vol. 60 (2011), pp. 499–519.

[6] See Decision 1/CMP.7, UN Doc. FCCC/KP/CMP/2011/10/Add.1, 12 March 2012, paragraph 1.

[7] Framework Agreement between the European Union and its Member States on the one part, and the Republic of Korea, on the other part (EU–Korea Framework Agreement), www.eeas.europa.eu/korea_south/index_en.htm (accessed 20 April 2012).

[8] Free Trade Agreement between the European Union and its Member States of the one part, and the Republic of Korea of the other part (EU–Korea FTA) [2011] OJ L127/6, 14 May 2011.

[9] Directive 2003/87/EC of the European Parliament and of the Council (EU ETS Directive) [2003] OJ L275/32, 13 October 2003, as amended to date.

adoption – most likely by the EU – of trade restrictive measures on product imports, with possible legal consequences under the FTA. At the same time, the Framework Agreement and the FTA provide the institutional framework in which such tensions can be resolved.

2 THE EU AND KOREA IN THE UNFCCC REGIME

2.1 *The status of the EU and Korea under the UNFCCC and the Kyoto Protocol*

An important feature of Article 24 of the Framework Agreement is that it applies 'without prejudice to discussions on climate change in other fora', including the UNFCCC. In this way, the treaty parties seem to acknowledge the primacy of other multilateral processes, with a special regard to the UNFCCC regime.[10] The latter is, in fact, not only the main international forum of climate negotiations, but also the central source of international law that addresses global warming. The regime is not limited to the UNFCCC and its Kyoto Protocol, but extends to a complex system of regulations developed by the COP over almost twenty years of activity. This is the main reason why lawyers often refer to the UNFCCC as a regime, rather than as a mere treaty, still bearing in mind that such a regime is largely part of the whole body of international law.[11]

Although both the EU and Korea are parties to the UNFCCC and the Kyoto Protocol, the legal status of the EU and Korea within the regime is differentiated. A key component of the UNFCCC and its Protocol is the divide between developed and developing countries, usually referred to as 'Annex I' and 'non-Annex I' countries.[12] Common obligations on all parties that stem from the treaties address, *inter alia*, the setting up of national inventories of anthropogenic emissions, cooperation for the diffusion of technologies and good practices, the communication of data on emissions to the COP and the formulation of national mitigation programmes.[13] Concurrently, both the UNFCCC and the Protocol apply a special and more onerous set of obligations on Annex I countries, consisting mainly in the implementation of mitigation policies and financial support to non-Annex I countries

---

[10] Other multilateral institutions where climate change negotiations take place are the G8 and G20. Even the UN Security Council has intervened, expressing its concern for the threats that climate change poses on peace and security; see the Security Council President's Statement, UN Doc. S/PRST/2011/15, 20 July 2011.

[11] See B. Simma and D. Pulkowski, 'Of Planets and the Universe: Self-Contained Regimes in International Law', *European Journal of International Law*, vol. 17 (2006), pp. 483–529.

[12] Annex I to the UNFCCC contains the list of developed country parties. It should not be confused with Annex B countries of the Kyoto Protocol, which, instead, are countries that agreed to binding emissions limitations and reductions.

[13] Respectively, UNFCCC, Article 4(1)(a)(c) and (j); and Kyoto Protocol, Article 10(b).

for their respective mitigation and adaptation activities.[14] While the EU Member States have the status of Annex I countries,[15] Korea belongs to the developing countries category, despite being an OECD member, possessing a fast-growing economy and being the world's ninth largest carbon emitter.[16] This has several consequences for EU–Korea bilateral relations in the field of climate change.

First, although being a party to the Kyoto Protocol, Korea has not been bound by any reduction goals during the first commitment period and is not expected to assume any under the second period, which starts in January 2013.[17] This is in sharp contrast to the EU. As a result, Korea has seen a sheer increment of its emissions.[18]

Second, Korea is eligible to be a host country of Clean Development Mechanism (CDM) projects on its territory, which makes it a recipient of climate technology investment from the EU.[19] The CDM is a flexibility mechanism of the Kyoto Protocol, which rewards Annex I countries' public and private entities, realising emissions reduction projects in non-Annex I countries with Certified Emissions Reductions (CERs). For each metric tonne of CO_2 equivalent reduction, a CER is issued in a project entity's virtual account. CERs can then be either sold on the carbon market or used for compliance in eligible emissions trading schemes (ETS), including the European one.

2.2 From Bali to Durban: the international negotiations for a post-2012 global agreement

Aware of the insufficiency of the Kyoto Protocol to effectively tackle the global rise of emissions, in 2007, the UNFCCC parties established a negotiating path, the Bali Action Plan, with the aim of reaching an 'agreed outcome' on pivotal issues for the climate regime.[20] Despite their different status in the

---

[14] See, respectively, UNFCCC Articles. 4(2)–(7) and 11; Kyoto Protocol Articles 2(3), 3(1) and 11.

[15] The EU is also a party to the UNFCCC and the Kyoto Protocol.

[16] See the IEA table on *Emissions from Fuel Combustion, 2011*, www.oecd-ilibrary.org/environ ment/co2-emissions-from-fuel-combustion-2011_co2-table-2011-1-en (accessed 21 February 2012).

[17] Decision 1/CMP.17, UN Doc. FCCC/KP/CMP/2011/10/Add.1, 15 March 2012, paragraph 1.

[18] Korea has almost doubled its aggregate greenhouse gasses emissions between the periods of 1990 to 2001. Furthermore, IEA projections place Korea at the top of emissions increase between OECD countries. See GHGs data at the official UNFCCC website, www.unfccc .int/ghg_data/items/3800.php (accessed 21 February 2012); and UNEP, 'Overview of the Republic of Korea's National Strategy for Green Growth', April 2010, p. 21, www.greengro wth.go.kr (accessed 21 February 2012).

[19] Kyoto Protocol, Article 12.

[20] They generally refer to: 1) individuation of an agreed long-term goal to achieve the scope of the Convention; 2) the scaling-up of mitigation efforts from all parties; 3) enhanced action in

UNFCCC regime, the EU and Korea actually share a similar perspective on the future of the climate change regime.

In UNFCCC's negotiations, the EU participates as a standalone negotiating entity. EU advocacy in reaching a global set of binding reduction goals by all countries, with the exclusion of the least developed countries (LDCs), has always been constant and in line with its internal climate change legislation.[21] On the other hand, Korea acts within the so-called Environmental Integrity Group (EIG), together with Switzerland and Mexico. Whereas the EIG includes two parties (Korea and Mexico) which do not have any binding reduction commitments under the Kyoto Protocol, this has not hampered the EIG from cooperating with the EU and calling for a binding pathway of global emissions reductions.

During four years of negotiations since the adoption of the Bali Action Plan, states have still not managed to reach a consensus on binding country levels of GHGs reductions. This, however, has not hindered some progress from being made. Among the various steps already taken,[22] parties have agreed to collectively mitigate emissions, in order to avoid a rise of average global temperature above 2°C from pre-industrial levels.[23] Furthermore, after the adoption of the 2009 Copenhagen Accord,[24] non-Annex I countries, including major emitters like China and India and, also, Korea, made individual pledges on their future mitigation efforts. In the UNFCCC, the pledges are followed and specified by National Appropriate Mitigation Actions (NAMAs), which generally consist of national policies or programmes aimed at reducing emissions in specific sectors within a country. With a recent decision at the 2011 Durban COP, UNFCCC parties set up an electronic NAMA registry, where non-Annex I countries can voluntarily submit their NAMAs and specify if, and to what extent, they would need international finance for their implementation.[25] NAMAs are relevant in the bilateral climate and trade context for being a potential driver of foreign direct investment in Korea and because of their potential to be linked with emissions trading schemes; this would happen through the generation of credits for emissions reductions in a similar fashion to the CDM.

As for the CDM, the Kyoto Protocol will commence a second commit-

---

adaptation; and 4) enhanced technology transfer. See Decision 1/CP.13, paragraph 1.

[21] By 2020, the EU is currently committed to reduce 20 per cent of its aggregate greenhouse gasses emissions from a 1990 baseline. See the European Council, 'Presidency Conclusions', 8/9 March 2007, CONCL 1, paragraph 32.

[22] See Rajamani, 'The Cancun Climate Agreements: Reading the Text, Subtext and Tea Leaves'.

[23] Decision 1/CP16, UN Doc. FCCC/CP/2010/7/Add.1, 15 March 2011, paragraph 4.

[24] The Copenhagen Accord is a non-binding document, of which the COP only 'took note' in its related decision. See Decision 2/CP15, UN Doc. FCCC/CP/2009/11/Add.1, 30 March 2010.

[25] Decision 2/CP.17, UN Doc. FCCC/CP/2011/9/Add.1, 15 March 2012, paragraphs 44–55.

ment period from January 2013, thus extending its obligations and flexibility mechanisms, at least up until 2017.[26]

Although uncertainty pervades the current status of climate negotiations, progressive achievements seem to have been reached in the COP. Independent studies have already found that the sum of state pledges in reducing emissions still falls short of what is actually required to stay within the 2°C goal.[27] Therefore, future negotiations will most likely seek to increase the level of commitment by states. As seen above, both the EU and Korea are playing a key role in these efforts, as both countries are leaving an open door to increased efforts in mitigation.[28] Furthermore, as will be explored below, Korea has been the first promoter of 'NAMA crediting', as a means of linking non-Annex I countries pledges with an expanded market mechanism that will generate emissions credits for developed countries and their regulated industries.

3 NATIONAL ACTIONS ON CLIMATE CHANGE

3.1 Introduction

Before delving into the ways in which the two partners can cooperate in relation to climate change, it is worth sketching out the current internal climate policies being pursued by the EU and Korea, with a focus on the significant features for bilateral relations.

3.2 EU climate change policy

The EU has always been at the forefront in the development of climate mitigation policies. The first significant effort has been the establishment of the EU ETS in 2003.[29] By transplanting its basic structure from the Kyoto Protocol regulations,[30] the trading scheme is aimed at setting an emissions cap on energy intensive sectors. Under this scheme, each Member State was delegated the task of assigning emission allowances for eligible operators on its territory.[31] Operators would be able to sell or purchase allowances

---

[26] Decision 1/CMP.7, paragraph 1.

[27] See UNEP, 'The Emissions Gap Report', November 2010, pp. 41–2, www.unep.org/publica tions/ebooks/emissionsgapreport/ (accessed 1 April 2012).

[28] The EU Council has committed to consider increasing the emissions reductions to 30 per cent from 1990 levels in the event of adoption of a new international agreement on climate. See European Council, 'Presidency Conclusions', paragraph 32.

[29] Emission Trading Directive 87/2003/EC.

[30] See UNFCCC Decision 18/CP.7, UN Doc. FCCC/CP/2001/13/Add.2, 21 January 2001.

[31] The assignment took place through National Allocation Plans: see Directive 87/2003/EC, Article 9. Each EU emissions allowance consists of a permit to emit 1mt of CO_2 eq: see Article 3(a) of Directive 87/2003/EC.

depending on their annual emissions targets, with the only obligation being to surrender a number of allowances equal to the quantity of GHGs emitted during the year. By providing the flexibility of choosing to reduce individual emissions or purchase surplus allowances, the overall aim of the EU ETS is, thus, to reduce the aggregate abatement costs and emissions.[32]

After its experience with the first allocations in the period 2005–8, and with the vision of increasing efforts in climate mitigation, in 2009, the EU adopted a comprehensive Climate and Energy Package,[33] endorsing the so-called '20-20-20' target[34] and comprising several directives that address, *inter alia*, a scaled-up EU ETS,[35] increased renewable energy production, the deployment of carbon capture and storage technologies and the reduction of emissions from sectors not covered by the EU ETS.[36]

From 2013, the amended EU ETS is to cover roughly 40 per cent of total emissions. The majority of allowances will be auctioned, rather than freely allocated, and the system of registries will be centralised.[37] For the remaining 60 per cent of emissions, the 'Effort Sharing Decision' imposes a reduction of 10 per cent from 1990 levels for the period up till 2020,[38] thus contributing to the '20-20-20' target.

From this brief analysis, it is clear that the EU has developed strong leadership in climate change,[39] not only because it occupied a leading role in bringing the Kyoto Protocol into force and making it effective, but also because it is the only major emitter, which, since 2003, has set forth a binding low-carbon path up until 2020,[40] with the presence of the EU

[32] D. H. Cole, 'Clearing the Air: Four Propositions about Property Rights and Environmental Protection', *Duke Environmental Law and Policy Forum*, vol. 10 (1999–2000), p. 111.

[33] For a thorough analysis, see K. Kulovesi, E. Morgera and M. Muñoz, 'Environmental Integration and Multi-faceted International Dimensions of EU Law: Unpacking the EU's 2009 Climate and Energy Package', *Common Market Law Review*, vol. 48 (2011), pp. 829–91.

[34] It refers to (1) a reduction of greenhouse gasses emissions of 20 per cent by 2020, compared to 1990 levels; (2) a 20 per cent share of EU energy consumption from renewable sources; and (3) a 20 per cent reduction of energy use through energy efficiency.

[35] Directive 2009/28/EC of the European Parliament and of the Council on the promotion of the use of energy from renewable sources [2009] OJ L140/63, 23 April 2009, amending the Directive 2003/87/EC.

[36] The directives of the climate and energy package can be found in the EU Official Journal L 140 vol. 52, 5 June 2009.

[37] EU ETS Directive, Articles 9, 10 and 19.

[38] Decision 406/2009/EC of the European Parliament and the Council [2009] OJ L140/136, 23 April 2009.

[39] M. A. Schreurs and Y. Tiberghien, 'Multi-Level Reinforcement: Explaining European Union Leadership in Climate Change Mitigation', *Global Environmental Politics*, vol. 7 (2007), pp. 22–4.

[40] The European Commission has also communicated its intention to adopt a strategy for an 80 per cent emissions reduction from 1990 levels by 2050; see European Commission, 'A Roadmap for Moving to a Competitive Low Carbon Economy in 2050', Document COM(2011) 112 final, Brussels, 8 March 2011.

ETS as its prime mitigation policy. Thus, facing the current reluctance of other major emitters to follow suit with binding emissions reduction goals, the EU has considered – and, in some cases, undertaken – unilateral measures with extraterritorial effect, in order to encourage the efforts of other states and actors. In other words, the EU has proposed indirectly applying emissions standards to industries and polluting sectors located in non-EU countries.

Among the measures already in place is the adoption of a Directive, which, from 2012, includes the aviation sector in the EU ETS. More importantly it covers all international flights arriving or departing from any airport on the EU territory.[41] As non-EU aviation companies are covered by an emissions cap for their routes in the EU, the compatibility of the EU legislation with international law has been challenged before the Court of Justice of the European Union. The Court found that none of the applicable international law[42] had the effect of quashing the Aviation Directive.[43] Although arguing for its incompatibility with the 'common but differentiated responsibilities' principle of the UNFCCC,[44] Scott and Rajamani recognise the extraterritorial character of this measure as it applies to flights, regardless of whether their emissions take place in or outside the EU airspace and, thus, constitute one of the targeted unilateral actions that the EU is putting forward.[45]

While the aviation case is explicative of the negative effects that EU unilateralism can generate, there are other potential unilateral measures that are already enshrined in the EU ETS Directive, which could also have negative effects on third states. One clear example is the potential restriction on the usage of CDM credits in the EU ETS. From 2013, only CERs generated from projects in least developed countries (LDCs) will be eligible for compliance in the EU.[46] Considering that the EU ETS amounts to roughly 85 per cent of the global carbon market,[47] this measure is likely to exert a strong effect on the future demand of CERs and, especially, on the role of CDM in major

---

[41] Directive 2008/101/EC of the European Parliament and the Council (Aviation Directive) [2008] OJ L8/3, 18 November 2008.

[42] The Court, for instance, stated that the Chicago Convention on International Civil Aviation would not be applicable to the case, since the EU is not bound by it, being the competence on those matters still on single Member States. Court of Justice of the European Union, C-366/10 *Air Transport Association of America and Others*, Judgement of 21 December 2011 (not yet reported).

[43] Ibid. paragraph 157.

[44] UNFCCC, Article 3(1).

[45] J. Scott and L. Rajamani, 'EU Climate Change Unilateralism: Including Aviation in the European Emissions Trading Scheme', *European Journal of International Law*, vol. 23 (2012), pp. 469-94.

[46] See EU ETS Directive, Article 11a(4).

[47] See World Bank, 'State and Trends of the Carbon Market' (2011), p. 9, www.worldbank.org (accessed 23 February 2012).

economies, such as China and India, which, to-date, have benefited the most from this flexible mechanism.[48]

Korea is also likely to be affected by this measure. According to a UNEP database, there are, to-date, 67 CDM projects already registered in Korea, with another 32 in the pipeline; of these projects, several are undertaken by EU entities.[49] Consequently, a limitation of CERs acceptance from non-LDCs will also result in a fall of demand of CERs from Korean CDM projects. However, according to the EU ETS Directive, there is an option for the EU to stipulate bilateral agreements with third countries – possibly Korea – for the acceptance of emissions reduction credits.[50] Article 24 of the Framework Agreement seems to offer fertile legal ground for a bilateral solution to avoid a future ban by the EU on Korean CERs. The Article, in fact, states that bilateral cooperation should be aimed, *inter alia*, at '[. . .] enhancing public and private sector financing instruments, including market mechanisms [. . .]' and at '[. . .] supporting, where appropriate, mitigation and adaptation action of developing countries, including through the Flexible Mechanisms of the Kyoto Protocol'.[51]

Despite this latter condition on CERs acceptance in the EU ETS, the same legislation contains a residual provision, which states that, once an international agreement on climate change is reached, only credits generated by participating states will be accepted under the EU ETS.[52] In such an occurrence, Korea will have to be a party to the new agreement, if it wants its emissions credits to be accepted in the EU ETS, notwithstanding any previous bilateral agreement on the matter.

The EU Directive also introduces controversial new 'carbon equalisation' provisions, which will be analysed below in the context of the EU–Korea FTA.

3.3 Korean climate change policy

Korea's first significant action in the field of national climate policy dates from 2010, when, after signing the Copenhagen Accord, the government submitted to the UNFCCC Secretariat a voluntary pledge that detailed

---

[48] The effects of this measure by the EU can be somehow mitigated by the option of bilateral agreements with third countries for the generation of emissions credits from projects. See EU ETS Directive, Article 11a(5).

[49] See UNEP/Risoe, 'CDM Pipeline', www.uneprisoe.org/ (accessed 23 February 2012).

[50] See EU ETS Directive, Article 11a(5).

[51] See EU–Korea Framework Agreement, Article 24(1)(d) and (g).

[52] See EU ETS Directive, Article 11a(7). It is noteworthy that, according to the European Commission, the recent prolongation of the Kyoto Protocol is not tantamount to an 'international agreement', as of Article 11a(5) of the Directive. See the informal Q&A document by the Commission, www.ec.europa.eu/clima/news/docs/additional_qa_06_01_2011_en.pdf (accessed 28 March 2012).

reducing greenhouse gasses emissions by 30 per cent from a business-as-usual scenario.[53] Concurrently, the government adopted a Framework Act on Low Carbon Green Growth,[54] which works as the fundamental piece of legislation to enact climate mitigation measures. The scope of the Act is not just related to climate change, but extends to interconnected matters (such as energy, economic growth and national environment)[55] and to a variety of sectors. The National Strategy for Green Growth, adopted by a presidential directive,[56] envisages a long-term path towards a sustainable economy and society. Thanks to Article 9 of the Framework Act, the government was able to adopt a five year plan, which details the broad vision of the National Strategy. Climate change mitigation occupies a prominent role in the plan, through the gradual setting of national targets in various sectors and the promotion of energy efficiency and renewable energy.

For the purposes of this chapter, two norms emerge for their potential relationship with bilateral relations with the EU. Article 3 of the Framework Act, in providing the principles for its future implementation, states: 'consideration shall be given to avoid weakening international competitiveness of domestic industries'. Furthermore, Article 46 empowers the government to establish a national emissions trading scheme and to adopt the 'necessary measures' to protect the international competitiveness of national undertakings participating to the scheme.[57] These provisions seem to echo the EU carbon equalisation mechanism of the EU ETS Directive, although they do not prescribe what specific measures the government should adopt.[58] With such legal background, in 2011, the government has drafted a bill for the implementation of the emissions trading scheme, which is currently waiting for approval by the National Assembly.[59]

[53] The official document is available at www.unfccc.int/files/meetings/cop_15/copenhagen _accord/application/pdf/koreacphaccord_app2.pdf (accessed 11 April 2012). It is important to note how the choice of the year-base is crucial in determining the final amount of reductions.

[54] Act No. 9931, 13 January 2010, online English version available at www.law.go.kr (accessed 28 February 2012). See, also, Global Green Growth Institute, 'Green Growth in Motion: Sharing the Korea's Experience', May 2011, www.gggi.org (accessed 1 March 2012).

[55] Act No. 9931, Article 3(1).

[56] Presidential Directive 239, 5 January 2009.

[57] Act No. 9931, Article 3(3).

[58] However, Article 42(5) of the Framework Act states that the government shall undertake individual assessments for each entity and also consult with them on matters related to international competitiveness.

[59] See J. Peetermans (ed.), *Asia and Beyond: the Roadmap to Global Carbon & Energy Markets*, IETA Report (2011), p.18, www.ieta.org (accessed 1 March 2012).

4 CLOSER COOPERATION ON CLIMATE CHANGE: OPPORTUNITIES AND CHALLENGES

4.1 Overview

The basis for EU–Korea bilateral cooperation in climate change can be found in Article 24 of the Framework Agreement, which specifies the areas where the duty of cooperation shall apply, without, however, detailing its modalities. For the purpose of this chapter, the relevant fields listed in the article are:[60]

> 1. Transition to a low-carbon society through the use of National Appropriate Mitigation Approaches (NAMAs).
> 2. Exchange of expertise in relation to emissions trading schemes.
> 3. Enhancing public–private partnerships and the use of market mechanisms for climate mitigation.
> 4. Supporting mitigation and adaptation also through the use of the Kyoto Protocol's flexibility mechanisms.

Overall, the scope of Article 24 seems limited to offering a solid legal and institutional framework for cooperation. Yet, only when it is implemented will it be possible to assess its effectiveness. Moreover, as will be seen below, the development of common policies in these areas is likely to have effects in bilateral trade and investment relations between EU and Korea. Thus, the pursuit of climate mitigation and adaptation measures could potentially come into tension with the provisions of other instruments, which are part of the EU–Korea legal framework.

In this part, the analysis will be focused on two specific policies listed in Article 24 of the Framework Agreement, policies, which, if implemented, could have significant consequences in terms of the bilateral relationship. These two fields of cooperation are:

> 1. The possible linkage between the European and future Korean emissions trading schemes.
> 2. The establishment of a crediting mechanism for the support of NAMAs.[61]

In addition, the so-called 'carbon equalisation mechanism' of the EU ETS will also be analysed for the purposes of FTA compatibility, since its implementation by the EU is likely to yield negative effects on bilateral trade.

---

[60] They are joint implementation, clean development mechanism and international emissions trading, respectively established under Articles 6, 12 and 17 of the Kyoto Protocol.
[61] See EU–Korea Framework Agreement, Article 24(a),(c) and (d).

4.2 Linking emissions trading schemes

As national emissions trading schemes are being developed in several countries, including Korea,[62] states and scholars are questioning the possibility of linking emissions trading markets.[63] Hypothetically, such links can be implemented in many forms.[64] In our context, a conceptual distinction emerges between unilateral and bilateral linkage, where a unilateral linkage would consist of a formal acceptance by only one scheme of emissions allowances issued from the other, whereas a full bilateral merger would imply a reciprocal acceptance of emissions allowances from the respective national schemes. Positive claims for this option relate to increased liquidity and enhanced flexibility for industries to abate mitigation costs.[65] The linkage of trading schemes involves complex cross-cutting considerations of an economic, political and legal nature. Here, only policy and legal concerns and possible consequences for trade arising from a linkage of the EU and Korean ETS will be canvassed, under the lens of the Framework Agreement and the FTA.

Tuerk et al. argue that sheer carbon price variations are unlikely to take place for the bigger of the two markets in a unilateral linkage between trading schemes which differ significantly in market size. Clearly, this scenario would apply in the case of the EU and Korea, whereby the EU ETS would take the part of the major market. Furthermore, this kind of link would 'de facto introduce price caps for the smaller scheme at the price level of the larger scheme'.[66] In other words, if a unilateral model is introduced, inevitably, the EU ETS would impose its carbon price on the Korean market. As for the full linkage option, Tuerk et al. also recognise the need for coordination, especially for what pertains to the harmonisation of national regulations.[67]

An example of undesired outcomes from an uncoordinated linkage, which can also be relevant for trade, would be an unbalanced allocation or auctioning of allowances, since it might affect the competitiveness of certain sectors. The imposition of emission caps on single industries in a trading scheme raises the operational costs for running their activities. In the EU,

---

[62] Existing schemes are taking place in the EU, Japan, New South Wales, Norway, Alberta and New Zealand. Other states that are considering adoption, apart from Korea, are the USA, Australia, Canada and Switzerland. See A. Roßnagel, 'Evaluating Links between Emissions Trading Schemes: An Analytical Framework', *Carbon and Climate Law Review*, vol. 2 (2008), pp. 394–5.

[63] The EU, for instance, advocates for the creation of an OECD state-wide ETS by 2015. See www.ec.europa.eu/clima/policies/ets/linking/index_en.htm (accessed 1 April 2012).

[64] See A. Tuerk, M. Mehling, C. Flachsland and W. Sterk, 'Linking Carbon Markets: Concepts, Case Studies and Pathways', *Climate Policy*, vol. 9 (2009), p. 343.

[65] See M. Mehling, 'Linking Emissions Trading Schemes', in D. Freestone and C. Streck (eds), *Legal Aspects of Carbon Trading: Kyoto, Copenhagen, and Beyond* (Oxford: Oxford University Press, 2009), pp. 110–1.

[66] A. Tuerk et al., 'Linking Carbon Markets: Concepts, Case Studies and Pathways', p. 343.

[67] Ibid.

if the caps, and, thus, the allocation of allowances, are not fine-tuned with the Korean ones, it is likely that distortive effects could take place on the comparative advantage of a domestic sector. Furthermore, as seen above, current domestic legislation allows for mechanisms to prevent such competitive distortions.[68] If these mechanisms are still in place after the linking of the EU and Korean ETS, then a unilateral action by one party is able to yield distortive effects on the integrated carbon markets and spread regulatory uncertainty among actors.[69]

Article 24 of the Framework Agreement provides fertile ground for bilateral coordination on the matter, as it aims to enhance cooperation in expertise exchange on the functioning of trading schemes. Such cooperation is already taking place, albeit in a less formal manner than the one envisioned by the Framework Agreement.[70] For instance, several EU countries and the European Commission have established an International Carbon Action Partnership (ICAP), with the specific aim of creating a forum of experts to discuss and address the design and integration of emissions trading mechanisms.[71] The Korean government has been participating as an observer since the adoption of its Framework Act on Green Growth. Although difficult to estimate, there is also evidence of informal technical engagement by single EU states' administrations, with the Korean government drafting its emissions trading legislation.[72] Overall, it emerges that in the complex policy task of linking emissions trading schemes, the bilateral Framework Agreement promises to work as an instrument of cooperation, so as to avoid the many legal uncertainties, including the ones related to trade.

4.3 Scaling-up bilateral FDI: from CDM to NAMAs

The use of the CDM in Korea proved successful, with the presence of some projects implemented by European entities. UNFCCC Parties, with Korea as one of the first promoters, acknowledging the potential of extending the conceptual basis of CDM from single projects to entire sectors of developing countries' national economies, have recently set up a NAMA registry, with the prospect of bringing about a scaled-up crediting mechanism. If

---

[68] See EU ETS Directive, Articles 10a(6) and 10b; Framework Act on Low Carbon Green Growth, Articles 46(3) and 45(5).

[69] See M. J. Mace et al., 'Analysis of the Legal and Organisational Issues Arising in Linking the EU Emissions Trading Scheme to Other Existing and Emerging Emissions Trading Schemes', May 2008, Foundation for International Environmental Law and Development, Institute for European Environmental Policy, World Resources Institute, pp. 58–9.

[70] See EU–Korea Framework Agreement, Article 44.

[71] See the ICAP political declaration, www.icapcarbonaction.com (accessed 29 March 2012).

[72] See House of Commons Energy and Climate Change Committee, 'The EU Emissions Trading System', 10th Rep. of Session 2010–2012, vol. 1, paragraph 55, www.parliament.uk (accessed 11 April 2012).

implemented, NAMAs might be a substantial driver of technology transfer, climate mitigation related FDI or other types of investment from the EU to Korea.[73]

Here, synergies between investment and potential climate regulations might stem from the FTA. Section C of Chapter 7 of the FTA is dedicated to the establishment of foreign investors in the respective countries. Assuming some NAMA crediting scheme takes the form of FDI or equity, Section C of the FTA liberalises investment in a range of highly polluting manufacturing sectors (such as chemicals, coke oven products and paper production),[74] by guaranteeing most favoured nation and national treatment standards and forbidding Parties to adopt quantitative limitations on foreign investments.[75] Thus, the FTA already provides fertile ground for the future development of NAMA crediting mechanisms in Korea, and it is mutually supportive of the Framework Agreement, in this regard. However, it is uncertain how targeted sectors that are not listed in the FTA would be treated, for the purposes of foreign investment. It is possible that the commitments on establishment could be expanded to include such sectors, using the institutional framework established under the FTA.

4.4 Carbon equalisation mechanisms

The current asymmetries between the EU and Korea's emissions targets can generate concerns amidst European manufacturers, regarding risks of carbon leakage and loss of comparative advantage for certain sectors. Carbon leakage is relevant at bilateral level, as it would consist of a 'relocation' of emissions from EU installations to Korean ones, due to the lack of, or less stringent, emissions standards.[76] With reference to recent bilateral trade statistics and to the EU ETS covered activities, the most relevant sectors of the EU economy that might be subject to carbon leakage seem to be chemicals and oven metals' production.[77] Parallel to carbon leakage, European manufacturers might face losses in competitive advantage in the global market, with respect to Korean manufacturers. If European producers face an additional cost for production, due to mitigation targets, then Korean producers would gain better positioning, in terms of exports in third countries.

---

[73] Mostly under the form of equity or debt.
[74] House of Commons Energy and Climate Change Committee, 'The EU Emissions Trading System', Article 7.10 and the table in Annex 7-A-2, Section 4.
[75] The prohibition on limitations is exhaustive and listed in FTA, Article 7.11.
[76] See N. S. Ghaleigh and D. Rossati, 'The Spectre of Carbon Border-Adjustment Measures', *Climate Law*, vol. 2 (2011), pp. 74–6.
[77] See Y. Decreux, C. Milner and N. Péridy, 'The Economic Impact of the Free Trade Agreement between the European Union and Korea', Report for the European Commission (2010), Tables 1.3 and 1.4, www.ec.europa.eu/trade/creating-opportunities/bilateral-relations/countries/korea/ (accessed 1 April 2012).

The EU ETS Directive provides two options for the EU to overcome these issues:

1. A free allocation of all allowances for sectors exposed to carbon leakage, with possible adjustments to that amount.[78]
2. An inclusion of importers of exposed products within the ETS cap.[79]

Both of these mechanisms pose potential problems, if considered from the perspective of international trade law.

In the first case, the measure might constitute a subsidy, both under the EU–Korea FTA and the WTO Agreement on Subsidies and Countervailing Measures (SCM Agreement). These two treaties generally take the same approach to the regulation of subsidies, with the FTA incorporating the rules in the SCM Agreement.[80] This begs the question of whether an adjustment mechanism, such as the one of additional free allowances allocation, can be interpreted as a prohibited or an actionable subsidy under Article 3 and 5 of the SCM Agreement. Without delving into an analysis of the legal components that qualify such subsidies as prohibited or actionable under that agreement, it suffices to recall that some authors already recognise this eventuality,[81] although the uncertain legal nature of emissions allowances make any definite assessment difficult.

The second option of including importers of products subject to carbon leakage in the EU ETS schemes could also amount to a unilateral measure affecting trade in the same fashion of the Aviation Directive,[82] given its extraterritorial effect. In this case, the only difference is that the entity obliged to submit allowances would be the importer of the product, most likely an EU-based entity, while in the case of the Aviation Directive, non-EU aviation companies are directly affected. Thus, the question is whether such a measure would be compatible with the FTA provisions.

Referring to the WTO regime, the European Commission has stressed the importance of framing the measure in a non-discriminatory manner, which might be a difficult policy task.[83]

---

[78] EU ETS Directive, Articles 10a(12) and 10b(1)(a).

[79] Ibid. Article 10b(1)(b).

[80] See EU–Korea FTA, Article 3.8.

[81] M. C. Cordonier Segger and M. Gehring, 'Trade and Investment Implications of Carbon Trading for Sustainable Development', in D. Freestone and C. Streck (eds), *Legal Aspects of Carbon Trading* (Oxford: Oxford University Press, 2009), p.88; and R. Howse and A. L. Eliason, 'Domestic and International Strategies to Address Climate Change: An Overview of the WTO Legal Issues', in T. Cottier, O. Nartova and S. Z. Bigdeli (eds), *International Trade Regulation and the Mitigation of Climate Change: World Trade Forum* (Cambridge: Cambridge University Press, 2009), p. 56.

[82] See Section 3.2 above.

[83] See European Commission, *Communication: Analysis of Options to Move Beyond 20% Greenhouse Gas Emission Reductions and Assessing the Risk of Carbon Leakage*, Document COM(2010) 265 final, Brussels, 26 May 2010.

A similar issue arises under the FTA. Article 2.6 of the FTA provides that none of the Parties may increase any custom duty from baselines established in the bilateral schedule of commitments, thus prohibiting any further imposition on imported products.[84] Therefore, if interpreted as a customs duty on imports, the obligation to hold allowances for products subject to carbon leakage would be in breach of the FTA. Conversely, resembling a provision of the 1994 General Agreement on Tariffs and Trade (GATT),[85] the FTA excludes from the category of customs duties any 'charge equivalent to an internal tax [. . .] in respect of the like domestic good or in respect of an article from which the imported good has been manufactured or produced in whole or in part [. . .]'.[86] This latter provision might apply to the carbon equalisation measure in the EU ETS Directive and, thus, make the scheme compliant with the FTA, inasmuch as its scope would consist of charging imported products at the same level of domestic ones, with the assumption that the coverage under the EU ETS would amount to an 'internal tax' under Article 2.6(a) of the FTA. If so, the measure should be implemented in a manner not violating national treatment obligations.[87]

Although the FTA has only provisionally come into force, the WTO regime can provide general guidance on the relationship between trade and climate. There is conspicuous literature on the field, highlighting how national climate policies can be incompatible with certain obligations of the WTO agreements, mostly related to the national treatment and most favoured nation principles and the general prohibition on quantitative restrictions of the GATT.[88] Studies span from carbon border-tax adjustments, to renewable energy production and labelling schemes.[89] There is also a significant track record of cases within the WTO dealing with the trade and environment nexus, some of them ending up in milestone (and highly debated) judicial decisions, such as *US–Shrimp*[90], *US–Tuna*[91] and *Brazil–Tyres*,[92] to name but a few.[93] In those decisions, the GATT's general

---

[84]   The schedule is included in Annex 2-A of the FTA.
[85]   GATT, Article II(2)(a).
[86]   EU–Korea FTA, Article 2.3(a).
[87]   Ibid. Article 2.8, as recalled by Article 2.3(a).
[88]   GATT, Articles I, III and IX, respectively.
[89]   See, generally, T. Cottier, O. Nartova and S. Z. Bigdeli (eds), *International Trade Regulation and the Mitigation of Climate Change* (Cambridge: Cambridge University Press, 2009).
[90]   *United States – Import Prohibition of Shrimp and Shrimp Related Products*, Appellate Body Report, 6 November 1998, WT/DS58/AB/R.
[91]   *United States – Restrictions on Imports of Tuna*, GATT Panel Report, DS29/R.
[92]   *Brazil –Measures Affecting Imports of Retreaded Tyres (Brazil–Tyres)*, Appellate Body Report, 17 December 2007, WT/DS332/AB/R.
[93]   For an in-depth analysis of such jurisprudence, see N. Bernasconi-Osterwalder, D. Magraw, M. J. Oliva, E. Tuerk and M. Orellana, *Environment and Trade: A Guide to WTO Jurisprudence* (London: Routledge, 2005).

environmental exemptions[94] worked as the main legal means to balance environment and trade interests.

In *Brazil–Tyres*, among other issues, the Appellate Body assessed if a trade restrictive measure that did not benefit the environment in the short-term would be, nevertheless, covered by the general exception of Article XX(b). The decision is relevant to understanding how a balancing exercise will be carried out. The Appellate Body stresses that to assess the necessity of a measure, it is sufficient to gauge the potential impact that such a measure might have in the future, without being compelled to provide quantitative data on its effectiveness. In its reasoning, the Appellate Body mentioned climate change incidentally, as a case where a prolonged period of time is required, in order to assess if and how a national measure has proven its environmental effects.[95]

Overall, despite the absence of a detailed jurisprudence in the field, states and international organisations are well aware of the possible negative impacts on trade that would stem from increased national mitigation efforts. The matter is further complicated if the international community continues delaying any agreement on the prevention, regulation and choice of forum for such conflicts, as this could lead unilateral actions, like the ones recently put in place by the EU. With regard to the bilateral relations between the EU and Korea, the parties will have to carefully cooperate to avoid unwanted tensions in specific sectors that are, or will be, subject to increased mitigation efforts and integrating policies. In this context, the institutional structure created by the EU–Korea Framework Agreement and the FTA is the perfect place to effectively avoid hurdles and foster integration.

5 CONCLUSION

This chapter has tried to address the highly discussed interaction between climate and international trade law from the perspective of EU–Korea bilateral relations, giving special regard to the most recent climate mitigation policies and the EU–Korea Framework Agreement and FTA. Despite the uncertainties in UNFCCC negotiations, the two bilateral treaties might offer future opportunities for cooperation, but they might also offer potential sources of tension, depending on the climate mitigation measure to be implemented. This may require an increased effort in institutional cooperation between the EU and Korea, in a way that will prevent undesired outcomes. In this regard, the innovative institutional framework of cooperation put forward by the Framework Agreement and the FTA might be the best place to balance climate mitigation and trade interests between two distant, yet so close, economies.

[94] GATT, Article XX(b) and (g).
[95] *Brazil–Tyres*, paragraph 151; it could even be asked whether such effects can ever possibly be quantitatively measured.

14

Cooperation in the Field of Personal Data Protection: One World, One Standard?

Il Hwan Kim

1 INTRODUCTION

On 24 January 2012, Google announced that, beginning 1 March 2012, it will synthetically manage all personal information obtained from around 60 of its services, including its search engines, e-mail (Gmail) accounts, YouTube and social networking services.[1] As the world's largest search engine, Google aims to provide more accurate and customised services, by checking the history of services that each Google account holder has been using. The company policy stipulates that it will no longer ask the user to give separate permission related to information integration. This announcement, however, is drawing fierce opposition from major civic groups in the United States.[2] They oppose Google's decision, because they are extremely worried about the company's 'monopoly on information power'[3]. They point out that the unilateral decision would make Google a kind of Big Brother, which will grasp all information about every individual, instead of providing users with a smart service, thus making internet use more convenient.

The AFP, on the other hand, reported, on 25 January 2012, that the European Union (EU) would require prominent internet companies, such as Google and Facebook, to step up the protection of users' personal information. If the revision takes effect, it will be applied to all twenty-seven EU Member States and to companies operating in those nations, even if their server is located in other areas. The measure is expected to be a hard blow on global corporations, such as Google and Facebook, which have made huge profits so far, by making use of their customers' information.

The knowledge information society is a society that produces knowledge based on information and communications technology. In other words, it is

[1] S. Grobart, 'Google's New Privacy Policy: What to Do', New York Times, 28 March 2012; the Korean Communications Commission and Korean Personal Information Protection Commission are currently investigating whether Google violates any personal information protection law.
[2] A. Efrati, 'Google Defends New Privacy Policy', The Wall Street Journal, 31 January 2012.
[3] Prema Katiyar, 'Google's New Policy Infringes privacy of millions of internet users', The Economic Times, 4 July 2012.

a society wherein information becomes the driving power for the creation of fortune and value. Therefore, in a knowledge information society, new responsibilities for the constitution and the government naturally emerge. That is, a knowledge information society requires the government to establish and maintain, more than ever before, the conditions for the establishment and execution of individuals' freedom and rights.

In today's information society, the regulation of personal information must be understood in the context of the debate on the risk that information technology development poses to humankind. Ever since the emergence of computers, there has been an increased fear that the state or private entities can gain access to a wide range of personal information through automated information processing and the ongoing collection of information. The protection of the privacy of individuals is one of the most important principles for a modern information society. This is because, in today's information society, the information possessor and the electronic-information processor exercise an overwhelming power, which has the potential to be abused. Therefore, while there is no doubt that the state or private companies must search, process and store the information that they need to perform their roles and responsibilities, it is also important that they must not collect, transfer or store information that they do not need, for such a purpose.

The most important issue at present is to raise the transparency of information processing to the greatest extent possible and to continue to guarantee the dignity and freedom of individuals, by normatively predicting technological development. Thus, the *Information Order* that we seek must be individual-oriented. To build an individual-oriented information system, it is necessary for all individual stakeholders to participate in its creation, from planning, through to building and operating, as well as the *ex post facto* protection of information. Accordingly, everyone should have the right to decide whether to make public one's personal information and whether to allow others to use such personal information.

As the information society advances, the demand for protection of personal information is significantly increasing in various countries. Everyone agrees that personal information in an information society should be protected.[4] Yet, in a world that has become one global market, the protection and transmission of personal information is no longer the problem of a single country or the regulatory issue of domestic law alone, but a global issue and of common interest to all people. This also means that the protection of human rights is no longer merely within the scope of the concept of rights, but is a global issue, related to trade and economic conditions. It follows that a collective and international effort to create a universally acceptable regulatory framework is necessary.

There are various indications of the need for data protection at the inter-

---

[4]   N. Singer, 'Just Give Me the Right to Be Forgotten', *The New York Times*, 20 August 2011.

national level in the agreements concluded between the EU and Korea. For example, the importance of data protection, in the context of electronic commerce, is explicitly recognised in the EU–Korea FTA, which provides that:

> The Parties agree that the development of electronic commerce must be fully compatible with the international standards of data protection, in order to ensure the confidence of users of electronic commerce.[5]

More generally, the need for cooperation on the protection of personal information is explicitly recognised in the EU–Korea Framework Agreement in Article 32:

> 1. The Parties agree to cooperate in order to improve the level of protection of personal data to the highest international standards such as that contained in the UN Guidelines for the Regulation of Computerized Personal Data Files (UN General Assembly Resolution 45/95 of 14 December 1990).
> 2. Cooperation on protection of personal data may include, inter alia, exchange of information and expertise.

However, such cooperation is made more difficult by the fact that, due to the differences in the legal traditions and constitutional laws of countries, the content and scope of personal information protection laws show a wide range of diversity. On the one hand, some countries, like the EU Member States, demand very high levels of data protection. On the other hand, other countries impose less stringent standards.

This chapter will discuss the current trends in the development of personal information protection laws, by comparing and contrasting the approaches taken by the EU and the United States. It will also explore how these differences have been overcome through cooperation between the relevant actors. Finally, the chapter will analyse laws recently enacted in Korea – a country that has already advanced into the information age and, thus, has encountered various types of issues relating to the protection of personal information.

2 THE EUROPEAN FRAMEWORK FOR PERSONAL DATA PROTECTION AND COOPERATION WITH THIRD STATES

2.1 The European approach to personal data protection

The EU and individual European nations accord a significant weight to the protection of an individual's private life and personal rights. This protection is achieved through a variety of legal instruments.

The protection of personal information is, in part, addressed through the lens of human rights law. Article 8 of the European Convention on Human

---

[5] EU–Korea Free Trade Agreement, Article 7.48(2).

Rights stipulates that: 'everyone has the right to respect for his private and family life, his home and his and correspondence'. Yet, under Article 8 of the European Convention on Human Rights, the state can interfere in an individual's private life, when it is:

> in accordance with law and is necessary in a democratic society in the interests of national security, public safety or the economic well-being of the country, for the prevention of disorder or crime, for the protection of health or morals, or for the protection of the rights and freedoms of others.[6]

Article 10 of the European Convention on Human Rights also stipulates the basic rights for freedom of expression, which could include the freedom to communicate information and ideology, without governmental intervention and limitation. Nevertheless, Article 10 is not interpreted as a general right to call for governmental agencies to make public the information that they possess. In other words, when the free information movement among individuals is interfered with by a public agency, it can violate paragraph 1 of Article 10, but this interference can be justified under paragraph 2 of Article 10. Ultimately, it is up to the European Court of Human Rights to formally declare the limits in exercising the rights stipulated by Article 8 and Article 10 of the European Convention on Human Rights.[7]

The right to respect for private and family life is now also recognised in the European Charter of Fundamental Rights, annexed to the Treaty on the Functioning of the European Union.[8] Moreover, the Charter of Fundamental Rights explicitly addresses the protection of personal information in Article 8, which provides:

1. Everyone has the right to the protection of personal data concerning him or her.
2. Such data must be processed fairly for specified purposes and on the basis of the consent of the person concerned or some other legitimate basis laid down by law. Everyone has the right of access to data which has been collected concerning him or her, and the right to have it rectified.
3. Compliance with these rules shall be subject to control by an independent authority.

These rights are obviously very abstract, and they require implementation, through specific laws dealing with the protection of personal information. Data protection was addressed through legislation adopted by the EU as early as October 1995, when the EU adopted Directive 95/46/EC on the pro-

---

[6] European Convention for the Protection of Human Rights and Fundamental Freedoms, Article 8(2).
[7] The European Court of Human Rights decided, in the case of *Gaskin v. United Kingdom* (Judgement of 7 July 1989, Series A, No. 160), that the privacy right stipulated by the European Covenant on Human Rights' Article 8 does not include general and positive access to information possessed by the government.
[8] Charter on Fundamental Rights, Article 7.

tection of individuals, with regard to the processing of personal data and on the free movement of such data.[9] The basic principles of the right, freedom and privacy of an individual included in the Directive were based on the contents of the 1981 Council of Europe Convention for the Protection of Individuals, with regard to Automatic Processing of Personal Data, aimed at protecting individuals in automatically processing personal information.[10]

The Directive is designed to protect the basic rights and freedoms of the public in each EU Member State, to safeguard their privacy right associated with personal information and to promote free distribution of personal information among the EU nations.[11] The Directive is commonly applied to both the public and the private sector. The Directive pushes ahead with a powerful personal information protection policy. The Directive requires EU Member States to enact their own legislation, implementing its terms.

The EU Directive is aimed at protecting the basic rights and freedom of an individual and his or her right to privacy, in relation to the treatment of personal information.[12] The rules in the Directive are also aimed at preventing an individual Member State from restricting or prohibiting the free flow of personal information under the pretext of protecting them.[13] The Second Chapter of the Directive, which consists of Articles 5 to 21, regulates the general rules of law governing the treatment of personal data. Accordingly, the purpose of collection and treatment of data should, first, be clear and legal, and it should be stipulated in the relevant enactment. Second, the collected data must be proper and relevant to this purpose. Third, the treatment of data should be fair; accurate and adequate information, with regard to the collection of data, should be provided to the principal agent of the information. Fourth, the treatment of data should be carried out according to its main agent's will, and it should follow the stipulated legal regulations. Moreover, when the collection and reprocessing of personal information is required, it should be revised and constitute the latest and most accurate information. All reasonable measures should be taken to reprocess, delete and correct inaccurate information, upon collection of the information. Each Member State should define the proper protection conditions for the designated personal information over a longer period of time, so that it can be used historically, statistically and scientifically.

Under the Sixth Chapter of the Directive, each Member State must establish regulators for personal information protection, who are in charge

---

[9]   Directive 95/46/EC of the European Parliament and the European Council of 24 October 1995 on the protection of individuals with regard to the processing of personal data and on the free movement of such data [1995] OJ L281/31, 23 November 1995.

[10] Available at www.conventions.coe.int/treaty/en/treaties/html/108.htm (accessed 14 June 2012).

[11] P. M. Schwartz and J. R. Reidenberg, *Data Privacy Law* (Washington, DC: Michie Law Publishers, 1996), p. 13.

[12] Directive 95/46/EC, Article 1(1).

[13] Ibid. Article 1(2).

of supervising the application of the adopted regulations. This includes the introduction of a reporting system on personal information protection and the resolution of personal information management disputes, as well as the right of those agencies to investigate violations of data protection laws. The regulatory bodies must be independent in implementing their duties.

All EU Member States implemented the Directive within the assigned timeframe, so there is a strong framework for the protection of personal information across all twenty-seven EU Member States. It should be noted that the European Commission proposed a draft European Data Protection Regulation on 25 January 2012, which would supersede the Directive and the national laws implementing the Directive, thereby establishing a single instrument, which regulates personal information protection across the EU.[14]

2.2 *The transmission of personal information from the EU to a third country*

The EU plays a leading role in adopting personal information protection laws, as is clearly exhibited in its personal information protection provisions discussed above. Not only has the EU been concerned with protecting data within EU Member States, but it has also been concerned with the risks posed by the transmission of personal information to third countries. For this purpose, Articles 25 and 26 of Directive 95/46/EC contain rules related to the transmission of personal data to third countries. The Directive stresses that each Member State should not infringe its own rules, when transmitting personal information to a third country. The third country, on the other hand, should observe the proper security level.

The EU evaluates the level of personal information protection of the third country, informs each Member State of its evaluation and prohibits a country from sending its own people's personal information to a third county which has not secured protection at an adequate level. The proper security level of the third country must be evaluated in every situation in the case of transmitting information. The vital issues to be considered are, in particular, the character of the data, the suggested treatment deadline, the country providing the data, the legal environment and the information protection guidelines and policies of the country receiving the information. The European Commission stipulates that if the third country fails to abide by the proper security level, Member States must be informed of its failure of compliance. Through this measure, Member States can prohibit any information from being sent to the third country in question. The rule means that the EU allows a third country – a non-European country – to distribute information, only when it implements the protection of personal informa-

---

[14] See www.mlawgroup.de/news/publications/detail.php?we_objectID=227 (accessed 23 March 2012).

tion at an adequate level. Therefore, the third country must set up adequate rules and security steps, requiring it to observe the purpose and character of personal information collection and make use of, to a certain degree, general laws and individual laws. As a result, the above-mentioned EU rules, concerning the transmission of personal information to third countries, could be perceived as a barrier to certain forms of commerce, particularly e-commerce, where it is necessary to transfer personal information.

2.3 Case study of cooperation between the EU and the United States of America

As a result of the rules described in the previous section, the transfer of personal information from the EU to the United States became an issue, because of the EU perception that: '[the] level of the United States' personal information protection falls behind' by the European standard.[15]

Although the US Constitution does not explicitly guarantee the right to privacy, the Supreme Court provides protection for various aspects of right to privacy through the interpretation of the Bill of Rights. The constitutional privacy rights have been developed by the Supreme Court in controversial cases, ensuing decisions on pregnancy, abortion and other private concerns.[16] While some argue that the right to privacy observed by the US Constitution can be integrated by a single and abstract principle or standard based on a certain fixed set of values, understanding its true nature remains extremely difficult.[17] Moreover, the openness and flexibility are both merits and demerits of the 'privacy' right created by the US Constitution. So whether privacy is seen either as a collection of numerous things or a single concept,[18] today's most persuasive theory is that we should take a closer look at the types of rights that the United States Supreme Court has considered to be worthy of protecting. They can be classified under three different headings: (1) the protection of physical space or area; (2) the individual ability to make a significant decision, without being interfered or disturbed; and (3) information privacy.[19]

The review of the relationship between the privacy rights of the US Constitution and the freedom of expression shows that the Constitution is

---

[15] F. H. Cate, 'The Changing Face of Privacy Protection in the European Union and the United States', *Indiana Law Review*, vol. 33 (1999), p. 228.

[16] See, for example, *Olmstead v. United States*, 277 U. S. 438 (1928); *Katz v. United States*, 389 U. S. 347 (1967); *Griswold v. Connecticut*, 381 U. S. 479 (1965); *Eisenstadt v. Baird*, 405 U. S. 438, 453 (1972); *Roe v. Wade*, 410 U. S. 113 (1973).

[17] See J. Kang, 'Information Privacy in Cyberspace Transactions', *Stanford Law Review*, vol. 50 (1998), p. 1204ff.

[18] See L. H. Tribe, *American Constitutional Law* (2nd edn) (Mineola, NY: The Foundation Press, 1988), p. 1303.

[19] Kang, 'Information Privacy in Cyberspace Transactions', p. 1202.

the foundation, not only of privacy rights, but also of the other pivotal rights confronting them. The First Amendment to the US Constitution is one of the most important rights, with regard to the government's infringement on the freedom of expression or publication. Any effort by the government to protect a right to privacy should also be in harmony with the First Amendment, if it is to pass Constitutional scrutiny. In reality, whenever the right to privacy collides with the rights of free expression in court, the latter prevails, practically without exception.[20] The benefits of free expression are always superior to those of privacy under the strict screening undertaken by the judiciary. When the rights of one who does not want his or her personal information to be published are in confrontation with those of someone who wants to publish it, then the court stands by the latter consistently. The rights of the latter are respected, as long as the government cannot prove the 'substantial' public benefits necessary to prohibit its publication.[21]

While a variety of laws and orders governing the use of personal information do exist in the United States, they have a general tendency to deal with a specific industry, economic field or concrete issue in either the public or the private sector. The laws in these individual areas are applied to a user of specific information, in the context of the use of specific information, a specific information type or a specific use of personal information. They are seldom related to consistently protecting any personal information from its collection, treatment and deletion. In particular, they have a strong tendency to prohibit the disclosure, rather than the collection, use and storage of personal information.[22] Moreover, in the US, personal information relies, to a large extent, on the judicial relief measures, through which each citizen who thinks his rights are infringed files a lawsuit, without being protected by the control and supervision of the state or an independent public body.[23]

In conclusion, the first reason why personal information is not protected in a consistent and proper way in the US is that a general and basic law presenting the general principles and standards of protection of personal information has not been adopted. The second reason is that the level or degree of personal information protection observed by each law widely varies, depending on the circumstances.[24] Certainly, whether personal information can be intensively protected in a specific field is unclear. However, the

---

[20] See, for example, Cate, 'The Changing Face of Privacy Protection in the European Union and the United States', p. 204.

[21] Ibid. pp. 203–5.

[22] F. H. Cate, *Privacy in the Information Age* (Washington, DC: Brookings Institution Press, 1997), p. 99.

[23] C. D. Raab and C. J. Bennett, 'Taking the Measure of Privacy: Can Data Protection be Evaluated?', *International Review of Administrative Sciences*, vol. 62 (1996), p. 545; P. M. Regan, 'Privacy Legislation in the United States: A Debate about Ideas and Interests', *International Review of Administrative Sciences*, vol. 62 (1996), p. 470.

[24] F. H. Cate, *Privacy in the Information Age*, p. 110.

present way to protect personal information separately in each area (without those principles and standards) inevitably has the disadvantage that the level and degree of protection can be very different.

It is clear that a fundamental difference exists between the personal information protection policy of the US and the EU. While the US supports the self-regulation of personal information protection policies of each industry, the EU Member States intervene positively in those that deal with personal information. This is the reason why the US attempted to negotiate with the EU, judging that the difference between the two sides' personal information protection policies could cause trade friction and undermine the transmission of personal information among states.

The US presents the Safe Harbor Principle as a solution to the problem. The Safe Harbor Principle is a step that the US Department of Commerce introduced, in order to satisfy the standard of 'adequacy' in transmitting information to third countries, as stipulated by the EU Directive.[25] This principle provides for new personal information protection standards, while maintaining the separate restrictions within each field and the existing personal information protection system commissioned by autonomous regulations. The Safe Harbor Principle was adopted to allow any organisation or related company to receive information transmissions continuously, as long as the US acknowledges that it takes adequate steps for personal information protection, by reporting to the Department of Commerce and ensuring that it will observe the agreement of its own accord. The Safe Harbor Principle stipulates the observance of notice, choice, onward transfer, security, data integrity, access and enforcement in protecting personal information.

3 THE CONTENTS AND CHARACTERISTICS OF KOREAN LAWS CONCERNING PERSONAL INFORMATION PROTECTION

3.1 *The constitutional law in Korea regarding the right to informational self-decision*

Unlike the US, which places freedom of speech ahead of an individual's right to privacy, and unlike EU countries, which stress an individual's privacy or personal right, the Constitution of Korea treats the protection of private life (Article 17) and the freedom of speech and expression (Article 21) with equal value. Thus, the judicial precedent and theory admit that the Korean Constitutional Court should affect a balancing test, so as to identify which basic right should precede the other, in each individual case.

In the information society, to judge whether the execution of information-processing systems violates the Constitution, one must judge whether such

---

[25] See www.export.gov/safeharbor/ (accessed 23 March 2012).

systems are handling personal information protected by the Constitution. If there is enough evidence justifying it, the Constitution allows the collection and processing of the corresponding information.

Regarding personal information protection, the Korean Constitutional Court has recognised the right to informational self-decision as a right that is not listed in the Constitution: 'the self-determining right to personal information is the right of the subject of information to determine to whom and in what scope his or her information is exposed and used'.[26] That is, it is the right of the subject of the information to determine the scope and usage of his or her personal information. Personal information, in this context, is any information that specifies an individual's character and subjectivity, such as the individual's physical information, beliefs, social standing and occupation. Therefore, it refers to all types of information that can allow others to recognise the individual's identity, including not only information on the individual's intimate or personal aspects of their life, but also personal information that has been formed in his or her official life or that has already been open to the public. Moreover, any act of surveying, collecting, storing, processing and using such personal information is considered, in principle, a violation of the self-determining right to personal information. The need to constitutionally approve the self-determining right to personal information as a new, independent and basic right is based on the change in social situations, which is discussed below. While general human rights, based on Article 17 of the Constitution on the secrecy and freedom of private life[27] and Article 10 of the Constitution on human dignity and value and the right to pursue one's happiness[28], or other constitutional provisions, which stipulate the need for a free, democratic and basic order, can be considered constitutional bases of the self-determining right to personal information, it would be impossible to completely include the contents to be protected by the self-determining right to personal information in each basic right and constitutional principle. Therefore, it appears to be inadvisable to limit the constitutional bases of this right to only one or two of the above basic rights

---

[26] 2005. 5. 26. 2004 Hun-Ma 190. Hun-Ma means constitutional complaint case filed by individual complainant(s) according to Article 68(1) of the Constitutional Court Act. Article 68(1) of the Constitutional Court Act provides that 'Any person who claims that his basic right which is guaranteed by the Constitution has been violated by an exercise or nonexercise of governmental power may file a constitutional complaint, except the judgements of the ordinary courts, with the Constitutional Court. Provided that, if any relief process is provided by other laws, no one may file a constitutional complaint without having exhausted all such processes.'

[27] Article 17 of the Constitution of the Republic Korea provides: 'The privacy of no citizen shall be infringed.'

[28] Article 10 of the Constitution of the Republic of Korea provides: 'All citizens shall be assured of human dignity and worth and have the right to pursue happiness. It shall be the duty of the State to confirm and guarantee the fundamental and inviolable human rights of individuals.'

or constitutional principles, rather, the self-determining right to personal information should be seen as 'an independent and basic right based on these articles and principles as the ideal foundations',[29] in other words, it is 'a basic right that is not enumerated in the Constitution'.[30]

3.2 Status and problems of personal information protection (PIP) laws

Since the late 1960s, several nations have enacted, or have been in the process of enacting, laws for PIP in the information society, so as to build a human-controlled information order. As each nation has different historical, political and legal traditions, each nation has its own way of finding a solution. In Korea, when the nation started to pursue information technology as a political policy in the 1980s, with, for example, the development of an administrative computer network, the concern regarding violations of privacy became paramount, leading to the passage of PIP laws in the late 1980s. The PIP laws pertain to both the public and the private sector.

The public sector was regulated by the Law Related to PIP in Public Organisations and to separate laws, such as the e-Government Law, the Residency Registration Law, the Law of Processing Public Resentment, the Government Service Worker Law, the Public Servant's Ethics Law and the Penal Law. In addition, to protect and supervise PIP in the public sector, the Ministry of Government and Home Affairs and other national administrations adopted a self-regulation control system.

The private sector, on the other hand, was regulated by the Law to Enhance the Usage of the Information-Communication Network and Privacy Protection. This Act is a general law in the private sector, which is considered to be a law to enhance the usage of an information-communication network. However, offline business subjects did not recognise that this law affected them. Moreover, it was difficult to recognise the law as a PIP law, because regulations, such as that on the prevention of internet violations and on the distribution of unsound information, co-existed. Indeed, personal data protection was also regulated by a series of separate sectoral laws, such as the Law of Using and Protecting Credit Data, the Real-Name Financial Transaction System Law, the Law of Medical Treatment, the Health and Medical Treatment Fundamental Law, the Law of Electronic-Communication Business, the Electric-Wave Law and the e-Commerce Fundamental Law. As a result of the sectoral approach, confusion in the legal system increased. Moreover, although the general law that applies to the private sector accommodates every international-level PIP principle, it was not being applied comprehensively in every sector. For example, department stores, beauty shops and fast food restaurants collect and use personal

---

[29] Ibid.
[30] Ibid.

information through membership, but are in a legal dead zone, because they do not collect and use personal information online. Because of the limited application scope of the law, there was a legislative loophole in the general law.

It can be concluded that the PIP supervision system was lacking in both the public and private sectors. While personal information collection and use are becoming more professional and diversified in the private sector, PIP violation, via information abuse, is on the rise.[31] Thus, the level of PIP requests needs active protection and not just passive protection, with measures such as the banning of the illegal use and provision of personal information.

3.3 *The main contents and characteristics of the Personal Information Protection Act 2011*

The Personal Information Protection Act (Act No. 10465), on which legislative discussions started in 2004, was announced publicly on 29 March 2011, and it has been in effect since 30 September 2011.

In the drafting stages of the Act, there were two different views in relation to the scope and format of the proposed legislation. One view emphasised a general-act system, whereby a general act is enacted for the public sector and another is enacted for the private sector, with additional special acts promulgated in each sector, if needed. In other words, the public and private sectors would have laws with different standards and scopes of application. Another view emphasised a combined-act system, which points towards the enactment of a combined law for privacy protection.

The Eun-young Lee Bill took the latter approach and applied the same PIP principles and standards to the public and private sectors. But there is a problem in applying precisely the same standard, because, in principle, people have the right to collect data and to freely establish contracts. The Hye-hoon Lee Bill addressed this issue by first setting a common standard for both sectors and then setting additional separate standards, which will be separately applied to each sector. In other words, it was adjudged that a common (framework) PIP Act should have a legislative form that encompasses both the public and private sectors, but has a different application for each sector.

The legislation also sought to ensure that PIP regulations develop in advance, or, at least, simultaneously, with the emergence of new information technologies. It did so through the establishment of an organisation that will control data processing. The plans for organising a PIP organisation are based on 'functional independence' and the 'efficiency of damage redemption'.

---

[31] For example, the number of reported personal information breaches in 2009 was 35,167. Moreover, 23,948 (68.1 per cent) operators were excluded from the application of law.

In its final form, the 2011 Act extends its regulatory targets to about 3.5 million public institutions and private businesses (about 3 million institutions and businesses are included in the government system), which signifies that the Act has resolved the legal dead zone. Moreover, the Act will regulate the common protective criteria and principles in collecting, using, processing and disposing of personal information, which used to be regulated by different legislative standards in different acts. In addition, the Act will further help boost the process of remedies for damage by guaranteeing the right to read, correct, delete and stop the process of collecting personal information and by introducing a notification and reporting system, in case personal information is leaked. It also introduces a collective dispute resolution system and group litigation that seeks to stop the infringement of rights. Furthermore, the Act will strictly control the process of using unique identification numbers, such as the resident registration number, and will provide the regulatory basis for the installation and restriction of CCTV systems.

The Act is expected to drastically strengthen the level of personal information protection by the government, as well as the prevention of incidents that infringe rights to privacy, by making obligatory the personal information impact assessment for public institutions. The Act will establish, under the President, the Personal Information Protection Committee, which will review and determine key policy issues and which will be granted the right to recommend corrective measures to any act of constitutional organisations, central administrative organisations and local governments that violate the law, as well as the right to present its yearly report to the National Assembly and to request necessary data. Finally, the Act expands the Personal Information Dispute Mediatory Committee to greatly strengthen its independence, with regard to its policies and decision-making processes.

4 CONCLUSION

The discussion and the subsequent move towards a new Personal Information Protection Act date back to 2003, during the advancement of the Korean information society. At the time, the debates were part of the process of seeking a *proper* law, which could guarantee the protection of personal information. Those debates raised philosophical concerns relating to the personal information law itself, that is, how the Act sets up the relationship between *protection* and the *use* of personal information, as well as legal issues concerning the proper format for the new law. Compared to the laws that have been discussed before, the new Personal Information Protection Act that was established in 2011 is considered a more advanced act that minimises the risks incurred from various types of leaks of personal information, and it contains various devices and means to protect the self-determining right to personal information. The present task is now to secure the legal use of personal information, based on the protections of the new Act. Accordingly, it is believed that the private sector must regulate itself, vis-à-vis the regulatory role of the Personal Information Protection Committee, which will be established soon.

A review of international and national standards for personal information protection shows that there are a variety of differences in the concrete legal regulations and the authority of regulatory agencies, because of each nation's distinct political, administrative and legal traditions and systems. Nevertheless, there is a common perception that personal information should be protected in an information society, and there has been a willingness to cooperate on the mutual recognition of standards.

It is suggested that the process of establishing the new Personal Information Protection Act provides excellent evidence that Korea is successfully addressing this issue, which is of common interest to all countries in the global information society. Indeed, the 2011 Act goes a long way to meeting the standards set by the EU in its own personal information protection laws.

As well as having an adequate national legal framework, it is also important to have channels of communication at the international level, in order to allow states to consult on these issues. For the EU and Korea, this is achieved, to some extent, through the 2010 Framework Agreement. Were any problems to arise in the transmission of protected personal information between the EU and Korea, it is clear that the Joint Committee established under the 2010 Framework Agreement could provide a forum for discussion of the problems.[32] Alternatively, a more specialised body could be created with the common institutional framework, so as to consider cooperation on personal information protection. Indeed, it is possible that this forum could also be used to negotiate more specific standards on personal information protection, which could lead to a more standardised approach between the two parties.

---

[32] Framework Agreement, Article 44.

Index